A World of Words

A World of Words

Language

and

Displacement

in the

Fiction of

Edgar

Allan Poe

Michael J. S.

Williams

Duke
University
Press
Durham and
London
1988

© Duke University
Press 1988
All rights reserved
Printed in the
United States of
America on acid-
free paper ∞

Library of Congress
Cataloging-in-
Publication Data
appear on the
last page of
this book

For
Sheelagh,
John,
and
Gavin

Contents

Acknowledgments   ix
Abbreviations   xi
Preface   xiii

I   "A World of Words"   1
II   "The Personage in Question": Self and Language   17
III   "An Unknown Quantity of X":
      Some Anxieties of Authority   45
IV   *"Duelli Lex Scripta, et Non, Aliterque":*
      The Struggle for Authority   62
V   "Word of No Meaning": Denial of the Symbol   80
VI   Voice and Text: Displacements of Authority   105
VII   Conclusion: Allegories of Reading   122
      Notes   153
      Index   179

Acknowl-

edgments

I would like to thank those people who have helped me in my work. I am particularly grateful to three generous friends: Robert C. McLean, Kathleen McLean, and Alexander Hammond. Robert McLean offered constant encouragement, perceptive criticism, and constructive advice at all stages of this study; Kathleen McLean skillfully edited many drafts and gave my prose any clarity it may now possess; and Alexander Hammond, to whom I am most indebted, freely gave ideas, criticism, hard work, enthusiasm, and humor—without his help, this study would never have been completed.

Others who have read all or part of the manuscript and offered valuable suggestions are James Davidson, Ralph Flores, and Joan Burbick; I owe a particular debt to Ulrike Koebke. My approach to Poe's work was influenced by ideas developed by Joseph Riddel in his seminar on American poetics at the 1981 summer session of the School of Criticism and Theory. Thomas C. Faulkner and Rhonda Blair of the Humanities Research Center, Washington State University, gave me much practical advice and help in preparing the manuscript.

Material from the preface appeared in slightly different form in *ESQ: A Journal of the American Renaissance;* the section "Some Words with a Mummy" originally appeared in *Poe Studies;* and the readings of "Shadow.—A Parable" and "The Gold-Bug" were first published in *American Literature.* I thank the editors of those journals for permission to republish.

Finally, my most enduring debt is to my family for their patient love and support.

Abbreviations

Unless otherwise indicated, the editions of Poe's works cited parenthetically in the text and notes are keyed as follows:

CW   *The Complete Works of Edgar Allan Poe,* ed. James A. Harrison, 17 vols. (1902; rpt. New York: AMS Press, 1965).

EAP   *Edgar Allan Poe: Poetry and Tales,* ed. Patrick F. Quinn (New York: Modern Library of America, 1984).

IV   *The Imaginary Voyages: The Narrative of Arthur Gordon Pym, The Unparalleled Adventures of one Hans Pfaal, The Journal of Julius Rodman,* vol. 1 of *Collected Writings of Edgar Allan Poe,* ed. Burton R. Pollin (Boston: Twayne, 1981–).

L   *The Letters of Edgar Allan Poe,* ed. John Ward Ostrom, 2 vols. (1948; rev. ed. New York: Gordian Press, 1966). Volumes are paginated consecutively.

M   *Marginalia,* ed. John Carl Miller (Charlottesville: Univ. Press of Virginia, 1981).

P   *Poems*, vol. 1 of *Collected Works of Edgar Allan Poe*, ed.
         Thomas Ollive Mabbott (Cambridge, Mass.: Belknap Press of
         Harvard Univ. Press, 1969).

TS   *Tales and Sketches 1831–1842; Tales and Sketches 1843–1849*,
         vols. 2 and 3 of *Collected Works of Edgar Allan Poe*, ed. Thomas
         Ollive Mabbott (Cambridge, Mass.: Belknap Press of Harvard
         Univ. Press, 1978–79). Paginated consecutively.

Preface

When Poe's remains were dug up and reburied in 1875, the *Washington Star* reported under the headline, "Walt Whitman at the Poe Funeral—*Conspicuous Absence of the Popular Poets*," that "about the most significant part of the Poe reburial ceremonies yesterday—which only a crowded and remarkably magnetic audience of the very best class of young people, women preponderating, prevented from growing tedious—was the marked absence from the spot of every popular poet and author, American and foreign. Only Walt Whitman was present."[1] There is some humor in the idea that Whitman probably wrote this account himself; more telling, however, is that its main thrust anticipated the fate of Poe's literary reputation in America: indisputably popular, particularly among the young, and yet segregated from the healthy "living" writers of the American canon.

The gestures of exclusion are well known: whether on moral, aesthetic, or psychological grounds, Poe has been consistently described as an other ("irresponsible," "vulgar," "abnormal") against which a version of normality has been defined. The most consequential gesture—that is, in the institutional context of the academic study of American literature—was that of F. O. Matthiessen, whose *American Renaissance* (1941) legitimized a period as the original moment of an authentic American literature, and canonized a group of American writers committed to "organic union between labor and culture" from whose company Poe was excluded as "hostile to democracy" and "factitious."[2] As Louis A. Renza remarks in a recent essay, Matthiessen figuratively reburied Poe among the footnotes to his book and so reaffirmed Poe's marginality to American literary history.[3] French Poe scholar Claude Richard claims with some justice that "if you approach American literature from the point of view of literary history, you'll meet [Poe] nowhere because he didn't fit into the 'picture.' "[4]

It is tempting to discover in Richard's observation a sense of Gallic proprietorship, or even to mistake it as an extension of the Baudelairean myth of Poe as neglected artist and alienated victim of crass American materialism. But we must allow Richard the past tense of "didn't"; his own studies show that he is certainly aware that since the efforts of, for example, Edward H. Davidson, Patrick F. Quinn, Robert D. Jacobs, and more recently, G. R. Thompson, Poe's works have received sustained American critical attention—much of it specifically aimed either at placing Poe firmly in his literary-historical milieu or at justifying his position in an American canon. Even Harold Bloom, whose antipathy to Poe's work is marked, confirms that Poe is "central," though he does so in terms that establish an opposition between Emerson ("life") and Poe ("negativity"): "Emerson . . . was and is the mind of America, but Poe was and is our hysteria, our uncanny unanimity in our repressions."[5]

Whatever we make of Bloom's assertion about the national psyche, however, "unanimity" hardly serves to characterize the state of Poe studies. What might be called the traditional view of Poe as a serious exponent of romantic visionary metaphysics still vies with the reading of Poe as romantic ironist, which, since it received its most systematic and persuasive articulation in G. R. Thompson's *Poe's Fiction: Romantic Irony in the Gothic Tales* (1973), has become increasingly influential.[6] Although the terms of this rivalry still tend to preoccupy many studies exclusively concerned with Poe—as indeed they emerge pe-

riodically in my own—recent years have seen an increasing number of
readings variously influenced by developments in contemporary literary
theory. Since "The Purloined Letter" is at least the nominal pretext for
the seminal exchange between Jacques Lacan and Jacques Derrida, this
fact merits no great surprise.[7] Indeed, as American literary critics have
adapted the concepts and procedures of Lacan and, more crucially,
Derrida to the task of revising received notions of American literary
history, they have found that Poe's texts, as Claude Richard observes,
"respond admirably to the new questions addressed to literature."[8]
Among those questions—posed with varying emphases in studies by,
for example, John T. Irwin, Joseph N. Riddel, and John Carlos Rowe—
are those raised by the relationship between language and the self, the
problematics of writing, the displacement or dispersal of origins, and
the nature of (inter)textuality.[9]

Although the present study remains alert to such theoretical issues—
they return repeatedly as themes for consideration—it is more centrally
concerned with the specific ways in which Poe's texts examine and reflect on the nature of their own signifying practices—that is, with the
degree to which language itself is a topic of those texts. Poe's tales, regardless of their ostensible character, consistently explore the conditions of their own meaning and the displacements implicated in any
act of signification. As the following readings will show, one major
source of anxiety is the attenuation of an (originating) authorial voice
once its text has been launched in time to undergo subsequent interpretation and reinterpretation.[10]

The chapters are arranged topically, and the texts with which each
deals are those that themselves foreground the particular issue under
consideration. But this order should not be regarded as an attempt to
establish a taxonomy for Poe's texts—which would be to engage in an
activity that the texts themselves expose as a manifestation of interpretive blindness. To cite one example: "Morella," here examined for
the implications it bears on Poe's questioning of "personal identity,"
could just as fruitfully have been discussed with "Berenice" and "Ligeia" in the chapter that explores Poe's interrogation of the limits of
the romantic symbol. The topical organization is essentially functional:
earlier chapters explore the assumptions out of which subsequent readings develop.

The first chapter offers a characterization of Poe's poetics, highlighting themes that return as motifs in the readings that follow. From Poe's skeptical qualification of the power of human creativity and his recognition of the arbitrary nature of language emerges an image of the writer trapped in the "world of words" and exploring its limits.[11] If Poe recognizes that we occupy "the prison-house of language,"[12] he is not always daunted by that insight; indeed, he can play inexhaustibly with this predicament. In the course of investigating Poe's analysis of the relationship between the subject and language, chapter 2 examines Poe's questioning of the conventional assumption that "personal identity" is both unified and stable, and suggests his awareness of the displacement of an authorial writing self by a self as it is written. Chapter 3 addresses the issue of authorial control over a text, and chapter 4 examines Poe's characterization of the relationship between author and reader as one of a struggle for authority.

The first chapters thus suggest Poe's acute awareness of the displacements at work in language—from origin, author, and univocal meaning—and of the interpretive anxieties to which they give rise. Chapters 5, 6, and 7 show the ways in which he exposes the illusions of those strategies of recuperation that such anxieties generate. The first demonstrates Poe's debunking of the redemptive possibilities of the romantic symbol; the second, his subversion of interpretation grounded in a recovered authorial voice; and the last, his circumscription of even those readings offered by apparent masters over the letter—Legrand, Dupin, and the narrator of *Eureka*. In the last instance, Poe declares himself what he has been by implication throughout his career, a skeptical demystifier of origins.

As should be clear from this summary, *A World of Words* offers not a definitive analysis of Poe's texts but an approach to reading them by way of the interpretive issues they already raise. In so doing, it suggests those features of Poe's texts that continue to disturb and disrupt efforts to achieve interpretive "mastery" over them, that refuse easy classification, and that defeat efforts to recover an authentic or "real" Edgar Allan Poe. The version of Poe that emerges in the course of this reading is an equivocal figure: fully aware of the radical displacements inherent in the use of language, he exposes the futility and necessary failure of idealist attempts to evade them, but nevertheless struggles to develop protective strategies by which to control their consequences for his own practice. Finally, these readings suggest that any project designed to recuperate a "truly original" and originating Poe will get little further than the sexton who, at Poe's first exhumation, lifted up Poe's skull and subsequently recounted that "his brain rattled around inside just like a lump of mud, sir."[13]

1

"A World of Words"

In "A Chapter of Suggestions" (1845) Poe declared that "the imagination has not been unjustly ranked as supreme among the mental faculties" (*CW* 14:187), and a glance through his literary journalism confirms that "imaginative" was among the most laudatory terms in his critical vocabulary. This, perhaps, is not surprising given his early reading of the *Biographia Literaria*;[1] in the "Letter to B——" with which he prefaced his *Poems . . . Second Edition* (1831), he wrote of Coleridge: "I cannot speak but with reverence. His towering intellect! his gigantic power! . . . In reading his poetry, I tremble, like one who stands upon a volcano, conscious, from the very darkness bursting from the crater, of the fire and the light that are weltering below" (*CW* 7:xlii). The only mention of the imagination in this letter is at that point where Poe introduces his major criticism of Coleridge; though he praises him as a "giant in intellect and learning," he suggests that Coleridge is too profound, for "learning has little to do with the imagination." He continues, in words that he will employ again in his career, by asserting that "as regards the greater truths, men oftener err by seeking them at the bottom than at the top; the depth lies in the huge abysses where wisdom is sought—not in the palpable places where she is found. . . . [Coleridge] goes wrong by reason of his very profundity" (*CW* 7:xxxviii–xxxix). Perhaps, then, there is no "fire and . . . light," only "darkness."

Floyd Stovall suggests that at this time Poe did not fully understand Coleridge—that his praise was that of "one who apprehends vaguely the mood and manner of Coleridge without understanding thoroughly his meaning and purpose," and his criticism was an attempt "to eradicate all traces of influence."[2] But the terms in which Poe establishes his criticism are nevertheless significant for a reading of his work. His rejection of "depth" as the locus of "truth," the assertion that metaphysical speculation yields only "abysses" of its own creation, foreshadows the nature of the narrator's plight in "Ligeia" (1836; *TS* 312) and anticipates the Dupin of "The Murders in the Rue Morgue" (1841; *TS* 545). Poe's opting for the "palpable places"—what Dupin terms the "superficial"—rather than the "depth" that is no depth, lies behind and is repeated by his qualification of the notion of the creative imagination.

In his Drake-Halleck review of 1836, Poe seems to echo Coleridge's famous definition of the primary imagination from chapter 13 of *Biographia Literaria;* there, Coleridge declares that "the primary IMAGINATION I hold to be the living Power and prime Agent of all human Perception, and as a repetition in the finite mind of the eternal act of creation in the infinite I AM."[3] Poe, on the other hand, emphasizes the secondary nature of human imagination; his phrasing is that "imagination is, possibly in man, a lesser degree of the creative power in God" (*CW* 8:283n.). His hedging—"possibly"—suggests a qualification of even the claim to secondariness, and the sentences immediately following rehearse the ground on which he will take issue with the distinction between fancy and imagination: "What the Deity imagines *is,* but *was not* before. What man imagines *is,* but *was* also. The mind of man cannot imagine what *is not.*" It is on this issue of imagination as creation that he asserts his departure from Coleridge in an 1840 review of Thomas Moore's *Alciphron:*

"The fancy," says the author of the "Ancient Mariner," in his *Biographia Literaria*, "the fancy combines, the imagination creates." And this was intended, and has been received, as a distinction. If so at all, it is one without a difference; without even a difference of *degree*. The fancy as nearly creates as the imagination; and neither creates in any respect. All novel conceptions are merely unusual combinations. The mind of man can *imagine* nothing which has not really existed. . . . It will be said, perhaps, that we can imagine a *griffin*, and that a griffin does not exist. Not the griffin certainly, but its component parts. It is a mere compendium of known limbs and features—of known qualities. Thus with all which seems to be *new*—which appears to be a *creation* of intellect. It is resoluble into the old. The wildest and most vigorous effort of mind cannot stand the test of this analysis. (*CW* 10: 61–62)

Robert Jacobs has shown the strong influence of Scottish Common-Sense philosophy on Poe's work, and it is at work here in Poe's heavily qualified definition of the powers of human creativity—a definition that remains relatively constant throughout his writings.[4] Using Coleridge as a pretext, he rejects the possibility of human creation *ex vacuo* on the same grounds that he had in 1836 rejected the convention of origination as "a mere matter of impulse or inspiration," arguing that "to originate is carefully, patiently, and understandingly to combine" (*CW* 14:73). The poet must use the given forms of the world in "*novel* combinations," but such forms are always implicated in previous "creative" efforts; they are, in now familiar terms, always textual and intertextual. The poet's combinations are "*of those combinations which our predecessors . . . have already set in order* (*CW* 11:73). This circumstance is reflected in "Ligeia," where the narrator has only the faded significance of inherited signs with which he tries to signify an "essence" that always escapes; it appears generally in Poe's practice, which echoes or deliberately cites previous texts—among them his own—and reflects the heightened awareness that he attributes to the "genius" to whom "there seems eternally beginning behind beginning" (*M* 149).

The end of such combination—according to Poe's 1842 Longfellow review—is "the *novelty*, the *originality*, the *invention*, the *imagination*, or lastly the *creation* of BEAUTY, (for the terms as here employed are synonymous) as the essence of all Poesy" (*CW* 11:73). But the site of such beauty is not the poem, since it is "precisely, not a quality . . . but an effect" (*CW* 14:197). Poe's terms frequently suggest that this effect is a form of transcendence—"a poem deserves its title only inasmuch as it excites, by elevating the soul" (*CW* 14:266)—but it is actually an induced awareness of the *failure* to transcend. It is felt, not in the plenitude of presence of the beautiful, but in an acute awareness of loss. In "The Poetic Principle" Poe extends a description he had first offered in the Longfellow review—of that "immortal instinct," a "sense of the Beautiful" (*CW* 14:273). Yet this sense does not have as its object the forms and sensations of this world—"which greet [the poet] in common with all mankind"—but rather it has as its object an absence; it is a "thirst unquenchable" that

> belongs to the immortality of Man. It is at once a consequence and an indication of his perennial existence. It is the desire of the moth for the star. It is no mere appreciation of the Beauty before us—but a wild effort to reach the Beauty above. Inspired by an ecstatic prescience of the glories beyond the grave, we struggle, by multiform combinations among the things and thoughts of Time, to attain a portion of that Loveliness whose very elements, perhaps, appertain to eternity alone. . . . We weep then . . . through a certain, petulant, impatient sorrow at our inability to grasp *now*, wholly, here on earth, at once and forever, those divine and rapturous joys, of which . . . we attain to but brief and indeterminate glimpses. (*CW* 14:273–74)

The grave marks the limit of knowledge; visions are only "indeterminate glimpses" circumscribed by mortality. The "thirst for supernal BEAUTY" is an "immortal" thirst in that it can never be quenched, since no "existing collocation of earth's forms . . . no *possible* combination of these forms" can satisfy it (*CW* 11:73). The relationship between "thirst" and the "supernal" is unclear—which has priority? Is the felt absence of plenitude a function of objectless, ever-frustrated desire? Once the "supernal Beauty" is conceived in terms of effect, the possibility arises that it is a product of "petulant, impatient sorrow" rather than its cause. The arousal of frustrated desire, the titillation of loss, becomes then the motive for poetry, which is defined above all in terms of poetic *feeling* or "Poetic Sentiment," and in which the supernal or the "transcendental" is internalized as a felt absence, implicated with the faculty of "Taste" (*CW* 14:273–74).[5]

Supernal beauty, the motive and object of all poetry, is at best an absent presence that escapes knowledge and language. The clearest and, perhaps, strangest articulation of what we might call this poetics of sublime loss occurs in "The Philosophy of Composition" (1846). Here Poe again insists upon the relationship between beauty—as "the excitement, or pleasurable elevation, of the soul" (*CW* 14:198)—and sorrow: "The *tone* of its highest manifestation . . . is one of *sadness*. Beauty of whatever kind, in its supreme development, invariably excites the sensitive soul to tears. Melancholy is thus the most legitimate of all the poetical tones." And, relentlessly following his assertion that "effects should be made to spring from direct causes" (*CW* 14:198), he arrives at his fittest topic: " 'Of all melancholy topics, what, according to the *universal* understanding of mankind, is the *most* melancholy?' Death—was the obvious reply. 'And when,' I said, 'is this most melancholy of topics most poetical?' . . . The answer . . . is obvious— 'When it most closely allies itself to *Beauty:* the death, then, of a beautiful woman is, unquestionably, the most poetical topic in the world' " (*CW* 14:201). By Poe's own account, then, the felt absence of beauty is best figured as death; and death—or the corpse—can signify only in terms of memory—here, *"Mournful and Neverending Remembrance"* (*CW* 14:208)—by which the past becomes a metaphor for that which is not present. The interrelations of beauty, death, memory, and failure of transcendence reappear throughout Poe's tales, and are bound up— as subsequent chapters will show—with the nature of language. In "The Philosophy of Composition," beauty and death are mutually implicated—most obviously in the figure of the beautiful woman—but his poetic as a whole is redolent of mortality.[6]

Poe's poetic displaces truth as the object of poetic language.[7] In "The Poetic Principle," he summarizes: "I would define, in brief, the Poetry of words as *The Rhythmical Creation of Beauty*. Its sole arbiter is Taste. With the Intellect or with the Conscience, it has only collateral relations. Unless incidentally, it has no concern whatever either with Duty or with Truth" (*CW* 14:275). He elsewhere asserts that there is a "radical and chasmal difference between the truthful and the poetical modes of inculcation" (*CW* 11:70). This chasmal difference is most obviously located in the denial of reference, the effacement of the extratextual world. Whereas the language that designs to make statements about the world should attempt to efface itself by being "perspicuous, precise, terse"—that is, by being transparently referential—"poetical" language represses reference in aspiring to an indefinite suggestiveness analogous to that of music.[8] Those factors that would subvert such suggestiveness are disqualified. Imitation is rejected as "mere repetition [which] is not poetry" (*CW* 14:273).[9] Nor should the poem be written to "inculcate a moral" (a procedure Poe labels "the heresy of *The Didactic*") but "solely for the poem's sake" (*CW* 14:271–72)—which is for the sake of the poetic *effect*. And allegory is deprecated as subversive of this effect because, by "psychal necessity," it disturbs the reader's "elevation" by demanding that "improper" connections be made between text and world, since it appeals to "our sense of adaptation . . . of the real with the unreal" (*CW* 13:148).

Both allegory and reference mark the belatedness of language, the temporal priority of the referent, and their rejection is a rejection of time; Poe's conception of poetic effect requires the suppression of temporal movement. However, just as memory is crucial to the evocation of figures of absence, so time necessarily inhabits the (timeless) lyrical moment. Poe's notorious refutation of the "long poem"—at one point he calls such a poem "a paradox" (*CW* 11:107) and at another declares that "it does not exist" (*CW* 14:266)—is, in effect, an attempt to deny time in the language of a poem and in the act of reading. The poem, "if truly fulfilling the demands of the poetic sentiment, induces an exaltation of the soul which cannot be long sustained. All high excitements are necessarily transient" (*CW* 11:107). The tension between the point of time's suspension and what he elsewhere calls "time's *endurance*" is clear (*M* 99). The poem—which induces the "elevating excitement" in the reader—requires language, which is necessarily temporal. Poe tries to accommodate duration and suspension in his requirement that a "rhymed poem" must not "exceed in length what might be perused in an hour" (*CW* 11:106); in "The Poetic Principle," he allows only half an hour. After this reading time, he claims, "revulsion" sets in, destroys the "effect," and so renders the poem "no longer such" (*CW* 14:266). On the other hand, he recognizes that "a poem *too* brief may produce a vivid, but never an intense or enduring impression. . . . Without a certain duration or repetition of purpose—the soul is never deeply moved. There must be the dropping of water upon the rock" (*CW* 11:107).

Here, clearly, the lyrical moment is subverted by the impingement of time as repetition—just as, in "The Philosophy of Composition," it enters as *"refrain"* which "depends for its impression upon the force of monotone—both in sound and in thought," in which "the pleasure is deduced solely from the sense of identity—of repetition" (*CW* 14: 199). Implicitly, this "monotone" of "sound and thought" meets the criteria of the ideal sign—signifier and signified are naturally one. Yet in "The Raven," as in Poe's works generally, such a sign is revealed as a function of interpretive desire and, like the lyric moment it here epitomizes, as subject to the vicissitudes of interpretation. The "monotone" is actually empty of significance: it issues from a "non-reasoning creature capable of speech" and is filled only by the active interpretation of the listener-lover, who situates it in the context of his own narrative, varying its "application."[10] The narrator is trapped in his inability to recognize the essential emptiness of the word, "Nevermore." What seems to be a potential incursion of meaning from a supernal realm is significant only in the context of the lover's narrative of loss. As the "application" varies, the "repetition" is a repetition with a difference, which must inscribe the passage of time.[11] Poe denies reference because its fundamental belatedness would kill the purely lyrical moment of ecstatic loss. Yet the language of poetry—as all language—is necessarily temporal, and the suspension of its movement can be only the silence of speech or the erasure of the page.[12]

Poe's effacement of reference in service of his "intentional effect of vagueness" may be, as John F. Lynen has suggested, part of a strategy to depict "words ceasing to exist in the process of becoming what they mean."[13] According to Lynen, "a word is destroyed by the meaningfulness which makes it a word. . . . In becoming a word, it has already started to merge with the reality it signifies." Such a description, however, does not seem to accord with, for example, the resolute materiality of Poe's language, with its musical rhythms, bizarre rhymes, and occasional emphasis on the obviously scriptive character of his words. Indeed, it is less a matter of the words merging with any "reality" that they signify than it is one of their being freed from their conventional significance to yield meaning according to the nature of the interpretive act performed upon them. This concept of the intrinsically empty signifier, which, we shall see, recurs in Poe's tales, is consonant with the rhetoric of effect. The suppression of reference, dependent on the recognition of the arbitrary relationship between signifier and signified, shifts the site of meaning from the relationship between word and world to that between reader and text.

Yet this is not to say that for Poe the signifier is always empty. In fact, in his discussion of the language of truth, which he resolutely opposes to that of beauty, we encounter another aspect of language that resists the reader's easy passage from signifier to signified: that is, its irreducibly figurative nature. The language of truth, he writes, must be "perspicuous, precise, [and] terse"; it must be transparently referential. Poe recognizes that such a language must be drained of metaphor, but as he writes he betrays his awareness that this is impossible. Poe claims that "the demands of truth are severe. She has no sympathy with the myrtles. . . . To deck her in gay robes is to render her a harlot. It is but making her a flaunting paradox to wreathe her in gems and flowers" (*CW* 11:70). But as he does so, he is deliberately "flaunting paradox." He uses the traditional figures for the figures of rhetoric—"robes" and "flowers"—to offer the truth that denies figuration, particularly metaphor, to the language of truth. He calls attention to this himself when he claims to be descending *from* metaphor—one of the "inessentials"—to maintain the difference between poetry and truth. This, however, is only a gambit to disguise the more subdued but still inescapable metaphoricity of his "simple and direct" language: "He must be blind indeed. . . . He must be grossly wedded to conventionalism who . . . shall still attempt to reconcile the obstinate oils and waters of Poetry and Truth" (*CW* 11:70). The basic assumptions—with a respectable pedigree extending at least to Aristotle's *Rhetoric*—that language is a transparent representation of an independent, preexistent "real" world, and that metaphor is a decorative, somewhat meretricious surplus that can be removed without significantly affecting the matter to be communicated, here begin to be undone. And, as we shall see repeatedly in Poe's tales, one factor that resists the imposition of a single interpretation on any signifier is just this proliferating surplus of meaning in words.

Thus each category of Poe's opposition between poetic language and denotative language is subverted by its own terms. On the one hand,

Poe advocates a resolute nonreferentiality and suspension of temporality in the attempt to evoke "glimpses" of the supernal; but, as we have seen, this project can evoke only a felt absence and is always subject to the inexorable movement of time. On the other hand, he advocates a transparent, referential, nonfigurative language that effaces itself before the world; yet his very phrasing of such a proposition betrays his sense of its impossibility given the irreducibly figurative nature of language. Ostensibly, the language of truth is directed toward the real world in time, and the language of beauty is closed off from that world and directed—if it is "directed" at all in the same sense—outward toward the timeless supernal. Each, however, is thwarted by the nature of language itself.

Poe's tales, in effect, assume a middle ground, a site on which different ideas about the nature of language and its relationship to the world are explored and their limitations established. As subsequent chapters will show, the tales repeatedly worry the questions raised by interpretation, and these questions—frequently dramatized as a struggle for mastery over the letter (most obviously, as prior commentary has recognized, in "The Purloined Letter")—are necessarily implicated in the nature of language. It is a commonplace that the romantics attempted to escape from what Hans Aarsleff has called the "linguistic relativism," most fully and most influentially developed by Locke, the main proposition of which was that of the arbitrariness of the linguistic sign.[14] Put simply, romantics struggled to assert a motivated language—whether by etymological research to recover an original natural language in which name and thing named were one,[15] or by affirmation of faith in the power of the romantic symbol to allow access to an ultimate, unmediated, extralinguistic reality.[16] According to Taylor Stoehr, "Poe and his narrators are practitioners of word-magic. They believe that there is a natural (or supernatural) connection between the word and what it names—not merely a conventional semantic relationship."[17] The casual linkage of "Poe and his narrators" should give us pause—particularly given the distance between them clearly established by commentators such as James W. Gargano[18]—and, as we shall see, when Poe entertains the possibility of the ideal sign he presents it as a function of interpretive desire. Those narrators who turn to the symbol as offering access to absolute being discover in it the disjunction between signifier and signified that they yearn to escape. They inhabit a world of signifiers that offer immediate access to neither extralinguistic reality, originating author, nor transcendental realm.[19]

So when Poe writes, in "Al Aaraaf" (1829), that "Ours is a world of words: Quiet we call / 'Silence'—which is the merest word of all" (*P* 104, ll. 126–27), we can take him quite literally. The act of naming the absence of sound displaces that which it names—quiet is broken by "Quiet"; and each further attempt—for example, " 'Silence' "—compounds the displacement as names name other names in an open-ended series of substitutions. According to this emphasis, the word "merest" carries with it the sense of boundary beyond which we cannot go, just as the "grave," as we have seen, marks the limit of knowledge.

In the course of his argument that Poe believed in "language as a means to transcendence," Stoehr cites at length an 1846 "Marginalia" entry on "the power of words."[20] Here Poe notes, "How very commonly we hear it remarked, that such and such thoughts are beyond the compass of words!" (*M* 98). On the contrary, he asserts, "I do not believe that any thought, properly so called, is out of the reach of language." Moreover, he goes on to assert his "faith in the *power of words*" to embody even "a class of fancies . . . [that] arise in the soul (alas, how rarely!) only at its epochs of most intense tranquility . . . and at those mere points of time where the confines of the waking world blend with those of the world of dreams" (*M* 100, 98–99). Such "fancies" occurring in the marginal state between waking and sleeping he seems to regard as crossing the margin between "Human Nature" and the "supernal"; they are "visions" of "the spirit's outer world." Stoehr's contention is that such visions do fall within "the compass of words," but rather different conclusions may be drawn from this passage.

First, Poe acknowledges that "thought, properly so called," is necessarily implicated in language: "I have never had a thought which I could not set down in words, with even more distinctness than that with which I conceived it:—as I have before observed, the thought is logicalized by the effort at (written) expression" (*M* 98). Writing, he in this way suggests, is not a merely secondary activity offering transparent access to prior thought, but itself is a shaper of thought, which, once written, becomes something different from the original "conception of the brain." Before the fancies can even be available to undergo such a displacement, they must be subjected to an even more radical series of transformations. They exist "but for an inappreciable *point* of time"; but for "absolute *thought* there is demanded time's *endurance*" (*M* 99). Consequently, Poe writes, he must "startle myself from the point into wakefulness—*and thus transfer the point itself into the realm of Memory*—convey its impressions, or more properly their recollections, to a situation where (although still for a very brief period) I can survey them with the eye of analysis" (*M* 100). Displaced into memory, into time, their essential nature is distorted, and though Poe writes that he does "not altogether despair of embodying in words at least enough of the fancies in question to convey . . . a shadowy conception of their character," his terms betray him (*M* 100). He will be offering only a "shadowy conception" of "shadows of shadows" (*M* 99)— an appropriate phrasing for the potentially endless displacements from any original point. Any "form, consequence, [or] precision" such a conception might have will be a product of the "act of indicting" itself rather than its relationship to the "fancies." In using this latter term, Poe effectively destroys his own argument for the power of words: "I use the word *fancies* at random, and merely because I must use *some* word; but the idea commonly attached to the term is not even remotely applicable to the shadows of shadows in question" (*M* 99). He subsequently foregrounds his terms by quotation marks—"I am aware of these 'fancies' . . . crowded with these 'shadows of shadows' "—and so underscores the interrelationship of language rather than its referential relationship to any prior "glimpse of the spirit's outer world" (*M* 99).

That Poe's interrogation of the power of words is not a naive celebration of "word magic," whereby a lost presence is recuperated in the "talismanic word,"[21] is evident in the so-called angelic dialogues. "The Conversation of Eiros and Charmion" (1839) is—according to the 1843 title—a dialogue "between two Departed Spirits" in the realm of Aidenn. This is that putative realm of "glories beyond the grave" (*CW* 14:273–74), for which, according to Poe's poetics, man yearns in exquisite earthly frustration. Here, "senses are bewildered . . . with the keenness of their perception of *the new*," and the hitherto "unknown" is now "known" (*TS* 456). This, then, is a visionary realm of new perception, free of earthly constraints; but its precise nature escapes the tale—reserved as it is for discussion "tomorrow" (*TS* 455, 456). Just as the term "conversation"—a familiar, even decorous naming of an angelic exchange—contains within itself the "converse" [L. *conversus*, turned about, transformed], so this angelic dialogue is concerned, can *only* be concerned, with the "world which has so fearfully perished" (*TS* 456).

Eiros's account of this destruction traces the movement toward an ideal absolute identity between a text—"passages in the most holy writings" (*TS* 457)—and the world. As this critical moment of identity approaches, the conventional interpretive strategies of men collapse: "We could no longer apply to the strange orb any *accustomed* thoughts. Its *historical* attributes had disappeared" (*TS* 459). As the comet violates the conventional structures of meaning, so it is interpreted in terms of effect—"It oppressed us with a hideous *novelty* of emotion"— that can be signified only metaphorically: "We saw it not as an astronomical phenomenon in the heavens, but as an incubus upon our hearts, and a shadow upon our brains" (*TS* 459). The climactic moment is that of absolute identity between word and world, signifier and signified: "the entire fulfillment . . . of the fiery and horror-inspiring denunciations of the prophesies of the Holy Book" (*TS* 461). This moment is the ironic consummation of romantic desires for a natural signification: the world is destroyed at the moment when word and world become one; and that moment also kills any angelic language—since for that "surpassing brilliancy and all-fervid heat even the angels in the high Heaven of pure knowledge have no name" (*TS* 461).

Charmion's request prompting this account—"Let us converse of familiar things, in the old familiar language of the world which has so fearfully perished" (*TS* 456)—is more than just an awkward device to justify the angels talking in English. On the one hand, in a strategy reminiscent of the "mere household events" of "The Black Cat" (*TS* 849), the distance between "familiar things" and the subsequent narration is staggering; yet the near-parallelism between "familiar things . . . familiar language . . . fearfully perished" suggests that the death of the world should in some way *be* "familiar." The implications of this are hinted at by the initial act of renaming that figures the spirits' transfiguration. According to Charmion, they must "forget" their "earthly name[s]" and speak to each other "henceforth . . . as" Eiros and Charmion (*TS* 455).[22] These angelic names are as arbitrary as their earthly counterparts, signifying only by mutual agreement. And it is this lack of motivation to the word, its displacement from its object that, on one level, is the topic of Eiros's discourse. Just as the absolute identity of word and world is the dissolution of both, so the "familiar language" of convention always has as its occasion the "death" of the world, since the latter can be figured only as that which is absent and irrecoverable.[23]

Poe's second angelic dialogue, "The Power of Words" (1845), explores the contrary possibility: that displacement from the world in effect allows the power of language to "create" new "worlds," although the terms themselves are heavily qualified. Like the "Conversation," this dialogue has "a guide and a follower—a mediator and a questioner,"[24] is conducted in "earth's familiar tones" (*TS* 1212), and is posited on the recent destruction of "the fair Earth" (*TS* 1215). The climactic passages are remarkable, and should be quoted in full:

> *Oinos.*—But why, Agathos, do you weep—and why, oh why do your wings droop as we hover above this fair star—which is the greenest and yet most terrible of all we have encountered in our flight? Its brilliant flowers look like a fairy dream—but its fierce volcanoes like the passions of a turbulent heart.
>
> *Agathos.*—They *are!*—they *are!* This wild star—it is now three centuries since, with clasped hands, and with streaming eyes, at the feet of my beloved—I spoke it—with a few passionate sentences—into birth. Its brilliant flowers *are* the dearest of all unfulfilled dreams, and its raging volcanoes *are* the passions of the most turbulent and unhallowed of hearts. (*TS* 1215)

The precise circumstances under which Agathos spoke his "passionate sentences" are unclear: perhaps they were uttered in the throes of frustrated sexual desire, but it is far more likely—because more consistent with Poe's poetics—that they were prompted by that "most poetical topic in the world," the "death . . . of a beautiful woman" (*CW* 14:201). It is usually assumed that Agathos "created" the star as angel, but if we bear in mind the fact of his "unfulfilled dreams" as we recall that both here and in the "Conversation" we are told that "there are *no* dreams in Aidenn" (*TS* 1212), it is probable that he was an "earthly" poet at the time. This would seem to be confirmed by his assertion that his "passions" were decidedly secular.

At first reading, this passage appears to offer a somewhat eccentric account of pure origination, in which an extreme version of the romantic dream of the purely literal word has been realized. Stoehr takes Agathos's assertions at face value and suggests that "this power depends somehow on the physical nature of the words themselves . . . their particular sound or look is intimately related to the characteristics of the thing they name."[25] However, a closer examination suggests that, rather than endorsing such an idea, Poe is merely entertaining it for examination. The literal *"power of words"* must not be taken too literally.

The straight reading must assume that the shift away from Oinos's similes—"like a fairy dream . . . like the passions"—is a shift to identity, marked by Agathos's insistence that "they *are!*—they *are!*" And yet—on a very obvious level—they are not. Agathos articulated his "unfulfilled dreams," not "flowers"; he spoke of his "unhallowed" passions, not "volcanoes." "Flowers" and "volcanoes" are figures— "flowers of rhetoric," if anything—in which he uttered his dreams and passions. They have become material in the way that the words of a text assume materiality—a condition emphasized here by the italics of *"are . . . are."* And this materiality is one mark of their existence independent of their author. Moreover, they remain resolutely figurative. Agathos, an author encountering his text, which has drifted independently through time, can only *assert* the identity of his "dreams . . . passions" and his words. His drooping wings are both a sign of his memory of their occasion and a sign of authorial anxiety—hence his attempt to reestablish the integrity of his connection with his creation. His assertion, however, must remain an assertion, since each new interpreter will, like Oinos, have to read his text figuratively in terms of "like" rather than *"are! . . . are!"*

A further qualification of Agathos's origination is offered by his earlier account of "the modes or . . . the methods of what, during mortality, we were accustomed to call Creation" (*TS* 1213). The Deity, he tells Oinos, "does not create," since "in the beginning *only,* he created," when "the first word spoke into existence the first law." The universe is a text whose author is irrecoverably absent. Those present instances that have "the *appearance* of creation" are in fact always "mediate" or "secondary"; by implication, man's "creations" are at most secondary, perhaps tertiary. Agathos's creation is, in Joseph Riddel's terms, "a figure of a figure . . . a mocking sign of the absence that is angelic or poetic repetition."[26]

Rather than offer a romantic complaint that the arbitrary nature of language renders it inadequate to "mystic" insight into the supernal realm, Poe implicitly closes off that realm. The very existence of what, in the 1848 "Marginalia" entry, he calls the "shadows of shadows in question" is radically in question. In an 1844 letter to James Russell Lowell, Poe suggests that the terms used to evoke the supernal are "*mere* word[s]": "I have no belief in spirituality. I think the word a *mere* word"; and, he adds, in terms reminiscent of his definition of imagination, "No one has really a conception of spirit. We cannot imagine what is not" (*L* 257). As Michael Davitt Bell has observed, just as Poe reduces spirit to matter, so he denies the existence of any "other" realm.[27] In *Eureka* (1848), Poe comments on "that merest of words, 'Infinity' ": "This, like 'God,' 'spirit,' and some other expressions of which the equivalents exist in nearly all languages, is by no means the expression of an idea—but of an effort at one. It stands for the possible attempt at an impossible conception" (*EAP* 1272). It points out the "*direction*" of man's effort, but its "*object*" is "forever invisible"; "Infinity" is thus a word "representative but of the *thought of a thought.*"

Moreover, he subsequently offers an analogy that, in effect, textualizes the universe: "In the construction of *plot,* for example, in fictitious literature, we should aim at so arranging the incidents that we shall not be able to determine, of any one of them, whether it depends from any one other or upholds it. In this sense, of course, *perfection* of plot is really, or practically, unattainable—but only because it is a finite intelligence that constructs. The plots of God are perfect. The Universe is a plot of God" (*EAP* 1342). The "plot of God" is inimitable and, as we have seen in the case of "The Power of Words," this condemns the plots of man to perpetual inadequacy to it. Ironically, since *Eureka* is a self-proclaimed "Art-Product" or "Poem," it thus denies its own adequacy even as it proclaims itself a "Book of Truths" (*EAP* 1259). More than this, however, as Joseph Riddel suggests, "the 'plot' of God is already a metaphysical or aesthetic concept, a kind of primary metaphor which is already an order of language. What lies behind or before the 'plot'—either God, unity, or nothingness—turns out itself to be a figural name for the non-figural."[28] Considered as "but the most sublime of poems" (*EAP* 1349), the universe enacts an absolute displacement from any originating act or divine authority. It is an empty signifier, representing the absence implicit in all representation and subject, like *Eureka* itself, to interpretation and reinterpretation. In this light we can make additional sense out of G. R. Thompson's statement that *Eureka* is "an elaborate art structure, which, like the Universe it describes, refers ultimately to nothing outside itself but the Nothing outside itself."[29]

II

"The Personage in Question": Self and Language

The "selves" that inhabit Poe's tales are fundamentally equivocal. His tales place in question the primary assumption of a unified self that lay behind Common-Sense philosophy, which, as Terence Martin has shown, permeated American intellectual discussion in the early nineteenth century.[1] Alarmed by the threat of solipsism that they perceived to be inherent in the metaphysical skepticism of Berkeley and, more particularly, Hume, and by the collapse of religious and moral values which they believed would be its consequence, Scottish Common-Sense philosophers attempted to provide a ground for the self's existence and its ability to achieve objective knowledge of the world. The two most influential representatives of this school, James Beattie and Thomas Reid, asserted that the self, as it responds to its perceptions, knows intuitively that it is itself real and unchanging, and that it is surrounded by a significant world. That is, perception is an act of valid belief in the reality of both subject and object.[2] The self is a unified, continuous, and responsible structure; in Reid's words:

All mankind place their personality in something that cannot be divided, or consist of parts. A part of a person is a manifest absurdity. . . . A person is something indivisible, and is what Leibnitz calls a *monad*.

My personal identity, therefore, implies the continued existence of that indivisible thing which I call myself. . . . I am something that thinks, and acts, and suffers . . . ; that *self* or *I* . . . is permanent.

The identity of a person is a perfect identity; wherever it is real, it admits of no degrees; and it is impossible that a person should be in part the same, and in part different, because a person is a *monad* and is not divisible into parts.[3]

The images of identity found in Poe's tales are quite different—fragmented or doubled rather than "indivisible," haunted by difference in time rather than "continuous," and sometimes incoherent rather than coherent. And always the question of personal identity is implicated in the ambiguities of the relationship between self and language, and the directly related issue of the fate of a self once it becomes written in the language of its text. Some tales are more explicit and literal than others in their line of attack on the assumption of a stable, essential self, but the interrogation of personal identity recurs consistently, regardless of any identifiable dominant mode—in the comic and satiric tales as well as in those apparently serious. The abrupt disassembly of body parts in, for example, "The Man That Was Used Up," the possibility of perfect repetition implicit in the concept of metempsychosis in "Morella," the frightening entertainment of an alien self in "The Imp of the Perverse," and the much-remarked motif of the doubled self in tales like "William Wilson"—all disturb that most fundamental and stubbornly-held conviction of the unity and stability of personal identity.

"A Predicament" and *"The Man That Was Used Up"*: The Body in Question

Bodies come apart quite frequently in Poe's comic tales—a process often unattended by the usual inconveniences. In "Never Bet the Devil Your Head: A Tale with a Moral" (1841), for example, Toby Dammit is an inveterate gambler whose favorite expression is *"I'll bet the Devil my head*" (*TS* 624); he loses both his bet and his head when he wagers a "little lame old gentleman" in black that he can "pigeon-wing" over a stile on a covered bridge (*TS* 627). He reckons without an iron bar hidden in the shadows above the stile, and his severed head is carried off by the devil, after which, according to the narrator, "he did not long survive his terrible loss." He dies, however, not because he happens to have no head, but because "the homoeopathists did not give him little enough physic, and what little they did give him he hesitated to take. So in the end he grew worse, and at length died, a lesson to all riotous livers" (*TS* 631).[4] In the course of offering an obvious burlesque of didactic fiction—here the moral tag is, naturally, "Never Bet the Devil Your Head"—the tale also plays with the relationship between language and the speaking self. The central event involves the literalization of a figure of speech—"*I'll bet the Devil my head*"—which, once uttered, invokes the decapitation of the subject. Thus, albeit crudely, the tale humorously illustrates what Poe elsewhere asserts: that "words . . . are murderous things" (*M* 81).

Dismemberment is often enough related to language in Poe's tales to suggest the possibility that fragmentation and, conversely, unity of character can be known only as effects of language rather than as preexistent conditions for it. The Signora Psyche Zenobia, in her tale "A Predicament" (the inset story of "How to Write a Blackwood Article" of 1838) undergoes a crisis of personal identity that is already potential in the distinction between "I" and the implicit possessive of "myself."[5] Having benefited from the advice of Mr. Blackwood—in itself a humorous depiction of the conventions of sensationalist writing—Psyche Zenobia searches for "such a scrape as no one ever got into before," one "adequate to the intensity of [her] feelings" (*TS* 340, 347). Having climbed a cathedral tower, she puts her head through "an opening in the dial-plate of a gigantic clock" to obtain a view of "the goodly city of Edina" (*TS* 352, 347). The "huge, glittering, scimitar-like minute-hand of the clock" gradually severs her head, teaching her "the literal import" of the phrase, the "*Scythe of Time*" (*TS* 353, 354). Undaunted, she provides a record of her sensations throughout the process.

At this point, Signora Psyche Zenobia's fate seems to offer a comic refutation of Thomas Reid's assertion that "a person is something indivisible, and is what Leibnitz calls a *monad*." Part of his argument is that amputation of a limb does not affect the identity of the person who endures it: "The amputated member is no part of his person, otherwise it would have a right to a part of his estate and be liable for a part of his engagements; it would be entitled to a share of his merit and de-merit" (Reid 203). The humorous suggestion that an amputated "part" might claim power over the "person" is taken up in "A Predicament." As the clock hand gradually increases "the cruel pressure" on her neck, one of Psyche's eyes pops out of her head and "lodged in the rain gut-ter which ran along the eaves of the main building" (*TS* 354, 355). She objects less to the actual loss of the eye than she does to its behav-ior—to "the insolent air of independence and contempt with which it regarded me after it was out." Indeed, the eye seems to have an inde-pendent existence in which, rather than be winked by her, it now has the power to make *her* wink:

> There it lay in the gutter just under my nose, and the airs it gave itself would have been ridiculous had they not been disgusting. Such a winking and blinking were never before seen. This behav-ior on the part of my eye in the gutter was not only irritating on account of its manifest insolence and shameful ingratitude, but was also exceedingly inconvenient on account of the sympathy which always exists between two eyes of the same head, however far apart. I was forced, in a manner, to wink and to blink, whether I would or not, in exact concert with the scoundrelly thing that lay just under my nose. (*TS* 355)

Only when her second eye drops out is she released from the control of her first. Even so, she is "not sorry to see the head which had occa-sioned me so much embarrassment . . . make a final separation from my body." Senses and body parts are now so dispersed and confused that it is no surprise that her sense of "selfhood" is uncertain: "I will candidly confess that my feelings were now of the most singular—nay of the most mysterious, the most perplexing and incomprehensible char-acter. My senses were here and there at one and the same moment. With my head I imagined, at one time, that I the head, was the real Signora Psyche Zenobia—at another I felt convinced that myself, the body, was the proper identity" (*TS* 355–56).

In these humorous tales, according to Edward Davidson, Poe "ridiculed what were later to be his most reasoned ideas of art."[6] G. R. Thompson traces more systematically Poe's "habitual mode of composition, the shift to opposites," whereby he burlesques his own compositional technique.[7] Certainly such self-consciousness reveals Poe's ironic distance from and an acute awareness of the fictionality of his own work. Furthermore, these tales explore crucial questions that permeate Poe's texts, regardless of how they are classified by those interested in such arrangements—arabesque, grotesque, comic, satiric, Gothic, burlesque, melodramatic, or hoaxical. In "A Predicament," for example, the unfortunate Psyche Zenobia confronts one of the classic issues of the problem of personal identity—that of the mind-body split. When the doubled Psyche Zenobia asserts that her feelings were "singular," there is surely no need to justify the reading of a pun in such a text. Her singularity is equivocal, since her "senses were here and there at one and the same moment"; moreover, the term collapses the temporal process by which her consciousness of her "proper identity" moves back and forth between body and head from one moment to another. Her predicament literalizes the distinction implied by language, in which a subject "I" can refer possessively to "myself'" as it can to "my head." The tale does not resolve the confusion, but the narrative point of view stays with "myself the body" as it extricates itself from the hole, impossibly retaining faculties of sight and hearing. Identity is implicitly only a narrative effect rather than a validating authority: the self, appropriately enough in a tale that foregrounds the "creation" of a literary persona, is only the written self diffused throughout the text, which, at best, offers only the temporary effect of singularity.

Another, related question is posed by the case of corporeal reduction. By how much can the material body be diminished, how many limbs and organs can be removed, before personal identity is altered or lost? In "The Man That Was Used Up" (1839), this question is raised in the context of the disjunction between a public identity created by a combination of "personal appearance" and gossip, and a personal identity made ambiguous by corporeal reduction.

The tale has been read as a satire directed at the contemporary enthusiasm for the gadgets of the mechanical age, an attack on the mindless celebrity worship of the "mob," and as a dismantling of either Vice President Richard M. Johnson or Brevet Brigadier General Winfield Scott.[8] Jonathan Auerbach has suggested that Poe "literaliz[es] the image of the self-made man" to show the degree to which such a figure "depend[s] on the public at large for his identity"; moreover, that as "a disposable commodity consumed by the public, the figure of the self-made man in fact serves to image the writer's own status in society."[9] Certainly, Auerbach's suggestion holds good, especially given Poe's repeated use of the then-common expression "to use up" to refer to reviewers' hatchet jobs on works they disliked;[10] Poe himself was accused by his rivals of being a "tomahawker," all "cutting and slashing." The *New Yorker* likened him to an Indian who "cannot realize that an enemy is conquered till he is scalped."[11]

This tale, in a movement quite typical of Poe's work, begins with the perception of an "appearance of mystery" (*TS* 378) and recounts the narrator's attempt to penetrate it. Here, the "mystery" is afforded by "that truly fine-looking fellow, Brevet Brigadier General John A. B. C. Smith," whose "presence" conveys a "*remarkable* something" for which the narrator strives to account (*TS* 378, 380). He makes a series of inquiries among his acquaintances—all of which, after cryptic encomia, are interrupted at the crucial point, "why, you know, he's the man—" (*TS* 382, 384, 385, 386). In frustration, he resolves to "go to the fountain-head," to visit the General and "demand, in explicit terms, a solution of this abominable piece of mystery" (*TS* 386). He discovers the General "dressing." Or, rather, he discovers an "odd-looking bundle of something" that squeaks the protest "I really believe you don't know me at all" (*TS* 386, 387). Gradually, as the "nondescript," with the aid of a "body servant," fits on in turn cork leg, arm, shoulders and bosom, wig, teeth, eye, and palate, it transfigures itself into the General—now the prosthetic man, "*the man that was used up*" (*TS* 389).[12]

Such a summary makes it clear that on one level the tale raises questions about the nature both of personal identity and of its status in the text.[13] Is the "odd-looking bundle of something" the General? Is the General merely a combined creation of artifice and gossip? The narrator begins by reciting a series of stock phrases that emphasize his assumption of the essential unity of the General's character: "There was something . . . remarkable . . . about the entire *individuality* of the *personage* in question. He was . . . of a *presence singularly* commanding. There was an *air distingué* [Poe's italics] pervading the *whole man*" (*TS* 378; emphasis mine). The narrator assumes that the unity of effect is motivated by a unity of essence; of course, he discovers instead that it is a product of the careful combination of elements which have already been "admirably modelled" (*TS* 379). In fact, the General is more artifact than man (a nomination that, as we shall see, itself causes problems for the narrator), and can be regarded as a parodic figure for the work of the poet—"combinations . . . *of those combinations which our predecessors . . . have already set in order,*" as Poe puts it in his 1842 review of Longfellow (*CW* 11:73). The implication that artistic creation is always a form of quotation is revealed in the narrator's wish that his "young and talented friend, Chiponchipino, the sculptor, had but seen the [General's] legs" (*TS* 380); presumably the sculptor would have delighted in such a model. But, of course, the convention that art imitates life is here ironized; the proposed original is already a copy modeled to surpass "the marble Apollo" (*TS* 379).

As the appalled narrator watches the transfiguration of the "nondescript" into the "General," he also hears a commentary on each device, so that the corporeal reassembly is paralleled by the reassembly (or glossing) of that public self that is the product of gossip. There is, the narrator admits, "a striking difference in the appearance of the personal man" (*TS* 388), but the very concept of the "personal man" has been disturbed by his discovery. Even the General's voice—that which crosses the boundary between inside and outside and is conventionally associated with the self—resumes its "clearness, melody, and strength" only by courtesy of a "somewhat singular-looking machine" (*TS* 379, 388).

The General is "remarkable" not only in his being composed of exquisite parts but also in his being the occasion for remarks; indeed, he is also composed of the fragments of gossip that, as Auerbach suggests, have created this "self-made" hero of the age. The same conventional phrases are repeated—"prodigies of valor," "terrible wretches," and (giving the lie to itself) "This is a wonderfully inventive age!"—in what we might call a mechanical process of image production.

The fragmentation of the General is also a literalization of his fate in the narrator's description of him. The temporality of language prevents any simultaneous apprehension of wholes; he must be described piece by piece. In fact, his condition literalizes the fate of all assumed independent unified identities in Poe's fiction as narrators strive to recuperate them in language that necessarily marks their dis-unity. Like Ligeia, they are recovered only as elements articulated by and through inherited cultural codes.[14] The problem of identity is, then, bound up in the problem of signification. In "The Man That Was Used Up," the narrator's attitude toward the sign is fundamentally conservative. At the outset he notes that the General's appearance "spoke of high breeding, and hinted at high birth" (*TS* 378); his emphasis on "breeding" and "birth" is obviously socially conservative, assuming a "natural" order of hierarchical relationships. But this reading also assumes a natural hierarchical relationship between signifier and signified, whereby the former is necessarily motivated by the latter and effaces itself in its favor. Furthermore, any disruptive element that might interfere with the reader's passage from one to the other—any ambiguity or "mystery"—can be readily cleared up by investigation which will yield "perfect understanding" (*TS* 389). What his search yields, however, is a "full comprehension" only of the arbitrary and artificial conventions by which significance is created; he discovers that these "natural" signs are symptoms of mechanical contrivance.

Although at the outset the narrator qualifies the word "remarkable" with the demurral, "this is but a feeble term to express my full meaning" (*TS* 378), his quest indicates his belief that a postulated unity of essence can be expressed in "explicit terms" (*TS* 386)—terms that signify distinctly neither more nor less than, from the narrator's point of view, they should. Yet his main difficulty is the surplus of meaning that is characteristic of language; he cannot escape "equivocation," whereby the same word changes meaning, carries various meanings with it into different contexts. To whom or what does "General" refer? To the "personal appearance" described so methodically? To the "nondescript," which escapes classification? Or to an indeterminate point somewhere between at which one becomes the other? One of the functions of the series of interrupted statements ("he's the man—") is to illustrate the possible range of "equivocation" in the word "man," in which figurative expression, general statement, proper name, and literary reference all lurk, and which come into play as the narrator tries to fix the word to the General and dissolve the mystery.

"Morella": *"too perfect* identity"

"Equivocation"—whereby one word signifies (at least) doubly—is also crucial to "Morella" (1835), in which the narrator's predicament turns on the double reference of the name "Morella," and the potentially endless equivocation inherent in the assertion, "I am here." This tale is one of several in which Poe employs the concept of metempsychosis to examine the puzzling nature of personal identity.[15] Clearly, the apparent translation of a "self" from one body into another must raise questions about the nature of that self and its conditions of existence—its *principium individuationis*" (*TS* 231). The narrator of "Morella" recounts the apparent transmigration of the identity of his dead wife, the formidably erudite Morella, into the body of their daughter, "to which in dying she had given birth" (*TS* 233). Although he had not loved Morella, he does love their daughter—despite his fascinated horror at her "perfect resemblance" to his dead wife. For ten years he cannot bring himself to give her a name, but eventually comes to believe that the "ceremony of baptism" might deliver him from what he calls "the terrors of my destiny" (*TS* 235). At the baptismal font, however, some "fiend" within him prompts him to name his daughter "Morella," upon which she collapses, responds "I am here," and dies.

It has been suggested that the narrator may be mad, that he may even have murdered both wife and daughter.[16] Certainly the status of his account of the duplication of Morella is rendered highly ambiguous, for he writes in the grip of an obsession he describes in his final paragraph: "The earth grew dark, and its figures passed by me, like flitting shadows, and among them all I beheld only—Morella. The winds of the firmament breathed but one sound within my ears, and the ripples upon the sea murmured evermore—Morella" (*TS* 236). So "Morella," which, on one level, contains an account of the development of the narrator's fixation, may just as well be a product of it. More is involved, however, than the question of the narrator's relative madness or sanity: the tale investigates the very idea of a self on which such judgments may be passed.

The narrator's account is punctuated by a series of moments that mark sudden reversals of his mood—characteristically from joy to fear—prompted by his approach to a "forbidden" knowledge. His study of "forbidden pages" enkindled in him a "forbidden spirit," and

Morella's musical voice "rake[d] up from the ashes of a dead philosophy some low, singular words, whose strange meaning burned themselves in upon my memory" (TS 230). The combination is at first
seductive, but then "joy suddenly faded into horror, and the most beautiful became the most hideous, as Hinnom became GeHenna." This
reversal foreshadows his sudden alienation from his wife—"the time
had now arrived when the mystery of my wife's manner oppressed me
as a spell" (TS 231)—and subsequently from his daughter—"the
heaven of this pure affection became darkened, and gloom, and horror,
and grief, swept over it in clouds" (TS 233). The last two cases offer a
suggestion as to the source of his fear. As Morella pined away, he notes,
he would feel pity for "an instant," but then "I met the glance of her
meaning eyes, and then my soul sickened and became giddy with the
giddiness of one who gazes downward into some dreary and unfathomable abyss" (TS 231–32); and of his daughter he writes: "That her
eyes were like Morella's I could endure; but then they too often looked
down into the depths of my soul with Morella's own intense and be-
wildering meaning" (TS 234). These two gazes locate his concern; we
do not need the obvious pun on I/eye, which recurs so frequently in
Poe's texts, to note that his terror is prompted by the abyss that opens
in the self once its sense of personal identity is displaced.

When the narrator recounts that he "abandoned [him]self" to his
studies, he is offering a literal as well as figurative statement (TS 230).
But what is this "self" that he deserts as he enters "the intricacies of
[Morella's] studies"? As he describes the way he came to a decision,
he implies that he took a level-headed, commonsense approach to his
work by asserting that he began only after he was "persuaded" that
"my convictions . . . were in no manner acted upon by the ideal, nor
was any tincture of mysticism . . . to be discovered . . . either in my
deeds or in my thoughts" (TS 230).[17] Such a view of himself as a reasonable, independent entity able to reflect on his own thought processes
is grounded, we subsequently discover, in his subscription to a Lockean
view of personal identity: "That identity which is termed personal,
Mr. Locke, I think, truly defines to consist in the sameness of a rational
being. And since by person we understand an intelligent essence having
reason, and since there is a consciousness which always accompanies
thinking, it is this which makes us all to be that which we call ourselves—thereby distinguishing us from other beings that think, and

giving us our personal identity" (*TS* 231). The narrator's carefully modulated tone and the logical markers of his sentences parallel the emphasis such a definition places on rationality and on the distinctions it makes between mind and world and between one mind and another. His endorsement of Locke might underlie what Halliburton has called the narrator's lack of "volition," his passivity;[18] it might also account for his attempt to govern the development of his daughter's character by secluding her and watching "with an agonizing anxiety over all which concerned" her, so that she "received no impressions from the outward world save such as might have been afforded by the narrow limits of her privacy" (*TS* 234, 235). Just as this attempt apparently fails to halt the return of his wife in the body of his daughter, so his investment in a Lockean definition of personal identity founders as its limitations are explored.

In the chapter of *An Essay Concerning Human Understanding* from which the narrator draws his summary, Locke repeatedly emphasizes that "it is impossible to make personal Identity to consist in any thing but consciousness; or reach any further than it does."[19] The narrator of "Morella" also emphasizes "the consciousness which always accompanies thinking" as constituting "that which we call *ourselves*" (*TS* 231). Thus the self is equated with an act of self-reflection, an equation based on the assumption that the self's motives and thought processes are available to its own scrutiny. This assumption is seriously questioned in several ways. Most obviously, when the narrator offers his account of the self-analysis that preceded his entry into his wife's studies, he hedges it with self-betraying qualifications: "In all this, *if I err not*, my reason had little to do. My convictions, *or I forget myself*, were in no manner acted upon by the ideal, nor was any tincture of the mysticism which I read, to be discovered, *unless I am greatly mistaken*, either in my deeds or my thoughts" (*TS* 230; emphasis mine). On the one hand, these phrases depict the element of conscious self-examination, but more important, their uncertainty suggests the possibility of error. If consciousness or memory constitutes the self, then how secure is that self constituted by the recollection of false memories?[20] More alarming, when memory is effaced, "I [literally] forget myself" and am another. Locke suggests that any interruption of the duration of "the same continued consciousness" (Locke 346)—for example, in amnesia, madness, or drunkenness—marks a boundary between two

different selves: "If it be possible for the same Man to have distinct in-
communicable consciousness at different times, it is past doubt the same
Man would at different times make different Persons" (Locke 342). In
this definition of personal identity as self-reflection, anything that is not
available to the consciousness is exiled and considered as other than
the self.

The vulnerability of a self so defined is suggested in the opening
paragraph of "Morella," in which the narrator performs just such a
gesture of exclusion: from his first meeting with Morella, he writes,
"my soul . . . burned with fires it had never before known; but the
fires were not of Eros" (*TS* 229). He denies that these fires were
erotic, and yet he "could in no manner define their unusual meaning,
or regulate their vague intensity." Clearly a part of himself is not open
to analysis. Similarly, after he denies the influence of "the ideal" or of
"mysticism," he feels a "forbidden spirit enkindling" within him. It is
"forbidden" in the sense of being prohibited by the rational definition
of selfhood to which he holds. He has temporarily "abandoned [him]-
self" to his wife's studies, and these release within him forces that
threaten the dissolution of this reasonable self. His sudden shift from
"joy" to "horror," by which what he perceived to be "the most beautiful became the most hideous," is prompted by his realization that he
has entered a realm of irrational and potentially violent forces.

In his fear, the narrator characterizes this part of himself in demonic
terms. The biblical allusion—"as Hinnom became GeHenna" (*TS*
230)—is clarified by Thomas Hobbes's *Leviathan* (1651): Hinnom
was a valley where "the Jews had committed the most grievous idolatry,
sacrificing their children to the idol Moloch"; in punishment, Josiah
burnt the priests on their altars. Thereafter, the place was a dumping
ground for "filth and garbage," and "there used to be fires made, from
time to time, to purify the air and take away the stench of carrion"; it
became known as "the place of the damned . . . Gehenna . . . usually
now translated Hell; and from the fires . . . there burning, we have
the notion of everlasting and unquenchable fire."[21] The narrator's analogy reflects the association of reason and law (here divine law), and his
horrified recognition that his studies have led him into a region "forbidden" by and to the reason—an act of prohibition designed to secure
its control of the self. But as the narrative progresses, this control—
based on Locke's sanguine assumption that "when we see, hear, smell,

taste, feel, meditate, or will anything, we know that we do so" (Locke 335)—crumbles as a part of himself he terms "fiend" or "demon" asserts its power. He writes that he "longed with an earnest and consuming desire" for Morella's death until *"with the heart of a fiend,* [he] cursed the days, and the hours, and the bitter moments" that intervened (*TS* 232; emphasis mine). And in his account of the ceremony of baptism he asks: *"What prompted me,* then, to disturb the memory of the buried dead? What demon urged me* to breathe that sound, which, in its very recollection was wont to make ebb the purple blood in torrents from the temples to the heart? *What fiend spoke from the recesses of my soul,* when . . . I whispered . . . the syllables—Morella?" (*TS* 235; emphasis mine). Thus the coherence of his conscious self-reflection is violated by subconscious forces that his Lockean definition attempts but fails to exclude from the self. Moreover, as Martin Bickman has shown, Morella herself can be read as having "her ultimate origin in the narrator's own psyche,"[22] and whether we follow Bickman's Jungian reading or a Freudian reading, Morella's return as a return of the repressed clearly operates as a fundamental critique of the narrator's concept of the self.[23]

Even as the narrator's account introduces elements that subvert his concept of self, his reaction to Morella's apparent return indicates the degree of his investment in it. According to Locke, because "consciousness of [a] past Action" is not "the same individual Action" but "a present representation of a past Action," there is no reason why "one intellectual Substance may not have represented to it, as done by itself, what it never did." Therefore "it must be allowed, That if the same consciousness . . . can be transferr'd from one thinking Substance to another, it will be possible, that two thinking Substances may make but one Person. For the same consciousness being preserv'd . . . the personal Identity is preserv'd." Locke admits this as a logical possibility, but suggests that "it never is so," for reasons that are "best resolv'd into the Goodness of God," who will not "transfer from one to another, that consciousness, which draws Reward or Punishment with it" (Locke 338).

To the narrator of "Morella" it seems as if this possibility has become a reality. He claims that he is disturbed less by the "strange . . . rapid increase in [his daughter's] bodily size" than he is by his conviction that her consciousness, her "mental being," is not appropriate to her experience, and so must be that of the first Morella: "Could it be otherwise, when I daily discovered in the conceptions of the child the adult powers and faculties of the woman?—when the lessons of experience fell from the lips of infancy? and when the wisdom or the passions of maturity I found hourly gleaming from its full and speculative eye?" (*TS* 233, 234). The return of Morella's consciousness in the body of her daughter would seem to offer the narrator an optimistic prognosis of the survival of a personal essence apart from the individual body. What then is the source of his terror?

At first, he can accept the child's "perfect resemblance" to "her who had departed," but the phrase "*perfect* resemblance" (emphasis mine) augurs the collapse of the difference inherent in the concept of similitude. He is comfortable with the daughter's like-ness to his wife—he "could bear" that "her smile was like her mother's . . . that her eyes were like Morella's"—but he is horrified by their "too perfect *identity*" (*TS* 234). What seems to be at stake here is the narrator's claim to a discrete personal identity defined, in part, by its difference from "other beings that think" (*TS* 231). His fear at the apparent perfection of identity between mother and daughter is rooted in his recognition that such perfect repetition collapses the differences between selves and subsumes them into an identity of a different conceptual order. Among the forbidden texts that "burned themselves in upon [his] memory" and that prompted his "disquisitions" on "theological morality" with his wife were "above all, the doctrines of *Identity* as urged by Schelling" (*TS* 231). These doctrines, he says, presented "the most of beauty to the imaginative Morella." It is at this point in his account that he offers his summary of Locke, as if asserting his credo in the face of threat. Certainly Schelling attacked Locke as antiphilosophical, asserting that his empiricism, like that of Francis Bacon, attempted "to measure the unlimited by the limited, and to extend the finite into the infinite."[24] Schelling's "doctrines of *Identity*" are of a different order from the concept of personal identity to which the narrator subscribes. Schelling's idealism asserts not distinctions between individual selves, but the undifferentiated identity of all reality as it rises from the Absolute. The fate of personal identity under these "doctrines" is suggested by the narrator of "Loss of Breath" (1835), who concludes a description of his sensations upon being hanged with: "In a very short time Schelling himself would have been satisfied with my entire loss of self-identity" (*TS* 79).[25] The narrator of "Morella" fears the "too perfect *identity*" of his wife-daughter because it collapses the concept of personal identity based on differences between "intelligent essence[s]" in favor of this all-embracing absolute "*Identity*."

This all-consuming "*Identity*" recalls the "ONE" of the epigraph taken from Plato's *Symposium*—"Itself, by itself solely, ONE everlastingly, and single" (*TS* 229).[26] The very redundancy here evokes the disparity between the language of the contingent world and the "ONE" that is inexpressible or, in the words of H. N. Coleridge—Poe's source here—"what cannot be translated." This raises the crucial issue of the role of signification and its implications for the climactic act of naming. According to Taylor Stoehr, the narrator's speaking of the name "Morella" is the "utterance of the unutterable," whereby the name mystically produces its reference as consequence.[27] Undeniably, as well as being the title of the tale, the "syllables—Morella" are repeated throughout the narrative, most obviously in the deathbed scene and in the final paragraph, in hypnotic incantation. The narrator does seem to believe that name and identity are interrelated, that one is motivated by the other. Hence his decision to name his daughter at the baptismal font—to fix her identity as different from that of her mother and so to arrest the process of translation. Concomitantly, when the name Morella springs to his lips, his belief leads him to assume that naming magically evokes and confirms the self of Morella as the child. This concept of the name—in which signified motivates and is present as signifier—is integral to the romantic dream of the ideal sign and as such is one aspect of the absolute "*Identity*" that the narrator fears.

When discrete selves are collapsed and subsumed into the "ONE," so the differences upon which signification depends are also erased: the consciousness of Morella does not merely inhabit the new body, but transforms it into a perfect repetition of the first. In this allegory of the sign, the signifier is necessarily motivated by the signified, indeed is identical with it. If the Absolute motivates all signifiers, then distinctions between them collapse—all bodies become Morella's body—and the contingent world dissolves in perfect repetition of the same: "And I kept no reckoning of time or place, and the stars of my fate faded from heaven, and therefore the earth grew dark, and its figures passed by me, like flitting shadows, and among them all I beheld only—Morella. The winds of the firmament breathed but one sound within my ears, and the ripples upon the sea murmured evermore—Morella" (*TS* 236).

However, the world signifies only the name Morella as mark of her absence. According to James W. Gargano, Morella's name contains "the resonant Latin root for 'death' and . . . the last four letters constitute a diminutive."[28] Gargano suggests that Morella may be seen as "an embodiment in little of the universal principle of recurring death." Without disputing this idea, perhaps we can also observe that she is associated with the annihilation of the contingent world that is a function of the yearning for the "ONE," and also with the necessary belatedness of ordinary language, which is itself a kind of death—the death of the object. The "baptismal font" is hard by the "ancestral vault"; the daughter-wife is named and dies. It is no surprise that there are no "traces" of the first Morella in the "charnel," since the charnel is language itself.

Moreover, because the self, as we have seen, is never ideally present to itself, even speech marks an absence—it will always be "expressions of the dead on the lips of the . . . living" (*TS* 234–35). The wife-daughter dies as she utters "I am here"—so offering a figure for her necessary displacement by her speech. "I" and "here" are strongly associated with the presence supposedly inhering in speech, yet they exemplify the distance of language from it—their meanings change according to speaker and occasion, and once the "personal identity" of the speaker is in doubt they remain resolutely enigmatic; the interpreter can fall back, like the narrator, only on an interpretation of them based on subjective fears and desires.[29]

"The Imp of the Perverse": "I arrested myself"

The interpretive problem faced by the narrator of "Morella"—that of identifying the "I" who speaks—is clearly most acute once the assumption of a self-consistent essence in control of his or her own voice has been undercut. The "fiend" who inhabits and displaces the reflective subject in "Morella" reappears repeatedly in Poe's work but is named most directly—though still inadequately—in "The Black Cat" (1843) and "The Imp of the Perverse" (1845). These have been described as "confessional" tales but, as we shall see, the notion of confession as a revelation of what has hitherto been hidden, as revelation of a secret essential self, is disturbed by this "imp." In "The Imp of the Perverse," the assumption that there is a clear, direct relationship between subject and voice, a relationship that allows an interpreter to track the subject down to where it lurks behind his words, is shown to be an optimistic fiction. The final image of the tale, in which the voice speaks despite the subject, and in which utterance is identified with death, introduces elements that radically complicate the process of interpretation and render its findings insecure.[30]

In an account that, as Sandra Whipple Spanier demonstrates, "both explores and embodies paradox,"[31] the narrator of "The Imp of the Perverse" (1845) attacks those "intellectual" and "logical" investigations of the self—phrenology is his main example—which, through the "arrogance of . . . reason" have overlooked one "radical, primitive, irreducible sentiment" in man (*TS* 1219). He repeatedly emphasizes that this impulse is "radical," "primitive," and "elementary," and that it does not "admit of analysis, or resolution into ulterior elements" (*TS* 1221); moreover, it is self-originating—"a *mobile* without motive, a motive not *motivirt*" (*TS* 1220). His vocabulary is that of one who has uncovered an essence on which to ground a consistent definition of personal identity; indeed, he claims that "beyond or behind this, there is no intelligible principle" (*TS* 1223). But this *"primum mobile"* (*TS* 1219) is itself hardly "intelligible"—it is, in fact, "incomprehensible": "a paradoxical something, which we may call *perverseness,* for want of a more characteristic term" (*TS* 1220). It is that which urges us to "act, for the reason that we should not"; accordingly, "the assurance of the wrong or error of any action is often the one unconquerable *force* which impels us . . . to its prosecution" (*TS* 1220–21). And, as the narrator's examples and his own confession demonstrate, this one irreducible "radical" ground to the self is paradoxically the urge to destroy that self.

The narrator's examples all invoke an opposition between rational self-preservation and irrational, perverse self-annihilation. The self is the locus of violent "conflict" between "definite" and "indefinite," "substance" and "shadow" (*TS* 1222). Yet it is "reason" itself that generates its antagonist; when, on the "brink of a precipice . . . reason violently deters us from [it], *therefore,* do we the more impetuously approach it." In fact, "to indulge for a moment, in any attempt at *thought,* is to be inevitably lost; for reflection but urges us to forbear, and *therefore* it is, I say, that we cannot" (*TS* 1223).[32] The conflict, then, is not a clear opposition between separable terms, since self-preservation and rational "reflection" are implicated with their dark aspects, self-annihilation and perversity, which always accompany them.

The difficulty of teasing these contradictory aspects of the self apart is paralleled by the difficulty of distinguishing their manifestation in language. In his first illustration, the narrator offers what seems to be a clear distinction between the languages of reason and perversity:

> There lives no man who at some period has not been tormented, for example, by an earnest desire to tantalize a listener by circumlocution. The speaker is aware that he displeases; he has every intention to please; he is usually curt, precise, and clear; the most laconic and luminous language is struggling for utterance upon his tongue; it is only with difficulty that he restrains himself from giving it flow; he dreads and deprecates the anger of him whom he addresses; yet, the thought strikes him, that by certain involutions and parentheses, this anger may be engendered. That single thought is enough. The impulse increases to a wish, the wish to a desire, the desire to an uncontrollable longing, and the longing, (to the deep regret and mortification of the speaker, and in defiance of all consequences,) is indulged. (*TS* 1221–22)

The language of perversity is here prolific, offering endless "involutions and parentheses," while that of reason is "curt," "precise," "clear," "laconic," and "luminous." As Spanier has noted, in this passage the narrator "perversely practices [the] circumlocution" he describes.[33] Indeed, the whole first section of the narrative—the disquisition on perversity—is characterized by such delaying proliferation, and the narrator points to this as supporting his claim to be a "victim" of perversity: "Had I not been thus prolix, you might either have misunderstood me altogether, or, with the rabble, have fancied me mad. As it is [that is, since he *has* been prolix], you will easily perceive that I am one of the many uncounted victims of the Imp of the Perverse" (*TS* 1224).

However, his subsequent account of his confession characterizes the language of perversity quite differently. When the "long-imprisoned secret" of his crime "burst" out, he "spoke with a distinct enunciation, but with marked emphasis" in "brief but pregnant sentences" (*TS* 1226). These terms recall the clarity and brevity of the language of reason rather than the prolix expression of the perverse. Moreover, they characterize the language of the last section of the narrative in which the planning and the murder are described economically—"I need not vex you with impertinent details. I need not describe . . ." (*TS* 1224)—and the narrator's collapse from "absolute security" (*TS* 1224) to self-betrayal is recounted rapidly in sentences that could well be called "brief but pregnant."

So there are two parts to this narrative—the explanation and illustration of perversity, and the confessional tale of successful murder and perverse confession; the style of one is "prolix," that of the other "brief but pregnant," and in each case the language accuses itself of manifesting the perverse impulse. This sense of a double voice is appropriate to a narrative that depicts the disintegration of a self's "absolute security" by the uncontrollable eruption into speech of a repressed part of that self.

The different linguistic manifestations of the perverse, in which words escape the control of and ultimately efface the speaking subject, suggest the possibility that perverseness as self-annihilation is closely implicated with language itself. The written word occupies a crucial position in the murder, since the narrator derives his method from "some French memoirs" where he "found an account of a nearly fatal illness that occurred to Madame Pilau, through the agency of a candle accidentally poisoned." The text prompts his action and, ironically, another text is present as mute witness to its fruition, since the victim dies "reading in bed" (*TS* 1224). Just as the "memoirs" generate his action, so do words apparently independently proliferate in his mind and lead to his deadly confession. Just as, he says, the "burthen" of a song or "snatches from an opera" return unprompted and repeatedly to our memory, so "I would perpetually catch myself pondering upon my security, and repeating, in a low under-tone, the phrase, 'I am safe' " (*TS* 1225). His former reflection on his "absolute security" and the illusory stability of selfhood that it implies become a difference from himself in language—he would "catch [him]self"; and one day, he notes in a prophetic phrase, "*I arrested myself* in the act of murmuring, half-aloud, these customary syllables" (*TS* 1225; emphasis mine). In "petulance" he repeats and extends the phrase: "I am safe—I am safe—yes—if I be not fool enough to make open confession!" The utterance of "these words" in "self-suggestion" enfigures his potential self-annihilation; his language confronts him "as if the very ghost of

him whom I had murdered—and beckoned me on to death" (*TS* 1225).
In his fear he attempts to obliterate language—he wants "to shriek
aloud," wipe out thought, and tear out his tongue; but "then, some invisible fiend, I thought, struck me with his broad palm upon the back.
The long-imprisoned secret burst forth from my soul" (*TS* 1225, 1226).

Significantly, the narrator claims that at the point of utterance "I
experienced all the pangs of suffocation; I became blind, and deaf, and
giddy"; as he spoke he was not conscious of doing so (in retrospect he
can note only that "they say that I spoke"); and when he had finished
he "fell prostrate in a swoon." His confession guarantees his own death,
and his experience of annihilation as he speaks prefigures his double
extinction—that as a character at the hands of the "hangman," and
that as an author displaced by his other self in the language of his story.
For this reason the end of his account is doubly fitting: "Today I wear
these chains, and am *here*. To-morrow I shall be fetterless!—*but
where?*" (*TS* 1226).

"The Tell-Tale Heart" and "William Wilson": Doubled Selves

Like the tales of radical dismemberment, those in which a subject dis-
integrates under the pressure of his sensed inner difference from himself
introduce a fundamental uncertainty into considerations of personal
identity. In a third group of tales, selves are not internally split but
apparently duplicated in the external world. Since Patrick F. Quinn's
extended discussion of the *doppelgänger* motif in Poe's work, doubles
have been detected in many of the tales.[34] In "The Tell-Tale Heart"
(1843), for example, in which we confront "the mind watching itself
disintegrate under the stress of delusion in an alienated world,"[35] the
mad narrator protesting his sanity is, in Quinn's term, "intrinsicate"
with the old man that he kills and dismembers. His crime seems motive-
less: "Object there was none. Passion there was none. I loved the old
man. He had never wronged me. He had never given me insult. For his
gold I had no desire" (*TS* 792). He returns obsessively to the old man's
eye—"I think it was his eye! yes, it was this!"—which, resembling
that of a "vulture," made his blood run cold; "and so . . . I made up
my mind to take the life of the old man, and thus rid myself of the eye
forever" (*TS* 792). According to the standard interpretation of the

tale, the "vulture" eye of the old man identifies him with time, and in him the narrator is attempting, ironically, to kill his own subjection to time, his mortality.[36]

As the narrator recounts the events of the night of the murder and speculates on the old man's feelings of terror, it becomes clear that the two are antagonistic forces of a divided self. When the old man cries "Who's there?" he is answered by silence, and the narrator knows that "he was still sitting up in the bed, listening;—*just as I have done, night after night*" (*TS* 794; emphasis mine). Soon, the narrator hears a groan and, he claims: "I knew it was the groan of mortal terror. It was not a groan of pain or of grief—oh, no!—it was the low stifled sound that arises from the bottom of the soul when overcharged with awe. *I knew the sound well.* Many a night, just at midnight, when all the world slept, *it has welled up from my own bosom,* deepening with its dreadful echo, the terrors that distracted me. I say *I knew it well*" (*TS* 794; emphasis mine). The identification of their experience of terror is followed by the "hellish tattoo" of the heartbeat, which, despite the narrator's claim that it is the old man's, could just as well be his own.[37] It precipitates his attack and, as he leaps into the room, both murderer and victim scream—his "loud yell" intermingles with the old man's shriek. Later, when he tells the police that "the shriek . . . was my own in a dream" (*TS* 796), he confirms the interrelationship.

On one level, the narrator's obsession with the old man's "Evil Eye" prefigures his subsequent dismemberment of the "stone dead" corpse, since he separates this eye from the old man and seems to attribute to it an independent existence and power.[38] He cannot "do the work" while the eye is closed, because it is "not the old man" who vexes him, but the eye (*TS* 793). In accord with the intermingling of identity, however, the old man's "Evil Eye" is that part of the narrator's self that he fears—his own "I," sensed as other than himself and hence evil.[39] When he notes that "*I* made up my mind" to "rid my*self* of the *eye*" (*TS* 792; emphasis mine), his phrasing invokes that doubling of "I" and "myself" already noted in, for example, "A Predicament." The addition of the homophonic pun is entirely appropriate in a text that, as David Halliburton has observed, attempts to masquerade as voice.[40] Consequently, the narrator's description of the old man's eye— it is always singular—offers a glimmer of a motive for the murder which is also self-murder.

His first description—"a pale blue eye, with a film over it. Whenever it fell upon me, my blood ran cold" (*TS* 792)—implies that it is the eye in itself that terrifies. But his description of its appearance in the "single dim ray" of his lamp on the night of the murder makes it clear that it is the "film" or "hideous veil" that evokes his horror: "It was open—wide, wide open—and I grew furious as I gazed upon it. I saw it with perfect distinctness—all a dull blue, *with a hideous veil over it that chilled the very marrow in my bones*" (*TS* 795; emphasis mine). The "eye" is "open—wide, wide open," yet it offers only a "hideous veil," which resists the gaze of the "I." Paradoxically, the identification of "I" and "eye" implies that he fears and is enraged by that in himself that he cannot "read," or understand, or penetrate. The room "as black as pitch with the thick darkness" recalls the Lockean model of the mind as *"dark Room,"*[41] and figuratively the narrator's entry— "every night, just at twelve"[42]—is his self-reflective discovery of an enigmatic and resistant alien self within.

So in killing the old man the narrator is attempting to kill his sense of himself as other than himself. Obsessed with the enigma of his "I," he kills the "eye." Now, after the event, he insists on his own sanity and offers support for his conviction: "Madmen know nothing. But you should have seen *me*. You should have seen how wisely I proceeded— with what caution—with what foresight—with what dissimulation" (*TS* 792). His narrative reenacts the gesture of the murder—even as it recounts it—by attempting to deny a part of himself. Yet his clarity of self-knowledge is delusory, evidence only of that difference from himself that is his madness. And all through the narrative, in ironic counterpoint to his boasting of his success in killing the "eye," the pronoun "I" recurs—"I . . . I . . . I . . ."—twenty-seven times in the first three paragraphs alone.

The last tale to be discussed under this rubric of "the personage in question" is the most obvious of the double stories, "William Wilson" (1839). This tale clearly examines the problematic relationship between the aspirations of an assumed imperial will and its self-generated double. In so doing, however, it also locates one source of the undercurrent of anxiety beneath the tales discussed so far—the subject's fear of displacement by, or even dissolution in representations of itself. The double appears to the narrator as a physical representation, an "image" that claims "absolute identity" with him; in destroying this image, the narrator is attempting to preserve the illusion of a self-contained, self-motivating identity. Moreover, in writing his account, the narrator tries to perpetuate his exercise of will by attempting to determine his readers' interpretation—"I would fain have them believe . . . I would wish them to seek out for me . . . I would have them allow . . ." (*TS* 427)—but, ironically, his inscription creates, in effect, a third "William Wilson," which, like his double, escapes his control and betrays him.

In "William Wilson" a distraught narrator recounts events in his dissolute life and the repeated thwarting of his projects by a figure with his own name and form. His frustration and resentment ensue in a desperate effort to free himself from his double's "arbitrary will" by stabbing him with "brute ferocity"; but then his dying namesake speaks in a voice that merges with his own: "*henceforward art thou also dead—dead to the World, to Heaven, and to Hope! In me didst thou exist—and, in my death, see by this image, which is thine own, how utterly thou hast murdered thyself*" (*TS* 448).

Such a tale clearly invites a psychological reading. Since the narrator has been without "virtue"—he has indulged in "wickedness . . . more than the enormities of an Elah-Gabalus" (*TS* 426–27)—between the time of this (self-)murder and the time at which he begins to write, and since the epigraph of the tale reads "What say of it? what say of CONSCIENCE grim, / That spectre in my path?" (*TS* 426), most critics have offered versions of a reading that identifies the second William Wilson with the first's moral conscience or superego, the death of which releases the instinctual id into willful indulgence of its desires.[43] According to this reading, the narrative is the attempt of the dying and remorseful William Wilson both to make sense of his past and to canvas "sympathy" from his "fellow men" (*TS* 427).

The governing opposition of William Wilson's account appears to be that between the subject's desire for dominion of his will over the world about him and those elements that resist such "arbitrary dictation" (*TS* 431). James M. Cox has noted the appropriateness of Wilson's "fictitious title" (*TS* 431), which he renders "Will-I-am Will's-son."[44] Indeed, in Wilson's account of his childhood he suggests that his "own will" usurped the position of his "weak-minded" parents, so that he became "in all but name, the master of my own actions" (*TS* 427). Later, at school, his "ardor," "enthusiasm," and "imperiousness" make him a "marked character" among his schoolmates and give him "ascendancy" over them (*TS* 431). Only his "namesake," he says, refuses "implicit belief in my assertions, and submission to my will," and in so doing thwarts his "arbitrary dictation" and "despotism" (*TS* 431). The narrator seems unwilling to make any compromise; the terms in which he reads existence admit only the polarities of dominator and dominated. In the omnipotence of his will he attempts to make the world conform to his desire—in a sense, to make it become a double of himself; yet, ironically, the double of himself takes the form of an other will and, in his uncompromising polar view of the world, he can only be either master or slave. Toward the end of his account he complains of the other's "inscrutable tyranny," of the "authority so imperiously assumed" over his own "natural rights of self-agency" (*TS* 445); it is in the name of these rights that he resolves "no longer to be enslaved" to the other's "arbitrary will" (*TS* 446) and, the next time they meet, he erupts "in an absolute frenzy of wrath" into violence (*TS* 447). The fundamental irony, of course, is that he is blind to the fact that the "stranger" he tries to escape is "an estranged part of himself."[45]

Otto Rank, in his essay "The Double as Immortal Self," suggests that the "fear of a real double . . . brings to us man's eternal conflict with himself and others, the struggle between his need for likeness and his desire for difference."[46] This certainly points to that tension in "William Wilson" discussed by, for example, Robert Coskren, between the "internal and the external self" manifested "in terms of a conflict between the individual and society."[47] But it also suggests another aspect of the narrator's fear—enamored of his own "singularity," he rejects that which would deny his difference from others, his "common" name, for example. Moreover, his fear of his double is just that—a fear of a physical representation of himself that he perceives as both the same as and as different from himself. Nor is its difference reassuring, since in its independence it reverses the assumed priority of subject to copy by not merely resisting his control but attempting to control him.

The narrator several times emphasizes his distaste for his own name. He claims to be "the descendant of a race whose imaginative and easily excitable temperament has at all times rendered them remarkable" (*TS* 427), and presents himself as being of "noble descent" (*TS* 431). Yet his name "was one of those everyday appellations which seem . . . the common property of the mob" (*TS* 431). He has, he tells us in terms whose pretensions seem designed to contradict their meaning, an

"uncourtly patronymic" and a "very common, if not plebeian, praeno-
mon" (*TS* 434). The words are "venom" in his ears because they
threaten his claim to superior singularity in the face of the anonymous
"mob." Hence, the appearance of a namesake makes him "doubly dis-
gusted with the name because a stranger bore it, who would be the
cause of its twofold repetition, who would be constantly in my presence,
and whose concerns, in the ordinary routine of the school business,
must inevitably . . . be often confounded with my own" (*TS* 434).
His resentment at this "twofold repetition" grows from his desire for
difference from those around him and from his related anxiety about
the relationship between self and name—on the one hand, he wants
there to be a direct, motivated relationship between the two, and, on
the other, he fears it, for if there is such a relationship then he is implicitly relegated to commonality with other men, the "mob."

That he desires such a simple, unambiguous relationship between
name and named is clear from the "fictitious" name he chooses, but his
desire for congruence between inner and outer, essence and appearance, is also seen in the narrative itself—in his "wonder and perplexity"
at the appearance of the Reverend Dr. Bransby, who was both principal
of his school and pastor of his church: "This reverend man, with countenance so demurely benign, with robes so glossy and so clerically
flowing, with wig so minutely powdered, so rigid and so vast,—could
this be he who, of late, with sour visage, and in snuffy habiliments, ad-
ministered, ferule in hand, the Draconian Laws of the academy? Oh,
gigantic paradox, too utterly monstrous for solution!" (*TS* 428–29).
Such can surely be only an insoluble paradox to one who believes that
outward appearance should consistently signify a stable inner essence.
If this is the case, it is no wonder that the narrator is horrified to confront an apparent physical duplication of himself; by this belief, the
double would throw his own existence into doubt.

He initially takes refuge in the idea of the superficial copy. His first
feelings of "vexation" thus grow stronger "with every circumstance
tending to show resemblance" between him and his "namesake" (*TS*
434). In his descriptions of the copy lurks the potential of an "identity"
that is both identical with himself and yet other than himself; ironically,
in emphasizing the otherness, he invokes the negation of the self that
he is trying to preserve. Just as he characterizes the events he depicts
as "drama" (*TS* 438, 446), so he describes the development of "re-

semblance" in the language of dramatic representation: "His cue, which was to perfect an imitation of myself, lay both in words and in actions; and most admirably did he play his part. My dress it was an easy matter to copy; my gait and general manner were, without difficulty, appropriated; . . . even my voice did not escape him . . . the key . . . was identical; *and his singular whisper, it grew the very echo of my own*" (*TS* 434–35). The very terms in which he describes the process trace the surrogation that he fears. At first, the fact of its being an "imitation" is emphasized by the use of expressions from the drama—the other took his "cue" and "most admirably did . . . play his part." But then the distinction between original and copy is progressively blurred—the clothes are "copied," the manner is "appropriated" and, finally, prefiguring the final speech, the voice is "identical."

That the "exquisite portraiture" is only noticed by himself the narrator justifies in language that confirms the aesthetic analogy, since it echoes Poe's own poetics: the narrator assumes that his namesake had been concerned only with his "intended effect," and that he had, with "the masterly air of the copyist," disclaimed "the letter" for the "full spirit of his original for my individual contemplation and chagrin" (*TS* 435). When the narrator, in a scene reminiscent of "The Tell-Tale Heart," creeps to the bedside of his sleeping rival to examine his "countenance" by lamplight, his reaction—no longer mere "vexation"—embodies his own sense of impending dissolution: "My breast heaved, my knees tottered, my whole spirit became possessed with an objectless yet intolerable horror" (*TS* 437). The precariousness of his identity is epitomized in the ambiguities of his question: "Were these,—*these* the lineaments of William Wilson? I saw, indeed, that they were his, but I shook as if with a fit of the ague, in fancying they were not" (*TS* 437).

When he flees, "awe-stricken, and with a creeping shudder," he is fleeing an estranged part of himself, but he is also fleeing the representation of himself that threatens to displace him. Upon each of the subsequent interventions of his rival he notes the "identity of apparel" between them, but willfully regards it as mere disguise. His blindness is apparent in his speculations: "I did not pretend to disguise from my perception the identity of the singular individual who thus perseveringly interfered with my affairs, and harassed me with his insinuated counsel. But who and what was this Wilson?" (*TS* 439); "Could he, for an instant, have supposed . . . that in this, my arch-enemy and evil genius, I could fail to recognise the William Wilson of my schoolboy days,—the namesake . . .?" (*TS* 445). The real question—both disguised and revealed by the double reference of the name—is always avoided because the answer is feared. If he is me, then who am I? Claiming "singularity" he repeatedly refuses to recognize the interplay of sameness and difference that constitutes identity and so courts annihilation.

The final confrontation, appropriately enough, takes place at a masquerade, to which the narrator has come to seduce a young wife who has already given him "the secret of [her] costume" (*TS* 446). His rival appears "in a costume altogether similar" to his own: "a Spanish cloak of blue velvet, begirt about the waist with a crimson belt sustaining a rapier. A mask of black silk entirely covered his face" (*TS* 447). Enraged, the narrator mortally stabs his antagonist, only to learn to his cost "the secret of [*his*] costume." In a series of vertiginous shifts the final paragraphs invoke a complex interplay between image and self.

The narrator is briefly distracted by a noise at the door of the room in which they have fought, and when he turns back to his "dying antagonist" he is astonished by an apparent "material change in the arrangements at the upper or farther end of the room": "A large mirror,—so at first it seemed to me in my confusion—now stood where none had been perceptible before; and, as I stepped up to it in extremity of terror, *mine own image*, but with features all pale and dabbled with blood, advanced to meet me with a feeble and tottering gait" (*TS* 447–48; emphasis mine). At the point of death, the distinction between self and image collapses—"it was Wilson, who then stood before me in the agonies of his dissolution. . . . Not a thread in all his raiment—not a line in all the marked and singular lineaments of his face . . . was not, even in the most absolute identity, *mine own*." At this point "Wilson"—the distinction between narrator and image has collapsed—offers the speech that concludes, "*see by this image, which is thine own, how utterly thou hast murdered thyself*" (*TS* 448). Blind to the other as intrinsic to himself, fearing the other as representation that will supplant himself, Wilson turns to murder—and in so doing ensures his own annihilation since it is only by means of his image that he could survive.

As the psychological reading of the tale suggests, the narrator has in effect created this image of himself that thwarts his will throughout the narrative. In writing his account, he creates another "William Wilson"—the tale—and in so doing attempts once more to assert his singularity; ironically, *this* double enacts the displacement he fears. His opening sentence—"Let me call myself . . . William Wilson"—is an act of self-naming that parallels the claim it contains (that of being "son" of his own "will"). Even as it does so, however, it raises the possibility of the double in the potential possessive of "myself," and reinforces it by the address to himself as "thou," later in the first paragraph. Moreover, since the self-naming occurs in the line under the title, "William Wilson," it suggests that in this case the double of himself is that image of himself that is inscribed in the tale.

The first paragraph foreshadows his later aspiration to singularity in that even in his self-condemnation he claims to be "unparalleled," the "outcast of all outcasts most abandoned" (*TS* 426). And in the second paragraph he attempts to impose his interpretation of events on his readers, even as he imposes "implicit belief in [his] assertions" on his schoolmates. He calls for the readers to "believe that I have been . . . the slave of circumstances beyond human control"—an evasion of responsibility that fails miserably. Just as the double *in* the tale testifies against him, so does his double that *is* the tale. And this double he cannot kill, since his writing self is displaced by his written self—which is the only one to survive the "Death [that] approaches" (*TS* 427).

III

"An Unknown Quantity of X": Some Anxieties of Authority

Anxieties about the nature of personal identity and the fate of the writing self inevitably impinge on the issue of literary authority. Throughout his career, Poe was acutely conscious of those factors inherent in his medium that displaced the author's control over the fate of his own work. On the most mundane level, his editorial responsibilities made him aware of the potential mutilation of manuscripts in their transference into print. In 1841—barely concealing a joke on symmetrical letters—he declared to Joseph Evans Snodgrass that "I am innocent of the elision in your quoted lines. Most probably the syllables were left out by our proof-reader, who looks over the articles after me, for such things as turned s's & o's, or battered type. Occasionally he takes strange liberties" (*L* 175). And in the same year he blamed a compositor for changes in the final form of a text, calling him a " 'genius' who takes much interest in these matters—and many unauthorized liberties" (*L* 188). The mutilation of a text in " 'setting' the MS. 'up' " is, of course, central to "X-ing a Paragrab" (1849). In this, Poe's last published tale, Touch-and-go Bullet-head, editor of the "Tea-Pot," is provoked by a rival to write a paragraph "as O-wy as O-wy could be." In what is perhaps a dig at Emerson's "Circles," Bullet-head defends the letter *O* as "the beautiful vowel—the emblem of Eternity,"[1] and produces an "unparalleled paragraph" in which almost every word has an *O* (*TS* 1371). However, when Bob the "printer's devil" comes to set the manuscript in type, he discovers that all his *O*'s have been "cabbaged,"[2] and so—following printers' convention—he substitutes the letter *X* for each one, and consequently produces a "mystical and cabalistical article" (*TS* 1373, 1374).[3] On the most obvious thematic level, then, "X-ing a Paragrab" dramatizes that element of risk, that "unknown quantity of X" that intervenes between the act of writing a manuscript and its final printed version and threatens to deflate by *X*-ing an author's sense of "conscious power" in composition (*TS* 1375, 1372). Poe's anxieties about such vagaries lie behind his celebration in 1845 of "the invention of *Anastatic Printing*"—a process by means of which he envisaged, "absolute *facsimiles*" of a writer's manuscript could be offered "to the public without the . . . interference of the type-setter" (*CW* 14:154, 155, 157).

Once in print, however, the text faced other threats. As a professional journalist, Poe had a strong sense of "literary property";[4] always short of money,[5] he tried in one frustrating period to escape journalism by obtaining a government appointment. In 1841, in a letter to Frederick W. Thomas, he used a telling economic metaphor: "I would be glad to get almost any appointment—even a $500 one—so that I have something independent of letters for a subsistence. *To coin one's brain into silver*, at the nod of a master, is to my thinking, the hardest task in the world" (*L* 172; emphasis mine). Economic figures also appear frequently in his discussions of purloined letters—plagiarism. In the following passage, written the year after "The Purloined Letter" (1845), he compares the "filcher of literary property" to the "ordinary pick-pocket": "The ordinary pick-pocket filches a purse, and the matter is at an end. He takes neither honor to himself, openly, on the score of the purloined purse, nor does he subject the individual robbed to the score of pick-pocketism in his own person; by so much the less odious is he, then, than the filcher of literary property."[6] Poe's obsession with plagiarism—"the most despicable species of theft"—is well known.[7] "Pinakidia" (1836) is laced with accusations of "pilferings"

(*CW* 14:38), and he devoted much energy and ingenuity to the detection of instances for his private *Chapter on American Cribbage,* offering *"exposés . . .* of the minute trickeries by which the thieves hope to disguise their stolen wares" (*M* 51).

As Robert Regan has shown, Poe was entirely capable of using the charge strategically for his own duplicitous ends;[8] even so, his aggressive concern was an aspect of his more general awareness of the problems facing an author in a period in which improvements in the mechanics of production and distribution of texts, the manipulation of the climate of reception by professional coterie journalists, and the rapid growth of a mass market all threatened to overwhelm the already dubious mastery of an author over the fate of his work.[9] The sheer number of texts in circulation allowed the "recondite, neglected, or forgotten books" to be plundered by "willful plagiarists," whose opportunities, Poe recognized, were multiplied by an international marketplace, since "in a foreign country . . . there [is] little probability of detection" (*M* 155). More than this, however, as book production increased, so did competition for readership. Early in his career, Poe depicted the author's struggle for an audience in terms of a struggle for power; in his "Letter to B———" (1836), he identified one of the main obstacles to an American writer as being that "he is read, if at all, in preference to the combined and established wit of the world. . . . It is with literature as with law or empire—an established name is an estate in tenure, or a throne in possession" (*CW* 7:xxxvi). It is not unreasonable—especially given the regal figure here—to perceive an analogy between Poe's notorious anxieties regarding the democratic "mob" and his own fears of literary anonymity among the "mob" of rival authors, his fears that his own works may be prematurely buried beneath the mass of competing texts.[10]

However, as Poe was aware, once published, the writer's work acquires an independent existence with only a tenuous relationship to its author. In the literary marketplace of his day it was particularly subject to the cut and thrust of the reviewer's pen, which, more often than not, was guided by private ambition or coterie interest.[11] In the opening paragraph of "Never Bet the Devil Your Head," Poe offers a series of humorous jibes at the critical presumption of completing a work of fiction by an act of interpretation that usurps the role of the author. In line with Poe's attacks elsewhere on the heresy of the didactic, his narrator entertains the proposition that "every fiction *should have* a moral; and, what is more to the purpose, the critics have discovered that every fiction *has*" (*TS* 621). He reviews a series of mutually contradictory interpretations of Melancthon and absurd ones of Homer: "Jacobus Hugo has satisfied himself that by Euenis, Homer meant to insinuate John Calvin; by Antinöus, Martin Luther; by the Lotophagi, Protestants in general; and, by the Harpies, the Dutch" (*TS* 621). Moreover, he claims, "modern Scholiasts are equally acute"; they discover and "demonstrate a hidden meaning in 'The Antediluvians,' a parable in 'Powhatan,' new views in 'Cock Robin,' and transcendentalism in 'Hop O' My Thumb.' " So a novelist need not worry about producing a moral since the critics will produce it themselves from "somewhere": "When the proper time arrives, all that the gentleman intended, and all that he did not intend, will be brought to light, in the 'Dial,' or the 'Down-Easter,' together with all that he ought to have intended, and the rest that he clearly meant to intend" (*TS* 621–22). In one sense, Poe perceives that the critic purloins authority from the author; however, in another, that authority has already been compromised by the very act of publication, in which the text becomes a pre-text for the proliferation of meanings—all that was intended, not intended, ought to have been intended, clearly meant to have been intended. Poe is discomfited by this situation but, aware of its ineluctable nature, he attempts to turn it to his own advantage as often as possible. His well-known predilection for hoaxing his readership is clearly a gesture compounded both of resentment at their presumed usurpation of his control over his "literary property" and of an attempt to retain ultimate control—even if it can be recognized only by an ever-narrowing circle of "insiders," which, at its minimal point, is reduced to a readership of one—himself.[12]

The ending of "X-ing a Paragrab," however, suggests that Poe recognized that the displacement he feared was inherent in the self-sustaining nature of writing itself, and that the proliferation of different readings of a text was a function of words, which always carry the potential surplus of meaning that threatens to overflow the constraints of intention. Once Touch-and-go Bullet-head's "mystical and cabalistical article" appears, the author, appropriately enough, disappears—"He had vanished, no one could tell how; and not even the ghost of him has ever been seen since" (*TS* 1374). He leaves behind his text and the "populace," whose "medley of opinion," without the controlling influence of their "legitimate object," the author, ranges through the punning possibilities of *X:* "an X-ellent joke," "X-uberance of fancy," "X-entric," "X-press . . . his X-asperation," "an X-ample to posterity," "driven to an extremity," "X-traordinary and in-X-plicable" (*TS* 1374–75). In another order of signification, "even the town mathematician . . . could make nothing of so dark a problem. X, everybody knew, was an unknown quantity; but in this case . . . there was an unknown quantity of X" (*TS* 1375). That is, the potential significance of *X* cannot be foreclosed; and, in confirmation, "Bob, the devil (who kept dark 'about his having X-ed the paragrab')" offers an interpretation based on yet another category of signs: "It was a clear case, that Mr. Bullet-head never *could* be persvaded fur to drink like other folks, but vas *continually* a-svigging o' that ere blessed XXX ale, and, as a naiteral consekvence, it just puffed him up savage, and made him X (cross) in the X-treme" (*TS* 1375). The fact that Poe himself was subjected to versions of this accusation adds a biographical point to the fate of the unfortunate Bullet-head's text.

The last chapter discussed the ways in which Poe's tales question the assumption of a unified self, implicitly entertain the possibility that any self, unified or dispersed, is an effect of language, and examine the displacements between the writing self and the written self. These concerns are all clearly interrelated, so much so that it is difficult to isolate any one issue for the purposes of analysis. One specifically literary anxiety raised by the threatened "dissolution" (*TS* 448) of the self is that regarding the fate of a single (originating) authorial voice in a text. David Halliburton has noticed the relative absence of direct speech in the tales, suggesting that this fact be read as an index of the narrators' isolation from their fellow men.[13] Thematically, his point makes sense, but this absence of speech can also be taken as an indication of the displacement of voice in the act of writing. Those voices that are depicted in the tales are at least distinctive, often—to use one of Poe's favorite terms—*outré,* and frequently in some way displaced: witness, for example, General Smith's voice box or the "ventriloquial abilities" (*TS* 1059) of the narrator of "Thou Art the Man" (1844).

The following brief discussion of "Loss of Breath" (1835) and more extensive analysis of "Shadow.—A Parable" (1835) focus on the issue of voice as addressed in two tales dating from roughly the same period in Poe's career but otherwise seeming to have nothing in common.[14]

The first is clearly a comic tale, a "burlesque," in G. R. Thompson's words, of "many of Poe's favorite themes, including alienation and the crowd, perversity, the *Doppelgänger*, burial alive, death-in-life, the absurd universe."[15] "Shadow," on the other hand, is usually linked with "Silence—A Fable," praised for its mystic or poetic style, and passed over without further comment. Studies of the Folio Club tales generally agree to admit "Loss of Breath" as one of those constituting the putative lost book and assign it to Blackwood Blackwood; but whereas Mabbott suggests that "Shadow" should be assigned to "the little man in black" (*TS* 206, n.2), Alexander Hammond would omit it.[16] There is no need in the present context to argue the merits of either case; it is sufficient to observe that analysis of "Shadow" indicates that it shares what Hammond has identified as the "central concerns" of the collection: "fiction and the literary process itself."[17]

Though the targets of the satire in "Loss of Breath" are multiple, the central situation reflects on and burlesques the identification of an authentic self with an originating, breath-inspired voice. Moreover, the narrator's final claim on "the attention of the reader," in which he asserts the impossibility of identifying a single "proper God" (*TS* 75), suggests an analogy with the attempt to recover a single validating voice from a text—a project that, according to "Shadow.—A Parable," is fraught with difficulty.

"Loss of Breath": "the lost object of my inquiry"

That the traditional relationship of breath and (often divine) inspiration was a favorite figure of the romantics is a commonplace. Since "How to Write a Blackwood Article" and "A Predicament" contain so many hits at the transcendentalists, Psyche Zenobia's name is appropriate—"Psyche, which is good Greek, and means 'the soul' " (*TS* 336). As Poe surely knew, *psyche* is also cognate with a verb meaning "to blow," hence the interrelation between breath and inspiration.[18] "Loss of Breath," as G. R. Thompson has shown, also makes specific thrusts at the transcendentalists—"the bug-bear speculations of transcendentalism" (*TS* 80)—and Mr. Lackobreath's predicament can be seen as a dig at the possibility of inspired original composition, at those who believe, as Poe puts it in his "Peter Snook" review of 1836, that "true originality is a mere matter of impulse or inspiration" (*CW* 14:73).

The narrative itself is based on the literalization of a figure; as in "The Man That Was Used Up" and "A Predicament," language is presented as prior to, indeed as determining, events in the world. The narrator is roundly cursing his wife "on the morning after [their] wedding" when, he writes, "to my extreme horror and astonishment, I discovered that *I had lost my breath*": "The phrases 'I am out of breath,' 'I have lost my breath,' &c., are often enough repeated in common conversation; but it had never occurred to me that the terrible accident of which I speak could *bona fide* and actually happen!" (*TS* 62). Just as in the tales of radical dismemberment parts of the body disperse the sovereignty of the whole by claiming their own identity, so here the breath is an object separable from its "owner"; like the "set of false teeth, two pair of hips, an eye, and [with what significance will become clear] a bundle of *billets-doux*" that Lackobreath finds during his search, breath can be mislaid. In the world of the text this loss is unattended by the usual fatal consequences; it is merely a handicap. Such playfulness, however, does not disguise the relatively serious point about the priority of language.

That Lackobreath's loss of breath is analogous to a loss of originality is suggested by the series of images that indicate his loss of potency. As David Ketterer has noted, we do not have to subscribe to Marie Bonaparte's identification of Lackobreath with "Poe in his impotent aspect"[19] to observe the equation of "breath with potency and its loss with impotence." Ketterer briefly summarizes the main support for such an equation: that it is the morning after the wedding night and things have not gone well; that the images of cities besieged—as in the first paragraph—are frequently figures for attempts to gain sexual entrance; that the subtitle—"Neither in nor out of 'Blackwood' "—has the force of innuendo, as does Lackobreath's failure to "ejaculate" his "new and more decided epithet" (*TS* 62) (to this we might add that Lackobreath withdraws to his room "to ponder upon some method of eluding my wife's penetration" [*TS* 64]); that he has a potent rival in Mr. Windenough; that his hanging is associated with erections and their lack; and, finally, that the "gaunt, tall, and peculiar-looking form" (*TS* 71) that

Lackobreath seizes by the nose and pulls into a sitting position may represent his own penis.[20]

Be that as it may, it is clear that after his loss Lackobreath laments his inability to produce the "new . . . epithet" and can only reproduce other roles, other voices. He discovers that he can talk if he drops to "a singularly deep guttural," since "this pitch of voice" depends "not upon the current of the breath, but upon a certain spasmodic action of the muscles of the throat" (*TS* 63). And in an attempt to avoid his wife's discovery he "committed to memory the entire tragedy of 'Metamora,'" in which "the deep guttural was expected to reign monotonously throughout." Subsequently, he is able to reply to any question "with some passage from the tragedy—any portion of which . . . would apply equally well to any particular subject" (*TS* 65). Lackobreath's strategy is successful only with his wife—thenceforward, either his "guttural ejaculations" go unheard or he loses the "powers of speech" entirely (*TS* 66, 67), with unpleasant consequences for his bodily parts. The tale records his sensations as he is subject to a series of physical indignities and torments that culminate in his being mistakenly hanged in place of the "mail-robber W——." In terms reminiscent of Mr. Blackwood's advice to Psyche Zenobia, Lackobreath observes that "to write upon such a theme [hanging] it is necessary to have been hanged" (*TS* 69), and proceeds to give such an account. That his narrative is primarily a blatant burlesque of the ludicrous predicament tales of *Blackwood's Edinburgh Magazine* we can see from passages like: "I heard my heart beating with violence—the veins in my hands and wrists swelled nearly to bursting—my temples throbbed tempestuously—and I felt that my eyes were starting from their sockets" (*TS* 78).[21] His memory seems "to have been endowed with quadrupled power"; and his absurd sensations absurdly give rise to philosophical speculations.

Neither comic intent nor effect is denied by the observation that both his memory and his speculations are dominated by prior texts. He recalls incidents of his past life—the trees in the forests where he hunted as a boy, the streets of the cities where he walked as a man—he emphasizes that "I could repeat to myself entire lines, passages, names, acts, chapters, books, from the studies of my earlier days" (*TS* 78). And when thoughts flood into his mind, they are all grounded in earlier writers:

dogmas in the old Aristotelians now generally denied, but not the less intrinsically true—detestable school formulae in Bourdon, in Garnier, in Lacroix—synonymes in Crabbe—lunar-lunatic theories in St. Pierre—falsities in the Pelham novels—beauties in Vivian Grey—more than beauties in Vivian Grey—profundity in Vivian Grey—genius in Vivian Grey—everything in Vivian Grey.

Then came like a flood, Coleridge, Kant, Fitche, and Pantheism—then like a deluge, the Academie, Pergola, La Scala, San Carlo, Paul, Albert, Noblet, Ronzi Vestris, Fanny Bias, and Taglioni. (*TS* 79)

The final tumble of names, in which philosophers, opera houses, dancers, and singers mingle, emphasizes both the secondary nature of his own consciousness and the quite arbitrary way in which it works. There is an added twist in the fact that, as Mabbott notes, the last names are derived from Disraeli's *Vivian Grey*, which Lackobreath has just eulogized.[22]

Giving no sign of life, he is buried alive in a "public vault"; managing to knock the lid off his coffin, he relieves his *"ennui"* by breaking open the other coffins and speculating about the mortality of their inhabitants (*TS* 70). Soon he discovers the object of his wife's "partiality" (*TS* 64), Mr. Windenough, who is "double-winded" (*TS* 73); from him, Lackobreath receives "respiration," and with the "united strength of [their] resuscitated voices" they shout until they are released from "the dungeons of the sepulchre" (*TS* 74).

As his present narrative shows, however, the recovery of breath is not the recovery of an originating inspiration. His opening paragraph of references to "holy writings," Diodorus, the siege of Troy, and Aristaeus foregrounds the fact that he must weave his own tale out of and against the texts that have preceded him (*TS* 62). Such is one implication of the tissue of quotations, citations, and stylistic parodies that constitute his account. It is a comic confirmation of the "true originality" that Poe opposes to the doctrine of inspiration in the quotation with which we began: "to originate, is carefully, patiently, and understandingly to combine" (*CW* 14:73).

A final comment on the conceit of the divine afflatus and the original voice is contained in the fact that the cries for help prompt Scissors, the Whig editor, to *re*publish "a treatise upon 'the nature and origin of

subterranean noises' " (*TS* 74)—the borborygmic associations are un-
avoidable; the treatise prompts "reply—rejoinder—confutation—and
justification" (*TS* 74–75), all of which are confounded by "the appearance" from the tomb of Mr. Windenough and Mr. Lackobreath—opposites whose difference has generated the "single voice." In this, perhaps,
lies the key to the narrator's final advice to the reader, in which he
suggests that instead of searching in vain to identify a single, correct
god to propitiate, he should make offerings "to the proper God" (*TS*
75). Analogously, the reader should not seek to identify a single, inspired, originating, and authorizing voice prior to a text.

If "Loss of Breath" suggests the reader must be content with ac-
knowledging the "proper" voice *in* the text without attempting to fix its
identity, "Shadow.—A Parable" shows, in the course of a more general
interrogation of the nature of signification, that such a voice is always
potentially plural, that the "dissolution" of the unified self noted in the
last chapter is paralleled by the dispersal of the author in the "unknown
quantity of X" that is expressed by the multitudinous voices of the text.

"Shadow.—A Parable": "the inflections of shadow"

The anonymous note appended to *The Narrative of Arthur Gordon Pym*
reads the figures of the chasms as constituting "an Ethiopian verbal
root—the root . . . 'To be shady'—whence all the inflections of
shadow or darkness" (*IV* 207). Poe's texts themselves have an umbral
quality, and "shady," with its connotations of deception to the point of
dishonesty as well as indeterminacy and gloom, is a gloss that could
easily be extended. They are the products of or inhabited by shady
characters who grasp—often in their own writing—at the shadows of
memory, try to interpret shadowy signs, and frequently confront that
indefinite representation of death that names itself as "*Shadow*" (*TS*
964).

This last, the conventional identification of shadow and death, recurs
often. The narrator of "Mesmeric Revelation" concludes an account of
his dialogue with the mesmerized and dying Vankirk with the question,
"Had the sleep-waker, indeed, during the latter portion of his discourse,
been addressing me from out the region of the shadows?" (*TS* 1040).
It is this region into which the narrator of "Shadow.—A Parable" is

preparing to journey—"I who write shall have long since gone my way into the region of shadows" (*TS* 188)—and from which the mutineers in *Pym* fear that Rogers's corpse has returned—as a "visitant from the world of shadows" (*IV* 111). In "The Colloquy of Monos and Una," shadow is the state to be passed *through:* Una says that "above all, I burn to know the incidents of your own passage through the dark Valley and the Shadow" (*TS* 608), and Monos describes his physical death— the "immortality" of "nothingness" (*TS* 617)—as "the strict embrace of the *Shadow*" (*TS* 616). This figure is, presumably, the same "Shadow" with which Ligeia "wrestled" so fiercely as to beggar description (*TS* 317, 318).

When Poe's narrators adopt the figure of Shadow, they are attempting to give substance to the unknowable—the moment of biological death that is either terminal point or threshold to another condition that is feared, or longed for, or both. To the living, Shadow both marks an absolute secret and, in itself, is indefinite and unknowable. According to the narrator of "The Premature Burial," "the boundaries which divide Life from Death, are at best shadowy and vague. Who shall say where the one ends, and where the other begins?" (*TS* 955); hence even to describe the indefinite margin between life and death as a "moment" is to adopt a self-deluding strategy of control. As will be seen, in Poe's "Shadow.—A Parable," this margin is the locus of an uncanny disruption of the conventional relationship between signifier and signified, shadow and substance. In the ideology of representation, the signifier is the shadow of the object by which it is motivated, the word is the shadow of its meaning, the living body the shadow of its spirit.[23] At death, however, the body remains as mute object, signifier of an unknowable signified that now, because unknowable, is termed shadow—the "Shadow" that the narrator and his companions apparently confront at the end of their wine-sodden wake.[24]

In one of the few commentaries on "Shadow.—A Parable," Joseph M. DeFalco compares it to "Silence—A Fable," noting that "Poe's reason for calling the one ['Shadow'] 'parable' and the other ['Silence'] 'fable' remains opaque."[25] Yet the term "parable," as well as meaning "comparison" or "illustration," can denote a "dark saying"[26]—an appropriate punning name for a narrative in which seven mourners, accompanied by an "enshrouded" corpse, sit around an "ebony" table in a "gloomy room" with "sable draperies" from among which a "dark and undefined shadow" emerges to announce, somewhat redundantly, "I am SHADOW" (*TS* 189, 190, 191).

The name "Parable" also locates one major concern of the tale—the relationship between a text and subsequent interpretations. "Shadow.—A Parable" questions the confident assumption that interpretation recovers a proper and unchanging meaning previously embodied in a text, emphasizing instead the reader's participation in the creation of meaning. Frank Kermode, in his analysis of parables, discusses what he calls their relative degrees of "darkness"—that is, their characteristic incompleteness, which calls for explanation and so demands a reader's engagement: "Parables are stories, insofar as they *are* stories, which are not to be taken at face value, and bear various indications to make this condition plain to the interpreter. . . . All require some interpretative action from the auditor; they call for completion; the parable-event isn't over until a satisfactory answer or explanation is given; the interpretation completes it."[27] Yet, as Kermode has shown, such completion is often ambiguous, and a reader's sense of interpretive mastery—of being an "insider" who understands appropriately rather than an "outsider" who is merely bewildered—is always equivocal. "Shadow.—A Parable" veers toward a skeptical recognition that meaning is potentially multiple, created by the projected fears and desires of different readers. The acts of interpretation described in the narrative—of the "prodigies and signs" in the plague-ridden world, of the corpse of "young Zoilus" in the room, and finally of the emergent "undefined shadow"—all confirm this recognition.

In Oinos's account of the events that preceded the company's sequestration with the corpse, he describes a world in which the "heavens," the "physical orb of the earth," and the "souls, imaginations, and meditations of mankind" are permeated with significance (*TS* 189). The natural world is read for "prodigies and signs," and to those "cunning in the stars"—among them, "me, the Greek Oinos"—"it was not unknown that the heavens wore an aspect of ill." All things are signifiers with the same signified, but that signified itself remains obscure: the "peculiar spirit of the skies," though manifested, remains hidden and corresponds to "those feelings more intense than terror for which there is no name upon the earth." Implicitly, this reading of the world derives from men's fear; astrology merely offers them a means of objectifying that fear by accounting in some way for the horrors of "the black wings of the Pestilence . . . spread abroad" (*TS* 189).[28]

Such is confirmed when we learn that although the enclosure of the room can shut out the physical signs—"the moon, the lurid stars, and the peopleless streets"—it cannot exclude "the boding and the memory of Evil" (*TS* 189). The sealed room is emblematic of its occupants' attempt to create a point outside the movement of time, to shut out mortality; yet their own consciousness of the past and fear of the future point to and generate their failure. According to David Halliburton, "Shadow.—A Parable" in this way anticipates "The Masque of the Red Death"; in both, an enclosed space that is at first positively protective becomes a claustrophobic site of death.[29] Oinos, in attempting to shut out death, actually seals it in; he creates a kind of demonic "sacred space," in which mortality, manifested in terms of "dead weight" and descent and present in the figure of the corpse, is already present and in which the figure of death emerges "not in an entry from without but an emergence from within."

The three main elements of the room—mirror, corpse, shadow—all raise the question of the nature of the relation of shadow to substance, signifier to signified, text to meaning. The possible solipsism of that reading of the world that glosses all things as manifestations of one unapproachable signified is confirmed by the image of the companions, sitting about a "round table"—recalling the phrase "the physical orb of the earth" and foreshadowing Oinos's discomfort at the "eyes of the departed"—which forms an "ebony mirror" wherein each sees "the pallor of his own countenance, and the unquiet glare in the downcast eyes of his companions" (*TS* 190).

Ironically, whereas the things of earth and faculties of mankind had previously been read as manifesting an unnamed "peculiar spirit," here the position of the signified is occupied by a material corpse. The "genius and the demon of the scene"—that which gives it significance— is "the young Zoilus enshrouded" (*TS* 190, 191).[30] This signified becomes, in turn, signifier as Oinos reads the "expression" of the dead eyes: "His eyes . . . seemed to take such interest in our merriment as the dead may haply take in the merriment of those who are to die. But although I, Oinos, felt that the eyes of the departed were upon me, still I forced myself not to perceive the bitterness of their expression, and, gazing down steadily into the depths of the ebony mirror, sang

with a loud and sonorous voice the songs of the son of Teios" (*TS* 190).
The hesitancy of "seemed . . . may haply," and "felt" suggests that
Oinos's reading is a projection of his own fears, a possibility that is reinforced by both the juxtaposition of the "eyes" and the "mirror" and
the triple pun of the phrase "I, Oinos, felt that the eyes. . . ." What he
"reads" is his fear of his own death, from which he recoils; and he
attempts by the power of his "loud and sonorous voice"—the symbol
of his individual "spirit"—to assert his existence in the face of mortality. Yet, although the songs are "those of the son of Teios," which
epitomize the denial of time,[31] his effort is undercut first by the simple
fact that they are not his own songs—his voice can only echo those
already sung by a man long dead—and second by the fading of his
voice in a foreshadowing of his inevitable death—at first "loud and
sonorous," his songs "gradually . . . ceased, and their echoes, rolling
afar off among the sable draperies of the chamber, became weak, and
undistinguishable, and so faded away" (*TS* 190). In the long process
of transmission, his utterance is just one of a series of fading echoes,
cut adrift from an original voice, destined to die among the shadows.

In Poe's work, silence is often associated with the image of the
shadow;[32] here, just at the point at which the last echo of the individual
voice dies, the shadow emerges: "And lo! from among those sable
draperies where the sounds of the song departed, there came forth a
dark and undefined shadow—" (*TS* 190). This shadow is dissociated
from any substance; though "a shadow such as the moon, when low in
heaven, might fashion from the figure of a man," it is "the shadow
neither of man, nor of God, nor of any familiar thing." In the homology
signifier/signified and shadow/substance, it is unmotivated signifier,
floating free because disconnected from any signified. Its displacement
from any identifiable original moment is emphasized by the figure,
"such as the *moon* . . . might fashion" (emphasis mine), which
stresses the displacement from an original creative source of "light."
It is "vague, and formless, and indefinite," and it is silent. Whereas the
corpse of "the young Zoilus enshrouded" offered a recognizably human
form onto which the narrator could project "expression" and significance, the shadow is just shadow, silent and unmotivated. The "seven
there assembled" dare not "steadily behold it,"[33] but instead again gaze
"continually into the depths of the mirror of ebony" (*TS* 191): "And
at length I, Oinos, speaking some low words, demanded of the shadow

its dwelling and its appellation. And the shadow answered, 'I am SHADOW, and my dwelling is near to the Catacombs of Ptolemais, and hard by those dim plains of Helusion which border upon the foul Charonian canal.' And then did we, the seven, start from our seats in horror, and stand trembling, and shuddering, and aghast" (*TS* 191). Even more horrifying than its words is the fact that "the tones in the voice of the shadow were not the tones of any one being, but of a multitude of beings, and, varying in their cadences from syllable to syllable, fell duskily upon our ears in the well remembered and familiar accents of many thousand departed friends" (*TS* 191). Confronted by this unmotivated shadow-text, Oinos attempts to place it, to establish some grounds for understanding its significance by discovering its place of origin and its name. He hopes that it will speak with a single authoritative voice that will give it unity, but it does not; the "multitude" of voices horrifies the "seven," each of whom hears in terms of his own memories of "departed friends."

At this moment of Oinos's discovery that a text either is mute or speaks with a multitude of voices that vary from reader to reader, the tale abruptly ceases. In fact this thematic treatment of the reader/text relationship repeats what has already been implied in the opening paragraph, the anxieties of which subvert any interpretation that purports to bring light into this shady tale: "Ye who read are still among the living; but I who write shall have long since gone my way into the region of shadows. For indeed strange things shall happen, and secret things be known, and many centuries shall pass away, ere these memorials be seen of men. And, when seen, there will be some to disbelieve, and some to doubt, and yet a few who will find much to ponder upon in the characters here graven with a stylus of iron" (*TS* 188–89).

This opening paragraph reveals an acute awareness both of the role of the reader in construing the meaning of a text and of the author's loss of authority over the meaning of his text as it is displaced through time. The direct address of the first sentence bluntly calls attention to the separate activities of reading and writing, and in so doing it points to the paradox between the claims to connection a written text makes and the actual distance implicit in it: "Ye who read are still among the living; but I who write shall have long since gone my way into the region of shadows" (*TS* 188). A sense of intimacy between reader and writer is established by the first clause, yet the second—strongly separated by the semicolon[34]—marks their difference and distance. The direct address, shared present tense, and parallel construction of "ye who read" and "I who write" seem to establish a connection, a common ground between writer and reader. Yet the phrases also clearly emphasize both the difference between their activities and—by the absence of pronoun referents—their anonymity. This difference is reinforced by the disrupted parallelism—between "are still among the living" and "shall have long since gone my way into the region of shadows"—where the different verb constructions subvert the shared present tense of "read" and "write" and draw attention to that temporal distance between reader and writer that parallels their different conditions, substance ("living") and shadow.

The temporal distance is also emphasized by the next sentence, in which the narrator predicts that "strange things shall happen, and secret things be known, and many centuries shall pass away, ere these memorials be seen of men" (*TS* 189). Two related issues are raised by his characterization of his writing as "memorials" to be "seen": first, it draws attention to the status of writing as material signs to be "seen" and subject to interpretive scrutiny; second, the term "memorial," though it draws on the traditional association of writing as aid to memory, has funereal associations that question the integrity of the relationship between "memorial" and what is memorialized. The narrator's final sentence develops this sinister aspect: "And, when seen, there will be some to disbelieve, and some to doubt, and yet a few who will find much to ponder upon in the characters here graven with a stylus of iron" (*TS* 189). Displaced from their origin, the "memorials" will be subject to a multiplicity of interpretations, and whereas the progression from "disbelief" to "doubt" might imply that the subsequent term will be "belief," it is not; the "few" only find "much to ponder upon"— which allows for yet a further variety of response. Once the "characters" have been "graven," they are subject to the vicissitudes of interpretation and reinterpretation. The inscription is displaced from its author and from its object; as such it is a "*grave*-n" figure of death, a "memorial" to its lack of motivation.[35] Confronted by such characters (signifiers displaced from their signifieds and displaced, too, from their putative author in place and time), the reader must try to discover a principle by which to interpret them—must try, for example, to fill the pronoun of "I who write" with a "me, the Greek Oinos" (me, the

Greek One). But the "stylus of iron" too easily metamorphoses into the many-voiced style of irony; the text, like the "SHADOW," is either silent or it speaks with too many voices.

Oinos's preliminary discrimination among the reactions of future readers to his account suggests the possibility of hearing many voices in *his* text, too; and, as is evident from the commentary on the tale, different voices *have* been heard. Is the tale "a serious and profound commentary of the power of the symbolized shadow of death to provoke terror and horror in the hearts of man," or an account of the "rite of purification" of the dead, or a parody of "pseudo poetic transcendental fictions"?[36] Is Oinos (One or Wine?) a sober and reliable narrator or is he drunk?[37] "Shadow.—A Parable" invites the analogy between the reader response to the text and the seven's response to the figure of the shadow. If, confronted by the narrator's ambiguous shadow-text, we ask "its dwelling and its appellation," we discover answers no more reassuring than those offered in reply to Oinos's question. Both text and figure are called, in dusky self-reference, "Shadow." Whereas the figure of shadow comes from the Catacombs, so the text issues from "the region of shadows" (*TS* 188). Furthermore, Oinos—"I who write"—like the "departed" Zoilus, like the "departed" friends, has followed the "departed" sounds of his voice; he has "gone [his] way into the region of shadows," leaving behind as "memorial" of his absence a shadow—the text—which can be made to speak with many voices. The triple pun at the "heart" of the tale—"I, Oinos, felt that the eyes"—which emphasizes the dissociation of signifier from signified, shadow from substance, thus enacts the displacement that underlies the anxiety of the first paragraph—that of the writing self as it becomes written. The narrative cannot be framed by a final return to the scene of writing; "Oinos" is now the multitudinous "I" of the text, constituted anew by each reader; his name marks only a departure and provides no authority for grounding interpretation in a single voice.

IV

"Duelli

Lex

Scripta,

Et Non,

Aliterque":

The Struggle

for

Authority

The likely degree of Poe's discomfort with and resistance to the loss of authority over the text is indicated by the tedious pertinacity of his argument in his 1836 article, "Maelzel's Chess-Player" (*CW* 14:6–37). Here, he attempts to prove that the famous chess-playing "Automaton" then touring America was not, in fact, a *"pure machine"* but the temporary residence of a chess-playing Mr. Schlumberger—a man "about the medium size," with "a remarkable stoop in his shoulders" (*CW* 14: 6, 35).[1] The idea of a *"pure machine,* unconnected with human agency in its movements" suggests a clear analogy to the image of the text displaced from its author. Each offers a disturbing prospect to an author such as Poe, who frequently referred to his own activity in combinative, constructive, and mathematical terms.[2]

Ironically, Poe's anxieties about the fate of his own work must have been compounded by his own practice. It is not surprising that an author who conceived of origination as combination (*CW* 14:73), and of combination itself as operating on *"those combinations which our predecessors . . . have already set in order"* (*CW* 11:73), should plunder his predecessors' texts wholesale, riddling his own texts with citations, concealed references, parodies, and burlesques. His hypersensitivity to the possible plagiarism of his own work can be seen as a strategy to cover his tracks on those occasions when he has taken risks;[3] but it is primarily an attempt to protect his own work from similar treatment.

Whatever his anxiety about plagiarism may have been, his 1844 preface to "Marginalia" reveals a willingness to explore an even more disturbing form of appropriation, one that reverses the conventionally assumed priority of (authoritative) text to (belated, hence secondary) reader and, moreover, threatens to erase the primary text altogether.[4] This preface purports to introduce selections of Poe's "marginal jottings" that were actually published in seventeen installments in various magazines. The preface was printed twice—in the *Democratic Review* (1844) and the *Southern Literary Messenger* (1849)—and, according to both Mabbott (*TS* 1112) and John Carl Miller (*M* xi), Poe almost certainly planned a collected edition.

In his "Letter to B———" (1836), he makes a caustic observation on the value of "the world's good opinion": "The opinion is the world's, truly, but it may be called theirs as a man would call a book his, having bought it; he did not write the book, but it is his; they did not originate the opinion, but it is theirs" (*CW* 7:xxxv). He thus emphasizes the difference between ownership and original authority. In the preface to "Marginalia," Poe offers two images of reading that mark the stages in the appropriation and effacement of the authority of the "volumes of my library" (*TS* 1115): possession of the book is the first step in a process of authorial negation.

His first image of the reader is that of himself—he writes that he always chooses books with an "ample margin," in which he is then able to pencil "suggested thoughts, agreements and differences of opinion, or brief critical comments in general" (*TS* 1113). Here is the traditional concept of the marginal note, fundamentally subordinate to the primary text that prompts it. Yet, we observe, it proliferates: "Where what I have to note is too much to be included within the narrow limits of a margin, I commit it to a slip of paper, and deposit it between the leaves" (*TS* 1113). The margin, pressured by the marginalia of the reader, is extended beyond the physical constraints of the book—a sign that the notes' purely supplementary nature is modulating. Moreover, such notes cannot serve as "*memoranda*," as reliable mnemonic devices to remind the reader of the content of the primary text, since " '*Ce que je mets sur papier*,' says Bernardin de St. Pierre, '*je remets de ma mémoire, et par consequence, je l'oublie;*'—and, in fact, if you wish to forget anything on the spot, make a note that this thing is to be remembered" (*TS* 1114). Indeed, in the next paragraph, Poe suggests that "the purely marginal jottings" are actually independent of the primary text: they "have a distinct complexion, and not only a distinct purpose, but none at all; this it is which imparts to them a value": "the *marginalia* are deliberately pencilled, because the mind of the reader wishes to unburthen itself of a *thought;*—however flippant—however silly—however trivial—still a thought indeed. . . . In the marginalia . . . we talk only to ourselves" (*TS* 1114).

Having, to all intents and purposes, divorced the marginal note from the original text, Poe offers a second image of himself reading: on a "rainy afternoon," he seeks "relief from *ennui* in dipping here and there, at random, among the volumes of [his] library" (*TS* 1115). The randomness, the wayward "dipping here and there," is in itself a subversion of the authority of any single book and a concealed confirmation of the paradoxical interrelationships of these volumes (all volumes). Moreover, rather than read any primary text, he reads "the numerous pencil-scratches" of his own notes, which, like his "dipping," impress him with their randomness—"their helter-skelteriness of commentary amused me" (*TS* 1115)—which emphasizes their almost anarchic independence from any controlling authoritative text. Believing that he would have derived even greater pleasure from examining another reader's marginalia, he conceives the idea of publishing his own.

He is aware of the most obvious problem—that of "transferring the notes from the volumes—the context from the text—without detriment to that exceedingly frail fabric of intelligibility in which the context was embedded" (*TS* 1115). His solution is no solution at all—if such be judged as a means of preserving the relationship of "context" to "text": "I concluded, at length, to put extensive faith in the acumen and imagination of the reader:—this as a general rule. But, in some instances . . . there seemed no safer plan than so to re-model the note as to convey at least the ghost of a conception as to what it was all about. Where, for such conception, the text itself was absolutely necessary, I could quote it; where the title of the book commented upon was indispensable, I could name it" (*TS* 1115–16). The "original" text is reduced to a faded "ghost of a conception," appearing among the marginalia only in the fragments of quotations and the subordinate position of the footnote to the (former) marginal note. In the terms Poe uses, "context" has become "text" and "text," "context," in a reversal that he anticipates in his question: "What then, would become of it—this context—if transferred?—if translated? Would it not rather be *traduit* (traduced) which is the French synonyme, or *overzezet* (turned topsy-turvy) which is the Dutch one?" (*TS* 1115).[5]

Lawrence Lipking has observed that Poe valued the marginal note precisely for its "complete independence from the text";[6] but then he suggests that it "offers the reader a kind of puzzle . . . a fragmentary clue to buried possibilities of meaning." His language here suggests that Poe demands that the reader rediscover and so reassert the priority of those primary texts that have been effaced. Poe, however, concludes with the declaration that "just as the goodness of your true pun is in the direct ratio of its intolerability, so is nonsense the essential sense of the Marginal Note" (*TS* 1116). Just as the pun epitomizes the surplus of meaning in the word, so the wayward marginal note, proliferating and claiming a brief authority—which will in turn give way to the "scribblings" of other readers—epitomizes the production of meaning by juxtaposition and difference rather than the recovery of meaning as a preexistent object.

Such a concept would seem to be consonant with Poe's rhetoric of effect. Yet, whereas the latter tends to cast the reader in a relatively passive role, subject to the designs of the author, the preface to "Marginalia" places him in a position of power over the text that becomes subject to his own construal. Indubitably, whereas Poe as reader would endorse such a position, Poe as author attempts to resist allowing his readers such power.

Poe's attitude toward his readers is, then, ambiguous: they are potential victims or lurking villains. On the one hand he fears the failure to gain a readership; yet on the other he resents the interpretive appropriation of his texts once they are out of his direct control.

One way he attempts to resolve this quandary is by means of the hoax—which pandered to the popular taste of the day while at the same time preserving his own sense of power. (While not in fact a pure hoax, the "Marginalia" project itself was duplicitous—Poe never made marginal notes in his own books; he composed some of the items specifically for the project, and most of the others he took from his own published reviews.) Such duplicity keeps readers perpetually hesitant to claim Poe's texts for their own. Similarly, almost all his texts are shot through with what we might call parodic self-criticism, which operates to ridicule and subvert his readers' premature satisfaction at having understood his tale. "The Premature Burial" (1844) offers a good example of the way in which this burlesque technique operates—especially since it closes with an act of aggression against the reader that is partially withdrawn as soon as offered, with the effect of undercutting even the security that such a gesture offers.[7]

"The Premature Burial": "bugaboo tales"

In "Loss of Breath," when Mr. Lackobreath is buried alive he complains amusingly of the dangers of "ennui."[8] Other Poe characters make more serious complaints when they suffer the same fate. Live burial occurs so often in his fiction that Marie Bonaparte speculates at length about Poe's own "womb-phantasy" anxiety,[9] and Daniel Hoffman writes that "Eddie . . . cannot shake himself free from the long shadow, the gasping breath, the feeling of fatal and foetal enclosure."[10] Biographical speculation aside, D. H. Lawrence makes the point that "all this underground vault business in Poe only symbolizes that which takes place beneath the consciousness."[11] In "Morella," for example, it evokes the psychological mechanisms of repression. The most productive analysis of this motif so far, however, is that of G. R. Thompson, who generalizes from it that "Poe's image of man is that of a forlorn, perverse, sentient being buried alive in the incomprehensible tomb of the universe."[12]

Poe's repeated use of this motif may indicate an analogous, specifically literary concern: the haunting fear of the author that his voice might be buried, his tale never told, or, once written, never read since it is buried in the welter of other texts with which it has to compete.[13] "Premature Burial" certainly hints at such a fear. The first part of the tale offers four examples of "direct testimony . . . to prove that a vast number of such interments have actually taken place" (*TS* 956). Jonathan Auerbach offers a suggestive parallel between this "narrative apparatus" and the devices that the narrator tells us in his own subsequent account he rigged up as a precaution against entombment.[14] If we accept this, we can also suggest that just as the apparatus in the coffin and the tomb are designed to ensure that the narrator's voice is heard once more, so the narrative frame is on one level designed to legitimate and so ensure a "hearing" for his own text.

The fear of the burial of utterance is reflected in the narrator's examples. In that which he claims he found in the " 'Chirurgical Journal,' of Leipsic"—a journal, he notes, that an American bookseller "would do well to translate and republish" (for which read "dig up")—the unfortunate victim "heard the footsteps of the crowd overhead [his grave], and endeavored to make himself heard." But it was only his movement of the earth that freed him and allowed him to speak "in broken sentences . . . of his agonies in the grave" (*TS* 958–59). The last "extraordinary case" the narrator offers is that of a Mr. Edward Stapleton, who was buried, dug up by body snatchers, and accidentally revived on the dissecting table by the application of a galvanic battery. Thereupon, he got off the table and spoke: "What he said was unintelligible; but words were uttered; the syllabification was distinct. Having spoken, he fell heavily to the floor" (*TS* 960). The narrator is intrigued by what "Mr. S." subsequently asserted: "He declares that at no period was he altogether insensible—that, dully and confusedly he was aware of every thing which happened to him, from the moment in which he was pronounced *dead* by his physicians, to that in which he fell swooning to the floor of the hospital. 'I am alive' were the uncomprehended words which, upon recognising the locality of the dissecting-room, he had endeavored, in his extremity, to utter" (*TS* 960–61).

The inability to cry out "I am alive" is one of the vital elements of the narrator's own fear. On the one hand, he is terrified of the physical situation: "The unendurable oppression of the lungs—the stifling fumes of the damp earth—the clinging to the death garments—the rigid embrace of the narrow house." But what raises him to a pitch of "appalling and intolerable horror" is the combination of "these things" both with the "memory of dear friends who would fly to save us if but informed of our fate" and with the knowledge that "of this fate they can *never* be informed—that our hopeless portion is that of the really dead" (*TS* 961). Moreover, the central image in the vision that appears in his dream is that of "the graves of all mankind" thrown open to reveal that "the real sleepers were fewer, by many millions, than those who slumbered not at all; and there was a feeble struggling; and there was a general sad unrest; and from out the depths of the countless pits there came a melancholy rustling from the garments of the buried" (*TS* 964). He hears no voices, only the muted sounds of struggle.

When, in the course of his own tale, the narrator reaches the climactic point of being convinced that he, too, has been buried alive, he writes that "I endeavored to shriek; and my lips and my parched tongue moved convulsively together in the attempt—but no voice issued from the cavernous lungs, which, oppressed as if by the weight of some incumbent mountain, gasped and palpitated, with the heart, at every elaborate and struggling inspiration." Finally, after great efforts, he succeeds, and "a long, wild, and continuous shriek, or yell, of agony, resounded through the realms of the subterrene Night" (*TS* 967). The result is unexpected—and chastening: " 'Hillo! hillo, there!' said a gruff voice, in reply. 'What the devil's the matter now?' said a second. 'Get out o' that!' said a third. 'What do you mean by yowling in that ere kind of style, like a cattymount?' said a fourth; and hereupon I was seized and shaken without ceremony" (*TS* 968). He learns that he has fallen asleep in a bunk on a boat carrying "garden mould"; his interlocutors are members of the crew.

This salutary reversal for the narrator is followed very soon by one for the reader. The narrator recognizes that he has been deceived by his own reading and, in "inevitable revulsion," he says, his soul "acquired tone . . . [and] temper." He "went abroad . . . [and] took vigorous exercise"; but he also notes that "I discarded my medical books. 'Buchan' I burned. I read no 'Night Thoughts'—no fustian about church-yards—no bugaboo tales—*such as this*" (*TS* 969). Such a sudden dislocation of perspective, as abrupt as the "Hillo!" of the gruff voice, exposes the fictional status of the tale and the degree to which the reader has been subject to it just as the narrator has been subject to his fictionally inspired obsessions.

Before noting the precise nature of the trap into which the reader has been led, it is necessary to point up a parallel between the inset tale itself and the narrator's delusion that he has been buried alive. In each, there is a shift of ground: J. Gerald Kennedy notes a movement from the "historical" to the "romantic" mode in the shift from the case "histories" to the narrator's "subjective" account;[15] within the narrator's account there is a parallel movement from his establishment of a context (his illness, fears, precautions) to the subjective experience of "the Night that endureth for evermore" (*TS* 967). The revelation that he is deluded is an implicit comment on the tale itself, but this is not confirmed until the second, analogous disillusionment of the reader.[16]

We have noted that the first half of the tale is designed to legitimize and so ensure a hearing for the narrator's own story. However, in so doing, the frame story flirts with the very danger it apparently seeks to avoid. The citation in detail of a series of testimonies—with names, dates, occupations, sources—and the evocation of the vast number of other versions—"It were an easy matter to multiply such histories as these" (*TS* 961)—threatens to bury the narrator's own account by, first, suggesting the sheer quantity of other, rival accounts and, second, taxing the reader's attention with the amount of detail and the fundamental repetitiousness of the cases. In fact, of the first half of the tale, Wayne C. Booth says: "We feel that something is wrong . . . it is difficult for us to resist boredom or annoyance."[17] What, then, keeps the reader reading? The narrative suggests its own unflattering answer, which adds a barb to the narrator's final gesture of withdrawal.

The narrator's opening paragraphs enact a series of gestures ostensibly designed to clear space for his own text. He first establishes a distinction between "legitimate fiction," which is the province of "the mere romanticist," and the "severity and majesty of truth" (*TS* 954, 955). Some themes, he asserts, are too "horrible" to be treated in fiction. For example, in accounts of "the Passage of the Berenisa, of the Earthquake at Lisbon, of the Plague at London, of the Massacre of St. Bartholomew, or of the stifling of the hundred and twenty-three prisoners in the Black Hole at Calcutta . . . *it is the fact—it is the reality—it is the history* which *excites. As inventions*, we should regard them with simple *abhorrence*" (*TS* 955; emphasis mine). Implicitly, then, his narrative will not be "legitimate fiction," but "history," since to "invent" such themes would inspire "abhorrence," and properly "offend" or "disgust" the reader.

In the next paragraph, he suggests that he will focus not on "vast generalities of disaster" but on "individual instances," since these are "more replete with essential suffering." This emphasis on the individual unit rather than on the mass reflects his claim for the reader's attention to his own text rather than others "in the long and weird catalogue of human miseries." But on what is such a claim based? On the degree of misery the narrative offers—"true wretchedness," "ultimate wo," and "the ghastly extremes of agony" (*TS* 955). His terms in these two paragraphs characterize the reader he will expose at the end— one who judges the *"mere* romanticist" severely (emphasis mine); who values the "propriety" of treatment; who endorses the "severity and majesty of truth" for its ability to "sanctify and sustain" "horrible themes"—but who is actually thus seeking to justify his private "thrill" and "most intense of 'pleasurable pain' " at the spectacle of human suffering.[18] Having appealed to the reader's complicitous sense of superiority in his condescension toward the products of the "mere romanticist," the narrator finally exposes him for what he is—a thrill-seeking consumer of "bugaboo tales—*such as this*" (*TS* 969).

Thus we can see that in "The Premature Burial" Poe attempts to demonstrate his authority in two ways. First, by evoking, parodying, and deflating prior texts, he offers what Kennedy calls "the last word on the subject" and so demonstrates his power over potential rivals.[19] Second, his strategic entrapment and exposure of the reader is an exercise in control and, perhaps, a vengeful expression of contempt for those who would reduce his work to one more instance of the pap of the day.[20]

"Von Jung, the Mystific": *"a refinedly peculiar case"*

In some tales, rather than embody his wary antagonism toward his readers in the narrative strategy of the tale, Poe introduces it thematically, offering characterizations of artist- and audience-figures and examining the relationships between them. Tales such as "The Man of the Crowd" (1840), "The Spectacles" (1844), "The Oblong Box" (1844), "The System of Doctor Tarr and Professor Fether" (1844), and "The Sphinx" (1846) can all said to offer humiliating images of various degrees of readerly incompetence.[21] Sometimes, however, antagonism flares into hatred, as it does in its most extreme form in "Hop-Frog" (1849). In this late tale, the deformed dwarf jester's resentment at his dependence on a cruel and boorish audience—the king and his ministers—culminates in his "*last jest*," in which, having convinced them to disguise themselves as orangutans, in costumes of tar and flax, he suspends his employer and his minions from a chandelier and ignites them, leaving "eight corpses [swinging] in their chains, a fetid, blackened, hideous, and indistinguishable mass" (*TS* 1354).[22] The king, who had "seemed to live only for . . . a good story of the joke kind" (*TS* 1345), also dies for one in a grisly "*novel*" invention that, in a manner reminiscent of Poe's earlier comic tales, literalizes the surplus of meaning in language. For the night of the "*fête*" the hall is fitted with "every kind of device that could possibly give *éclat* to a masquerade" (*TS* 1347); "*éclat*," of course, means a burst of brilliance, perhaps with connotations of *éclairer*, "to light up," and "*fête*" has echoes of *fétide*, "stinking." The king, then, is literally "fêted" during the masquerade.[23]

In other tales, too, Poe threatens to make a monkey out of the reader. One of these, "Von Jung, the Mystific" (1837), characterizes the relationship between author and reader in terms of a duel for "domination" (*TS* 294). On the one hand, Von Jung is an author figure whose power in large part derives from his skill as a reader; on the other hand, his antagonist, Hermann (for which, possibly, we can read Herr Mann = Mr. Man = Everyman), is defeated because of his reading incompetence. What is at stake in the conflict is the opposition between two views of language—one that recognizes that it operates by convention and is fundamentally arbitrary; another that believes in the perfect congruence between word and world and believes that language is natural.

Given Poe's delight in the art of the hoax, it is understandable that David Halliburton should suggest that "a story like 'Mystification' [the title of the 1845 *Broadway Journal* version] is not only about the mystifying impulse in the Baron Ritzner Von Jung but the mystifying impulse in Poe himself."[24] Halliburton is not the only critic to detect autobiographical resonances in the tale; Edward Davidson, however, suggests that it is in the description of Von Jung's victim, Hermann, rather than in the Baron himself, that we should see hints of a self-portrait in which Poe "made sport of himself."[25] Such observations are justified by the obvious parallels between Von Jung's love of "*grotesquerie*," which depends on his skillful manipulation of appearances

(*TS* 293), and Poe's own literary techniques.[26] Von Jung is presented—in contrast with the obtuse boor Hermann—as an exemplary reader capable of discerning the "key" to an obscure text and of interpreting it accordingly (*TS* 303). This ability is the prime source of his power, and it is complemented by his own control over language and his consequent ability to manipulate his chosen victim. Indeed, his *"art mystifique"* may justifiably be termed authorship, for the tale offers what can best be described as a fantasy of authorial domination over the reader's reception of a text; it is, as it were, Poe's fair warning to his audience that to approach his tales as Hermann approaches the obscure text on the *duello*—thoughtlessly confident in the stability of unexamined assumptions about language—is to risk being made a monkey of.

Even a brief review of the tale shows the central role played by texts and interpretation. The action turns on the relative failure and success of interpretive acts by Hermann and by Von Jung. The Baron Ritzner Von Jung is introduced by the narrator as a man of mysterious powers that enable him to dominate those around him without their ever being able to enter the "mystery which overshadowed his character" (*TS* 295). The narrator claims a privileged status for his own knowledge of Von Jung and suggests that the Baron's talent for *"mystification"*—in which the ability to manipulate appearances plays a large part—results from "an almost intuitive knowledge of human nature, and the most wonderful self-possession" (*TS* 295). As an illustration of the Baron's talent, the narrator offers an account of his confrontation with one Hermann, who "contrived to bear, . . . among a particular set at the university, a reputation for deep metaphysical thinking, and . . . for some logical talent" (*TS* 297).

Hermann is a duelist with many victims, but, says the narrator, "it was upon his minute acquaintance with the etiquette of the duello, and the *nicety* of his sense of honor, that he most especially prided himself" (*TS* 298). Von Jung deliberately initiates a quarrel on this very subject, reacts to an insulting reply by hurling a decanter of wine at Hermann's image in a mirror (to fulfill, he tells him, "all the spirit, if not the exact letter, of resentment for your insult"), and by this "refinedly peculiar" gesture provokes the outraged Hermann to withdraw (*TS* 300). The latter consults his library of works on the code of the duello and reads to the narrator a section from "a pretty thick octavo, written in barbarous Latin by one Hedelin, a Frenchman, and having the quaint title, *'Duelli Lex scripta, et non, aliterque'* "; the passage, he assures the narrator, applies to this case—even though the narrator could understand "not one syllable of the whole matter" (*TS* 301). Hermann sends the narrator to Von Jung with a written demand for either an explanation or a duel, but the Baron, without reading it, is aware of its contents, and hands the narrator his "already written reply":

> "With perfect certainty . . . of being comprehended, I beg leave, in lieu of offering any sentiments of my own, to refer you to the opinions of the Sieur Hedelin, as set forth in the ninth paragraph of the chapter on *'Injuria per applicationem, per constructionem, et per se,'* in his *'Duelli Lex scripta, et non, aliterque.'* The nicety of your discernment in all the matters here treated of will be sufficient, I am assured, to convince you *that the mere circumstance alone of my referring you* to this admirable passage, ought to satisfy your request, as a man of honor, for explanation." (*TS* 302)

Hermann, in turn, reconsults the book and considers the "explanation offered [to be] of the fullest, the most honorable, and the most unequivocally satisfactory nature" (*TS* 303).

Bemused—for he is still unable "to gather the least particle of definite meaning" from the passage—the narrator seeks an explanation from Von Jung, who explains that he had in fact "purposely thrown the treatise in Hermann's way two or three weeks before" and that the secret lay in Hermann's vain refusal to admit that he did not understand "anything and everything in the universe that had ever been written about the duello" (*TS* 303, 304). In fact, "the language was ingeniously framed so as to present to the ear all the outward signs of intelligibility, and even of profound analysis, while in fact not a shadow of meaning existed, except in insulated sentences" (*TS* 303). However, once a "key" was adopted—"leaving out every second and third word alternately"—the passage yielded "a most horribly grotesque account of a duel between two baboons."

If the gulling of Hermann is anything to go by, Von Jung's "epoch" of "domination" (*TS* 294) is implicitly enabled by the reading strategy of his community of victims, a strategy that seems to be based on a belief in a natural, direct relationship between signifier and signified.

A concomitant assumption of such a belief is that any one signifier signifies only singly, and this clearly determines the reading of Von Jung
accepted by members of his own household. Even they, according to
the narrator, accept his appearance and manner at face value and associate him only with "ideas . . . of the rigid and august" (*TS* 296);
such readers see that Von Jung's lips "rested one upon the other" in
such a way as to convey "*entirely* and . . . *singly*, the idea of *unmiti-
gated* gravity, solemnity and repose" (*TS* 294; emphasis mine). Rather
than recognize the relationship between these "ideas"—the use of the
word almost implies a spatial location in the readers' minds—and their
own interpretive activity, they assume that they are directly and necessarily motivated by an essential identity that is Von Jung.

The assumption that any one signifier signifies only singly is clearly
faulty; in the narrative this assumption seems related to the fact that
the community is a closed system "within the limits of the *uni*versity"
(*TS* 293; emphasis mine). Here a particular code operates, that of
"young men of wealth, of high connection, of great family pride, and
all alive with an exaggerated sense of honor" (*TS* 296–97). Like all
those with vested interests to protect in an aristocratic culture, they assume that the hierarchical position they occupy is a natural rather than
a cultural product. By the same token, the signifiers by which they live
are assumed to have single necessary signifieds that are unquestioned.
Hence, "while [Von Jung] was pronounced by all parties at first sight
'the most remarkable man in the world,' no person made any attempt
at accounting for this opinion. That he was *unique* appeared so un-
deniable it was deemed not pertinent to inquire wherein the uniquity
consisted" (*TS* 293). In the 1845 version, "impertinent" is substituted
for "not pertinent," so suggesting connotations of social impropriety
and further emphasizing the cultural nature of the code, which, implicitly, has generated the successive misreadings of Von Jung.

"P——" exposes and undercuts the assumptions built into this code
more directly in his remarks about Hermann's reputation and appearance. This "original," he notes, had "contrived to bear, . . . among a
particular set at the university, a reputation for deep metaphysical
thinking, and, I believe, for some logical talent" (*TS* 297); according
to the narrator, however, he was in fact "one of the greatest asses in
all Christendom" (*TS* 297). In his description of Hermann's head he
implies that such a misreading is a result, in part, of a phrenological

interpretation of his features—for such an interpretation assumes exactly that correspondence between outer configuration and inner essence, between signifier and signified that has led to the communal misreading of Von Jung:

> The upper region was finely proportioned, and gave indication of the loftiest species of intellect. The forehead was massive and broad, the organs of ideality over the temples, as well as those of causality, comparison, and eventuality, which betray themselves above the os frontis, being so astonishingly developed as to attract the instant notice of every person who saw him. The eyes were full, brilliant, beaming with what might be mistaken for intelligence, and well relieved by the short, straight, picturesque-looking eyebrow, which is perhaps one of the surest indications of general ability. (*TS* 298)

In case we have missed the emphasis on the act of interpretation in such phrases as "gave indication of," or "what might be mistaken for," the narrator reaffirms that in fact Hermann "really was a fool" (*TS* 298), and hence that the phrenological reading is at odds with the truth. Whether or not we accept the narrator's version of Hermann, his divergence introduces a measure of doubt and suggests that the meaning yielded by the phrenological code is a function of the code itself, rather than the object it purports to describe.

The assumption that such codes are natural and necessary rather than conventional and fundamentally arbitrary also underlies the students' faith in the code of the duello, which is the ritual enactment of their "pride" and "honor," and hence of their position in society (*TS* 297). The "received code" of the duello stands for the inherited constructs by and through which they confirm their identities, and which they assume to be natural and transhistorical. Hermann, in his unquestioning acceptance of the authority of those "musty volumes" that he consults for guidance, is the extreme case who becomes a victim of his own fetish. The linguistic implications of his attitude toward the code are brought into higher relief by the motto that Poe added to the *Broadway Journal* version of the tale in 1845: "Slid, if these be your 'passados' and 'montantes,' I'll have none o' them.—" (*TS* 292). The quotation marks draw attention to a prior act of naming that is an integral part of the development of a code (here, that of the duello); the possessive pronoun suggests the element of subjectivity in such an act; and the refusal of the final clause suggests the existence of other possible applications of the terms, thus implying that each linguistic version of reality is a human construction that necessarily functions by the exclusion of alternatives—in essence, that signification is the product of arbitrary human construction rather than a feature of the natural order. This analysis is confirmed by the title of the quizzical text—*"Duelli Lex scripta, et non, aliterque"* (*TS* 301)—which Mabbott translates as "The Law of Duelling, written and unwritten and otherwise" (*TS* 305, n.10).

Von Jung's power of *"mystification"* is a function of his control over language. His victims believe that their signifying systems are natural and so are constrained by them; Von Jung recognizes their fundamentally arbitrary and conventional nature and so is able to manipulate their signs to his own ends. Since his audience believes that signifiers are motivated by their signifieds, Von Jung is able to determine their interpretation of his attitude by manipulating his appearance. He is a master performer who, in the process of drawing Hermann into his coils, can manifest a "total . . . alteration of countenance" from "the quizzical expression which was its natural character" to one "cadaverously white" in which he is "apparently striving to master his emotion" (*TS* 299). Similarly, he can exploit their analogous assumption that a man's choice of specific verbal devices necessarily corresponds to, is motivated by, and so reveals an inner character, by his manipulation of his "discourse."[27] In the conversation about the duello he is at first "silent and abstracted," but "at length seemed to be aroused from his apathy, took a leading part in the discourse, and dwelt upon the benefits, and more especially upon the beauties, of the received code of etiquette in passages of arms, with an ardor, an eloquence, an impressiveness, and an affectionateness of manner, which elicited the warmest enthusiasm from his hearers in general" (*TS* 297). The others believe, but the narrator is "staggered" by Von Jung's performance, since he "well knew him to be at heart a ridiculer of those very points for which he contended, and especially to hold the entire *fanfaronnade* of duelling etiquette in . . . sovereign contempt" (*TS* 297).

Von Jung's discourse, as we have seen, issues in a confrontation and an exchange of insults with Hermann. Mabbott has suggested that the Baron's name, Ritzner, is related to the German verb, *ritzen*—"to scratch or to crack"—and that it is thus appropriate for the joke-cracker, Von Jung (*TS* 304, n.1). But the Baron cracks more than jokes; we subsequently learn that he has cracked the code of "the everlasting treatise '*Duelli Lex scripta, et non, aliterque,*' " and here, at the climax of his exchange with Hermann, he cracks the mirror when he "hurled the decanter full of wine furiously against the mirror which hung directly opposite Hermann; striking the reflection of his person with great precision, and of course shattering the glass into fragments" (*TS* 300). This action is emblematic of Von Jung's procedure throughout. Most obviously, as Von Jung himself points out, it "deviate[s] . . . from the general usage among gentlemen"—that is, it transgresses the social code to which the others subscribe; the insult cannot be accounted for by the etiquette of the duello and Hermann, the self-avowed expert, can only characterize it as "refinedly peculiar." More than this, however, the shattering of the "reflection" both figuratively rehearses the Baron's disruption of the mutually validating texts that are the authority for the code of the duello and functions as an appropriate image for his subversion of the assumption of the motivated sign.

Von Jung requests that Hermann "will forgive me for the moderate tax I shall make upon your imagination, and endeavour to consider, for an instant, the reflection of your person in yonder mirror as the living Mynheer Hermann himself." He then suggests that his "discharge" of the decanter at the "image" will "fulfil all the spirit, if not the exact letter" of his resentment at Hermann's insult and remove the need for "physical violence" (*TS* 300). In both the acting out of a scene and the content of that scene, Von Jung invokes the mechanisms of representation and displays the contradictions inherent in them. The authority of the duello is grounded in texts—the "musty volumes" that Hermann consults in an attempt to puzzle out the "refinedly peculiar" nature of the insult (*TS* 300–301). It is they that would dictate and give meaning to the action normally following on "similar cases of personal affront." Von Jung "deviate[s]" by acting out a scene that represents the action, calling on Hermann to read in it the same meaning ("spirit") that he would read in the original ("letter") (*TS* 300). Yet Hermann, the absolutely literal reader, can only claim to find the meaning of the representation in a text that he actually cannot understand—the "*Duelli Lex scripta, et non, aliterque*" (*TS* 301). Von Jung has implicitly reversed the natural authority of the signified over the signifier, the assumption of which dictates Hermann's reading of the world. Hermann believes that the duello texts naturally ground and give significance to actions. Von Jung's representation undercuts this belief by imposing itself on Hermann's reading of those prior texts; he wants to find a ground that motivates the action he does not understand, and so he does: in a text that has all "the outward signs of intelligibility" but "not the least particle of definite meaning."

Within the scene that the Baron acts out, he suggests an even more radical critique of Hermann's literalism. He offers the reflection as an exemplary mimetic sign, in which signifier (the "image") and signified (the "living Mynheer Hermann") are fused. Yet he does so in terms that insist upon the difference between them, and he draws attention to the fact that the disjunction can be overcome for an "instant" only by an exercise of the observer's imagination. In other words, he implies that the ideality of the sign is itself a human creation rather than a function of any necessary relationship with its object. The logical manifestation of this ideal sign would be, as in the Swiftean allegory, the object itself; the destruction of the sign would be the destruction of the object. In part, this is the lesson that Von Jung enacts for Hermann; by smashing the image he literally smashes the literal, and reveals the conventional nature of the link between sign and referential world. Hermann's survival *should* show him the inherent weakness of his assumptions.

Finally, we must note a series of parallels that suggest that Von Jung's action reflects on the narrator himself as well as Hermann. Just as Hermann claims an insider's knowledge of the code of the duello, so the narrator claims a similiar insight into the Baron's character. Early in his narrative he claims that he "knew all that it was necessary to know of the character of the Baron Ritzner Von Jung" (*TS* 293), and he repeats versions of this claim throughout his tale: he alone knows the Baron to be capable of a joke; he alone knows that Von Jung is "at heart . . . a ridiculer of those very points for which he contended" in his discourse on duelling; and he alone has seen "the quizzical expression" that is the "natural character" of the hoaxer's face (*TS* 299). Based on this knowledge, this "insight into [Von Jung's] mental conformation," the narrator offers us an "anecdote" that will, he claims, illustrate his true nature. In other words, he invites the reader to make an easy passage through the signifier (his tale) to the signified (Von Jung's "true" character), and yet the action of his narrative implies that the assumption of just such an easy passage is a form of blindness born of conceit and stupidity. With this in mind, we note that the role the narrator himself plays in the events of the tale is that of a mechanical transmitter of texts he does not understand in a situation he does not understand. These reflections in themselves are sufficient to cast in doubt his characterizaton of Von Jung as the single original author of events, an author whose influence is "all-pervading and magical" (*TS* 294).

Von Jung's artistry is of a different order; in a world that is pervaded by previously written texts, originality is not origination but combination and manipulation. Von Jung is able so to create by reason of his recognition of the arbitrary nature of language and hence of texts; he can violate and subvert the immediate authority of the already written, but he cannot escape prior texts. To a certain extent they are his medium. Even his act of *"grotesquerie"* is already written in the history of his family, "every member of which (at least as far back into antiquity as any certain records extend) was more or less remarkable for talent of some description,—the majority for that species of *grotesquerie* in conception of which Tieck, a scion of the house, has given some vivid, although by no means the most vivid exemplifications" (*TS* 292–93). Moreover, of course, his power over Hermann involves his ability to manipulate a book already written—a joke already played, according to his provenance for the text, by Hedelin, in the manner of Du Bartas.[28] The final irony is, perhaps, embodied in Von Jung's fate: a master-manipulator of texts, he is subject to inscription—in the annals of the university and in the narrative itself, from which only constructed versions of the Baron can ever be recovered.

V

"Word of No Meaning": Denial of the Symbol

The ideology of the symbol, as Paul de Man has observed, has long pervaded post-romantic approaches to literary texts and has determined "the polarities that shape the value judgments implicated in these discussions: such familiar oppositions as those between nature and art, the organic and the mechanical, pastoral and epic, symbol and allegory."[1] To this list we might add the dualistic conception of language in which the fully motivated ideal sign as a natural and divinely sponsored instrument is valorized over the conception of the linguistic sign as an arbitrary human construct. Certainly, romantic writers often contrast the conventional nature of ordinary language, in which no necessary relationship pertains between sign and the natural world, with an idealized language of immediate presence in which word and world are one—that is, with a language that aspires to the power of the "*Logos*, that was in the beginning, and was with the thing it represented, and was the thing it represented."[2]

This is Coleridge's formulation, and it clearly repeats the formula he adopts in his well-known and apparently unqualified opposition between symbol and allegory. In *The Statesman's Manual* (1816) he writes:

> Now an Allegory is but a translation of abstract notions into a picture-language which is itself nothing but an abstraction from objects of the senses; the principle being more worthless even than its phantom proxy, both alike unsubstantial, and the former shapeless to boot. On the other hand a Symbol . . . is characterized by a translucence of the Special in the Individual or of the General in the Especial or of the Universal in the General. Above all by the translucence of the Eternal through and in the Temporal. It always partakes of the Reality which it renders intelligible; and while it enunciates the whole, abides itself as a living part in that Unity, of which it is the representative.[3]

In this opposition, the romantic symbol is, to adopt Hazard Adams's term, "miraculous,"[4] which is not surprising, given its place in Coleridge's argument that the particulars of the Bible are "symbols, harmonious in themselves, and consubstantial with the truths, of which they are the *conductors*."[5]

Even in other, less overtly theological texts, the "miraculous" features of the romantic symbol are asserted. As its etymology suggests, the word "symbol" evokes the restoration of something torn apart;[6] it reclaims the total unity of the transcendental sign that had been disrupted by arbitrariness. To a fragmented, contingent world, the symbol offers a form of redemption: both part and index of infinity, this "purely" motivated sign ostensibly offers access to the ineffable realm of the spirit beyond rational comprehension. Expressing what it alone can express, it cannot be translated into ordinary language, but signifies by effect on the sensitive/poetic soul alive to the possibilities of the transcendental.[7]

Such a concept is seductive, which perhaps accounts for its prominent position in subsequent interpretations of romanticism. Yet, as Paul de Man argues, the assertion of the superiority of the symbol over allegory is implicitly a denial of time and as such can be regarded as "self-mystification"—a strategic attempt to defend the self from its "authentically temporal predicament."[8] Indeed, in "The Rhetoric of Temporality," de Man demonstrates that early romantic discourse on the symbol/allegory distinction—including that of Coleridge in *The Statesman's Manual*—is heavily qualified; and he locates what he calls the "true voice" of romantic literature in allegory, in which the primary relationship is not between allegorical sign and its meaning but that between sign and previous sign "with which it can never coincide." Allegory, thus defined, "necessarily contains a constitutive temporal element," and "designates primarily a distance in relation to its own origin, and, renouncing the nostalgia and the desire to coincide, it establishes its language in the void of this temporal difference."[9]

The valorization of the symbol is an expression of the desire to spatialize time in an attempt to transcend the inescapable temporality of discourse. Even a text like Hegel's *Aesthetics*, which seems to offer a theory of aesthetics based on just such a valorization—for example, in the well-known definition of the beautiful as "the sensory appearance [or manifestation] of the idea"[10]—in fact simultaneously undoes the theory of the symbol. As de Man demonstrates, it derives to a great extent from emphasis on the metaphor of "interiorization," according to which "aesthetic beauty" is understood as "the external manifestation of an ideal content which is itself an interiorized experience, the recollected emotion of a bygone perception."[11] According to de Man's analysis, the progression from perception to thought in Hegel is dependent on the faculty of memorization, which takes the form of inscription: "the idea . . . makes its sensory appearance . . . as the material inscription of names," and in such appearance we are dealing only with signs.[12] Consequently, says de Man, "what the *Aesthetics* calls the beautiful turns out to be . . . something very remote from what we associate with the suggestiveness of symbolic form"; it is, he observes elsewhere, "essentially prosaic."[13]

Such qualifications of the concept of the romantic symbol, of the ideal sign in which signifier and signified are supposedly one, establish a context in which to place Poe's own profound reservations. Indeed, as is suggested in chapter 1, Poe's whole project denies the viability of such a sign, implying that its formulation is merely the product of an interpretive desire that is a form of monomania. The narrators of "Berenice" (1835) and "Ligeia" (1838) are each in the grip of such desire; obsessive idealists, they yearn for the plenitude of the "spiritual" and refuse to accept the arbitrary nature of language in a contingent world; they claim instead a symbolic ligation with absolute being, a transcendental realm, or an original moment. Their narratives, however, demonstrate the futility of their claim and identify the quest for the symbol as the impossible project of a deluded mind.

"Berenice": "tous ses dents étaient des idées"

"Berenice" seems to offer a warning against itself; that is, as we read we are drawn into the "library chamber" and are there offered what, on one level, is a cautionary tale of the effects on the balance of the mind of "loiter[ing] . . . in books" (*TS* 209, 210). The narrator implicitly locates the cause for his susceptibility to monomania in the library. It is here, he writes, in "the very regions of fairy land— . . . a palace of imagination— . . . the wild dominions of monastic thought and erudition," that a "total . . . inversion took place in the character of my commonest thought. The realities of the world affected me as visions, and as visions only, while the wild ideas of the land of dreams became, in turn, not the material of my every-day existence, but in very deed that existence utterly and solely in itself" (*TS* 210). This opposition between "the realities of the world" and "the wild ideas of the land of dreams" is one that, as Terence Martin shows, contemporary moralistic critics of fiction repeatedly made, based on the "metaphysical assumption . . . that true reality is limited to the actual, that is, to actually existing being."[14] They feared the power of imaginative writing to disturb and subvert the ability of the impressionable mind to make judgments about such a reality. Egaeus's account of his disease, his ludicrous fixation on and "frenzied desire" for Berenice's teeth,[15] and the implied final act of violation and disfigurement, offer a bizarre confirmation of such fears.[16] And yet the narrative also implies that the search for a pre- or extratextual "reality" is doomed to frustration. Egaeus's plight is that he is born into a world already inscribed with records of attempts to transcend it, a "world-as-text" in which the arbitrary nature of language precludes signification of the transcendental, which is infinitely displaced by chains of signifiers. His obsession with and seizure of Berenice's teeth is Poe's ironic comment on any attempt to possess the symbol and so gain access to the realm of the ideal.

David Halliburton draws attention to the acute sense of enclosure in the narrative.[17] In the original version of the tale, which first appeared in the *Southern Literary Messenger* (March 1835), Egaeus makes a grisly excursion to "the bed-chamber of the departed," where, behind the curtains of the bed, he is enclosed "in the strictest communion with the deceased" in an "atmosphere . . . redolent of death"; there, the "enshrouded dead" offers him a "species of smile" from which he "rushed forth a maniac" (*TS* 217). But in the 1845 version, after a series of revisions that, according to David E. E. Sloane and Benjamin Franklin Fisher IV, shift the emphasis of the tale "from the corruption inherent in the surroundings to the psychology of the narrator,"[18] Egaeus remains hermetically confined in his chamber, the boundaries of which, Halliburton notes, "are identical with his consciousness."[19] Egaeus explicitly draws attention to this identification as he relates the onset of his fixation on Berenice's teeth: "The shutting of a door disturbed me, and, looking up, I found that my cousin had departed from the chamber. But from the disordered chamber of my brain, had not, alas! departed, and would not be driven away, the white and ghastly *spectrum* of the teeth" (*TS* 215).[20] Subsequently, chamber and consciousness are again conflated when Egaeus recounts how, in the grips of obsessive meditation, he "sat motionless in that solitary room— . . . and still the *phantasma* of the teeth maintained its terrible ascendancy, as, with the most vivid and hideous distinctness, it floated about amid the changing lights and shadows of the chamber" (*TS* 216). Clearly, any distinction between the room in which he sits and the chamber of his brain is lost in this chamber of "changing lights and shadows," which is either and both.[21]

When Richard Wilbur notes the recurrent motifs of "*enclosure* or *circumscription*" in Poe's tales, he prefers the latter term "because it is Poe's own word, and because Poe's enclosures are so often more or less circular in form."[22] "Circumscription" is appropriate to "Berenice," however, for another reason: with its connotations of *inscription* it hints at Egaeus's situation, since the chamber he occupies and that figures forth his consciousness is "the inner apartment of the library" (*TS* 214); he is both written, and written around.

The congruence between chamber and consciousness is also, implicitly, one between consciousness and text, and it exploits the analogy between writing as collective memory and individual memory as text. Egaeus, born in the library, is born into an inscribed world—"Here died my mother. Herein was I born" (*TS* 209). This world constitutes his earliest memories, which are "connected with that chamber, and with its volumes" (*TS* 209), and, as we have already seen, his consciousness and his chamber are interchangeable. Just as the "gloomy, gray, hereditary halls" contain signs of the past that must, in effect, be read, so too, do the "gray ruins of [his] memory" (*TS* 209, 210). But both kinds of inscription, written text and the text of memory, are products of an act of radical selectivity that must betray the object, and both are subject to temporal displacement and the loss of the object that motivated them.

Such radical selectivity is clearly seen in the collection of "volumes" in the "chamber," which, Egaeus suggests, provides the most convincing confirmation of the naming of his family as a "race of visionaries" (*TS* 209). The volumes by their very exclusiveness and their single focus on the "visionary" project draw attention to their arbitrariness and to the monomania that selected them.[23] Moreover, Egaeus in the grips of his "disorder" subjects them to an even more stringent selectivity—they "partook . . . in their imaginative and inconsequential nature, of the characteristic qualities of the disorder itself" (*TS* 213).

The inevitable temporal drift of signs away from their referents is implicit in the second paragraph of Egaeus's narrative. On the most obvious level, he is surrounded in his "paternal halls" by signs and texts: "Our line has been called a race of visionaries, and in many striking particulars—in the character of the family mansion—in the frescos of the chief saloon—in the tapestries of the dormitories—in the chiselling of some buttresses in the armory—but more especially in the gallery of antique paintings—in the fashion of the library chamber—and, lastly, in the very peculiar nature of the library's contents—there is more than sufficient evidence to warrant the belief" (*TS* 209). The order in which he offers his evidence follows a movement inward—from the general character of the house, through the main rooms, to the central library; concomitantly, the signs themselves increase in the complexity of their inscription—from fresco, tapestry, and chiseling to paintings and texts. Several displacements are revealed in this paragraph that bear on Egaeus's situation. He suppresses his paternal name in favor of the nomination, "race of visionaries";[24] yet this naming is called into question by the ambiguity of the final clause— do such signs offer "evidence" that his "line" *was* such a race, do they confirm the existence of the "belief" that prompted the past act of naming, or, doubly remote, do they warrant only the "belief" that his family was called such? This ambiguity is intensified because the very existence of the "race" is supposed only through the subsequent interpretation of signs that signify, first, its present absence and, second, a past desire for what was/is absent—the transcendental realm that is the desired object of the visionary.

At different points in his narrative Egaeus shows an awareness of linguistic characteristics that contribute to the impossibility of recovering an original, motivating object from a written text: "Misery is manifold. The wretchedness of earth is multiform. Overreaching the wide horizon as the rainbow, its hues are as various as the hues of that arch—as distinct too, yet as intimately blended. Overreaching the wide horizon as the rainbow! How is it that from beauty I have derived a type of unloveliness?—from the covenant of peace, a simile of sorrow?" (*TS* 209).[25] His self-interrogation in this opening paragraph embodies a recognition that any statement about the world necessarily bears the freight of prior acts of interpretation. The making of the simile draws with it the previous figure of the rainbow as "covenant," and the repeated "as" constructions emphasize that even those statements that presume to translate original perceptions of the world are always necessarily made in terms of something else.[26] "Original" perceptions are displaced along chains of signifiers that themselves are figurative translations of always already figurative perceptions. Egaeus's desire for the ideal sign is a desire to escape this figuration, which, as we shall see, ironically issues in a "disfiguration" of a different order (*TS* 218).

Subsequently, among the characteristic symptoms of his monomania that Egaeus describes is the tendency to "muse for long unwearied hours, with [his] attention riveted to some frivolous device on the margin or in the typography of a book" (*TS* 211). If we bear in mind the congruence between text and world and text and consciousness, his shift to the "margin" is emblematic of his desire for transcendence— which is a desire to escape the contingent world and its arbitrary linguistic sign. (An ironic comment on such a desire is subsequently provided by the fact that Berenice's "disfigured body" is discovered on the "margin" of the grave [*TS* 218].) And his single-minded obsession determines his reading, which yields only itself: "Few deductions, if any, were made; and those few pertinaciously returning in upon the original object as a centre" (*TS* 212). Moreover, trying to free himself from language, he repeats "monotonously, some common word, until the sound, by dint of frequent repetition, ceased to convey any idea whatever to the mind" (*TS* 212). Yet all this does is reaffirm the arbitrary nature of language, reaffirm that there is no necessary relationship between sound and significance.

This absence of motivation—here between referent and word—recurs in the relationship between events and their traces in Egaeus's memory. When he struggles to account for the time between "the setting of the sun [when] Berenice had been interred" and midnight, when "it seemed that I had newly awakened from a confused and exciting dream" (*TS* 217), he explicitly identifies the traces of the past accessible to consciousness as a kind of text: "But of that dreary period which intervened I had no positive, at least no definite comprehension. Yet its memory was replete with horror—horror more horrible from being vague, and terror more terrible from ambiguity. It was a fearful page in the record of my existence, written all over with dim, and hideous, and unintelligible recollections. I strived to decypher them, but in vain" (*TS* 217–18). Traces on the "fearful page" of memory are, like words, liable to the drift away from the referents, subject as they both are to the displacements of time. The tale as a whole reveals the disjuncture between the contingent world and absolute being, between word and referent, and between present self and past self. Egaeus's monomania desperately focuses upon the disconnected traces in the world, language, and memory in an attempt to recover putative validating origins from the "dim, and hideous, and unintelligible."

That this project has the aspect of a nostalgic longing for ideal presence is clear if we compare this occasion of "hideous, and unintelligible" recollection with ostensibly more positive acts of memory. Early in his narrative, he claims that "it is mere idleness to say that I had not lived before—that the soul has no previous existence. You deny it?— let us not argue the matter. Convinced myself, I seek not to convince. There is, however, a remembrance of aerial forms—of spiritual and meaning eyes—of sounds, musical yet sad; a remembrance which will not be excluded; a memory like a shadow—vague, variable, indefinite, unsteady; and like a shadow, too, in the impossibility of my getting rid of it while the sunlight of my reason shall exist" (*TS* 209–10). Halliburton describes this as "a dreamlike memory, with . . . platonic

overtones, . . . a haunting reminder of a pre-existence in which, could
he recover it, he might again be happy and whole."[27] Ketterer concurs,
terming it a "dimly remembered arabesque state," with which Egaeus
seeks reconnection by marriage to Berenice, the "sylph amid the shrubberies of Arnheim."[28] It is clear, however, that Egaeus's claim for prior
existence is supported entirely by a willed act of interpretation of
traces in his memory—traces that, like those that are "dim and hideous," are "vague, variable, indefinite, unsteady." Radically adrift
from any validating source, they are "shadow." Implicitly, this "previous existence" stands for any prior self before the present moment of
consciousness, and the assumption of continuity is revealed as an ideal-
ization analogous to Egaeus's clinging to belief in the previous ideal
existence of his "soul."

As Ketterer notes, there seems to be a parallel here with Egaeus's
memories of the young Berenice: "Berenice!—I call upon her name—
Berenice!—and from the gray ruins of memory a thousand tumultuous
recollections are startled at the sound! Ah, vividly is her image before
me now, as in the early days of her light-heartedness and joy! Oh, gorgeous yet fantastic beauty! Oh, sylph amid the shrubberies of Arnheim! Oh, Naiad among its fountains!" (TS 210). The most important
point for our purposes is that the image is a displacement, standing
"as" the "Berenice" of the "early days." Egaeus desperately wants to
assert that the name is a symbol in which Berenice is present; but
words cannot bridge the displacement over time, indeed they mark it—
the "gray ruins" are not redeemed by the "image before me now." The
significance of the displacement in time is brought home by the next
sentence—"And then—then all is mystery and terror, and a tale which
should not be told" (TS 210–11). The image is further displaced by
the tale itself, with its fundamental narrative movement through time—
"And then—then . . ." It is this movement that he tries to deny
through his belief in the previous life of his own soul, a belief that reflects his desire for exemption from time, from the natural cycle of
birth, decay, and death.

His fear of this process, of its implication with signification, is
made clear in his description of Berenice's "fatal disease": "the spirit
of change swept over her, pervading her mind, her habits, and her
character, and, in a manner the most subtle and terrible, disturbing
even the identity of her person!" (TS 211). As he catalogues those as-

pects of Berenice that are subjected to this "change"—her mind, habits, and character—we are justified in asking what makes up the culminating "identity of her person," the alteration of which so disturbs him. His earlier statement on his having "lived before" implies an identity of selfhood with "soul," but his obsession with the change in Berenice locates her identity of person in her fleshly body: "My disorder revelled in the . . . startling changes wrought in the *physical* frame of Berenice—in the singular and most appalling distortion of her personal identity" (*TS* 213). His confusion is one between the constructed ideal of "fantastic beauty" for which he yearns, and the evidence of Berenice's natural subjection to time. His reaction is extreme because the disjunction between his ideal and the contingent world subject to death is complete—*any* evidence of change would be to him a "revolution of [a] horrible . . . kind" (*TS* 211).[29]

His reaction to the evidence of temporality bears a direct relationship to his experience with language: "Alas! the destroyer came and went!—and the victim—where is she? I knew her not—or knew her no longer as Berenice!" (*TS* 211). "Berenice" is his name for the image of "fantastic beauty" that he cherishes, resistant to change. His refusal to recognize the victim as Berenice is a symptom of his longing for a natural, unchanging relationship between name and named, between word and referent, and it is a refusal to accept the arbitrary nature of language in a contingent world.

It is this refusal that explains his dentophilia and establishes a context for his exclamation: "Of Mademoiselle Sallé it has been well said, '*Que tous ses pas etaient des sentiments*,' and of Berenice I more seriously believed *que tous ses dents étaient des idées. Des idées!*—ah, here was the idiotic thought that destroyed me! *Des idées!*—ah, *therefore* it was that I coveted them so madly!" (*TS* 216).[30] His obsession with the teeth reflects his desire for a purely motivated sign that does not just re-present, but actually *is* the idea in material form. Possession of such a sign, he feels, "could alone ever restore me to peace, in giving me back to reason" (*TS* 216). But this "reason" is that associated with his nostalgia for the ideal realm (*TS* 210). He thus invests his very sanity in his perception of the teeth as symbols offering access to such a realm, and his monomania is an ironic comment on the romantic desire for the transcendental, supernal oneness attainable through the symbol.

teeth

In his monomania, the narrator claims for the teeth the power of perfect, self-contained signification. The final paragraphs, however, reveal this claim to be a deluded symptom of frustrated desire. The most obvious way in which it does this is in its reduction of the teeth to their simple materiality: they are merely "thirty-two small, white, and ivory-looking substances . . . scattered to and fro about the floor" (*TS* 209). His inability to name them as "teeth" is a culmination of his progressive dissociation from language in these paragraphs—which begins with his inability to "decypher" the text of his own memory and continues with his bewilderment at the "words . . . of the poet Ebn Zaiat" and his puzzled account of the "broken sentences" of his "menial." Finally, when his servant "directed [his] attention to some object against the wall," he has to look at it "for some minutes" before he can name it as "a spade." The "white substances" take their place among a series of signs—the texts, the muddy and bloody garments, the "impress of human nails" on his hand, and the "instruments of dental surgery"—*between* which relationships must be established by an interpretive act before their significance can emerge. In effect, these paragraphs offer us a paradigm for the reading process by which we attempt to reconstruct the diegetic realm, the implications of which are confronted more directly in "Ligeia."

"Ligeia": "The charnel character to the figure"

Much of the commentary on "Ligeia" has focused on the "hideous drama of revivification" of the ending (*TS* 328). Does Ligeia return from death to inhabit the corpse of Rowena and thus provide an exemplum of the power of the human will to cross the ultimate boundary,[31] or is the event the narrator's monomaniacal or drug-induced hallucination?[32] Is the tale a straightforward account of supernatural events, or is it an "allegorized jest" or hoax of literary conventions?[33] James Schroeter, a self-proclaimed "rational" critic who argues for a supernatural reading, characterizes the debate in terms of attitudes toward language—between those who accept the narrative as a "straightforward and literal expression of Poe's meaning" and those who read its events as "symptoms of a deeply buried meaning."[34] (That is, language is either an unproblematic vehicle of prior meaning, transparent to the inquiring eye, or it presents obstacles to the recovery of meaning that

are ultimately overcome by an appropriate interpretive strategy of recuperation. This distinction is not really an opposition at all, for each
case presupposes the critic's faith that meaning exists prior to and is
separable from the text that embodies it—that only an adequate critical operation is required to draw it forth. I do not argue for the text as
resistant symbol/icon, eluding all interpretations by being significantly
mute, but I do contend that the text itself refuses the closure implied
by single interpretations and that this refusal is one of the implications
of the fate of Poe's narrator's search for *the* ultimate meaning of Ligeia.

"Ligeia" is an equivocal text, one that can be shown to display all
the characteristics of "hesitancy" that Tzvetan Todorov identifies with
the genre of the fantastic.[35] My concern is with the strategy of interpretation adopted by the narrator of the tale, and with its failure. In
the first part of his account the narrator attempts to re-present his "lost
love," and in so doing uses a vocabulary appropriate to the central
romantic concept of the symbol. But this vocabulary is ultimately inadequate, and it is apparent that he, like Egaeus, is caught in the web
of language in which texts, words, and images refer back and forth to
each other. The pure signifier, the ideally motivated sign for which the
romantics yearned, and the symbol in which they put their faith, is ultimately silent, an empty signifier filled only by the interpreter's desire.

In his essay, "Freud's Masterplot," Peter Brooks observes that "narrative always make the implicit claim to be in a state of repetition, as
a going over again of a ground already covered: a *sjuzet* repeating the
fabula, as the detective retraces the tracks of the criminal."[36] Here
Brooks uses the terms of the Russian formalists—he elsewhere uses the
correspondent *récit* and *histoire,* "plot" and "story"—to point to the
fundamental claim of narrative to be an act of repetition in language
of events "in the world of reference."[37] This conventional distinction
between present writing and past events is subverted in a series of equivo-
cations at the outset of "Ligeia," which is by no means a straightforward
narration of recollected events. The narrator's failures of memory draw
statements about the past into the realm of present speculation, and
subsequent narrative characteristics indicate that he is creating or interpreting the figure of Ligeia as he writes. The double reference of
"Ligeia," which names both the tale and "the lady," emphasizes that
she is his creation in the process of narration and that her existence
prior to that given her by the text is indeterminable.

Richard Wilbur calls the first paragraph a "paroxism of noninformativeness,"[38] drawing our attention to the fact that it lacks the kind of information conventionally expected of first paragraphs and dwells instead on the failure of memory and its supplementation by present speculation and assertions of belief. The narrator's absence of memory—"I cannot, for my soul, remember . . ."; "I cannot *now* bring these points to mind . . ." (*TS* 310)—has the effect of focusing on this *now* of failed recollection and of writing. His subject here is less the past than its loss and his inability to recover it.

The narrator begins with the loss of a beginning. He cannot remember the "how, when, or even precisely where, [he] first became acquainted with the lady Ligeia" (*TS* 310). In face of this loss of an assumed first point and its defining context, he shifts his emphasis to speculate about possible causes of his loss. Perhaps "much suffering" during intervening "long years" has effaced his memory of a beginning; or perhaps there was no single point, no recallable origin to the series of "paces so steadily and stealthily progressive that they have been unnoticed and unknown" (*TS* 310). These alternatives are left unresolved, equally true or equally untrue or both, at the moment they are written. The second point about which he speculates is the loss of a different kind of beginning: "And now, while I write, a recollection flashes upon me that I have *never known* the paternal name" of Ligeia (*TS* 311). The one "fact" that he remembers, "but indistinctly," cannot satisfy his desire for recovery of the past—it is a condition of ignorance, a remembered lack of Ligeia's "paternal name," and implicitly of her validating origins. He attempts to supplement this remembered ignorance by speculation about "the circumstances which originated or attended it." Was it, he wonders, "a playful charge on the part of my Ligeia, . . . a test of my strength of affection, . . . or was it rather a caprice of my own?" (*TS* 311). But these alternatives are effaced as soon as offered—the circumstances have been "utterly forgotten" (*TS* 311).

In place of unequivocal statement of prior facts and circumstances he can offer only assertions of belief: "Yet *I believe* that I met her first and most frequently in some large, old, decaying city near the Rhine. Of her family—I *have surely* heard her speak. That it is of a remotely ancient date *cannot be doubted*" (*TS* 310; emphasis mine). The certainty insinuated by the last two sentences collapses in the subsequent "recollection that I have *never known* [her] paternal name," and in face of the fact that to the amnesiac all prior time is "remotely ancient." In this case, certainty is displaced by a recollection of ignorance; but the narrator's belief in "some large, old decaying city near the Rhine"—no matter how vague its object—returns in the narrative as reaffirmed fact when he subsequently claims that after Ligeia's death he "could no longer endure the lonely desolation of . . . dwelling in the dim and decaying city by the Rhine" (*TS* 320). The juxtaposition of these two statements of belief, given equal value at the point of writing, and their subsequent different fates—one denied, one repeated as fact—unsettles the status of his discourse and disturbs the distinction between repetition and creation; like the positing of unresolved alternative speculations, it emphasizes that the most important action in this tale involves the narrator's composition of it, that the crucial drama involves his entrapment in the web of language as he struggles to "embody" Ligeia in words, a struggle that reveals that creation *is* repetition, is necessarily belated.

Other features of his narrative support this conclusion—some more strongly than others. One is that whereby figurative statements subsequently return on the level of action: for example, the narrator's metaphoric description of the beauty of Ligeia's face—"It was the radiance of an opium dream"—returns as his slavery "in the trammels of opium" (*TS* 311, 320);[39] and Ligeia's coming and going "as a shadow" returns as the "faint, indefinite shadow" that the narrator perceives beneath the censer in Rowena's bridal/death chamber (*TS* 311, 325). This interpenetration of figure and action undercuts the truth value of his statements about events and suggests that action in the narrative may be considered the literalization of its initial figures rather than the re-presentation of prior events.

Moreover, the text stresses how the narrator's present act of writing is implicated in his attempts to remember and his struggles to fill the gaps by speculation born of desire: the process of writing itself seems to blur the distinction between memory and supplementation, repetition and creation, re-composition and composition. For example, when the narrator first draws attention to the process of composition, he insists that it is "now, while I write," that he perceives his ignorance of Ligeia's paternal name. The distinction between past and present is similarly disturbed when the narrator writes of the all-encompassing nature of Ligeia's learning and the excitement, delight, and hope with which it filled him: initially he seems to be clearly referring to events of the past; and yet, he writes: "How singularly—how thrillingly, this one point in the nature of my wife has forced itself, *at this late period only*, upon my attention! . . . I *saw not then what I now clearly perceive*, that the acquisitions of Ligeia were gigantic, were astounding" (*TS* 315–16; emphasis mine). Such statements raise obvious questions about the truth status of his extended account of Ligeia's learning and his previous experience of it; they similarly emphasize the willed character of many of the events that the text offers as recorded memories.

An analogous undecidability is introduced by another characteristic strategy of the narrator—that whereby he typically moves from a speculative statement of desire to a subsequent assumption of its truth, offering it as firm factual ground on which further statements are built. For example, he says at first of the "strangeness" that he identifies as the essence of Ligeia's beauty, that he has "tried *in vain* to detect the irregularity and to trace home [his] own perception of 'the strange'" (*TS* 312; emphasis mine); then, after his obsessive cataloguing of forehead, hair, nose, lips, teeth, and chin, he declares that it "*might have been* . . . that in [the] eyes of my beloved lay the secret" (*TS* 312–13; emphasis mine); finally, his statement is definite: "The 'strangeness' . . . *which I found* in the eyes . . ." (*TS* 313; emphasis mine). Such a movement subverts the claim of his statements on the past and implies that they cannot be measured against any clear-cut notion of truth prior or external to the text the narrator is producing in the present of its composition.

Thus the narrative itself is predicated on an interrelated series of displacements from a presumedly original visionary past. For the more optimistic romantics, memory operated as a metaphor for origins,[40] but Poe emphasizes the fundamental disjunction involved in its uncertainties and insists on the enclosing embrace of the arbitrary "world of words." The narrator's project is an attempt to transcend such an embrace, but it paradoxically reveals its own impossibility.

The terms in which the narrator offers his description of Ligeia betray the related assumptions on which they are grounded. He traces the essential "strangeness" of her beauty to that "something more profound than the well of Democritus—which lay far within the pupils of my beloved" (*TS* 313).[41] He develops a "passion to discover" this "something," assuming that he needs only to read through the ostensible manifestations of her beauty (*TS* 313). He believes that her surface is an index of her inner presence—that is, he endows her with the characteristics of a motivated sign.

Moreover, the narrator couches his description of Ligeia in terms that suggest that she was of this world and yet offered access to a transcendental realm beyond it. He describes her "person" and its fleshly parts but does so in what we could call semes of divinity. He invokes the "majesty" of her "demeanour" and claims that her beauty offered a "spirit-lifting vision . . . wildly divine"; the contours of her forehead indicated a "majesty . . . divine," and the curve of her nostrils spoke her "free spirit"; her mouth was the "triumph of all things heavenly" (*TS* 311–12). His attempt to recover her in language is an attempt to recover a lost proximity to the realm of the spirit.

To the narrator, Ligeia represents an original "spirituality" and the possibility of access to absolute truth. He links his yearning for an original with that for a full knowledge when he describes one of "the many incomprehensible anomalies of the science of mind": "In our endeavors to recall to memory something long forgotten, we often find ourselves *upon the very verge* of remembrance, without being able, in the end, to remember. And thus how frequently, in my intense scrutiny of Ligeia's eyes, have I felt approaching the full knowledge of their expression—felt it approaching—yet not quite be mine—and so at length entirely depart" (*TS* 313–14). For him, Ligeia is the focus of both desires; in her, he believes, the realm beyond memory and beyond knowledge was/is accessible.

The narrator characterizes Ligeia as a mentor figure, under whose guidance he could have penetrated to a "wisdom too divinely precious not to be forbidden!" (*TS* 316). In a significant juxtaposition he calls her "the partner of my studies, and finally the wife of my bosom" (*TS* 311).[42] He claims that her learning was preternatural—"immense . . . gigantic, . . . astounding"—and encompassed "the classical tongues . . . the modern dialects of Europe . . . [and] *all* the wide areas of moral, physical, and mathematical science" (*TS* 315–16). Because of the "infinite supremacy" of the learning of this encyclopede,[43] he submitted himself to her "guidance through the chaotic world of metaphysical investigation." Consequently, he claims, "as she

bent over me in studies," that he felt "that delicious vista by slow degrees expanding before me, down whose long, gorgeous, and all un-
trodden path, I might at length pass onward to the goal of a wisdom
too divinely precious not to be forbidden!" (*TS* 316). But just as the
significance of her "expression" eludes him in the first part of the narrative, so does ultimate revelation of this sense of absolute knowledge,
of "divine wisdom" made accessible in and through Ligeia, elude him
in the second part. Though he believes that his expectations had been
"well-grounded" and that her "presence, her readings alone," had rendered "vividly luminous the many mysteries of the transcendentalism
in which we were immersed," the ground shifts from under him as she
nears death, and "wanting the radiant lustre of her eyes, letters, lam-
bent and golden, grew duller than Saturnian lead" (*TS* 316).

(This lost "divine wisdom" is analogous to that "full knowledge" of
her expression for which he longs.)His description emphasizes the in-
tensely subjective nature of his hopes: "With how vast a triumph—
with how vivid a delight—with how much of all that is ethereal in
hope—did I *feel* . . . that delicious vista . . . expanding before me"
(*TS* 316). This echoes his earlier discussion of the meaning of her
expression, in which it is the *felt effect* of "strangeness" that he tries to
"trace home." In doing so he encounters more strangeness—"strange,
oh strangest mystery of all!":

> I found, in the commonest objects of the universe, a circle of anal-
> ogies to that expression. . . . in the survey of a rapidly-growing
> vine—in the contemplation of a moth, a butterfly, a chrysalis, a
> stream of running water. I have felt it in the ocean; in the falling
> of a meteor. I have felt it in the glances of unusually aged people.
> And there are one or two stars in heaven—(one especially, a star
> of the sixth magnitude, double and changeable, to be found near
> the large star in Lyra) in a telescopic scrutiny of which I have
> been made aware of the feeling. I have been filled with it by cer-
> tain sounds from stringed instruments, and not unfrequently by
> passages from books. (*TS* 314)

Lawrence Buell has studied the use of catalogue rhetoric by the American transcendentalists, and locates its dominant impulse in "the sense
of the underlying identity of all things in the universe as manifesta-

tions of the divine plenitude."[44] He also notes the sense of terror and of chaos beyond control that is the dark side of such a rhetoric.[45] The unifying element of the narrator's analogical tracings is located not in their motivating spirit but in their effect on the narrator, in the "sentiment such as I felt always aroused within me by [Ligeia's] large and luminous orbs"—that is, in the effect of "the strange." However, the relationship of cause and effect is not straightforward, for he feels the effect only after he has internalized Ligeia's beauty— "subsequently to the period when Ligeia's beauty passed into my spirit, there dwelling as in a shrine" (*TS* 314). His subjective sense of "the strange," of otherness that escapes definition and analysis and for which there can be no adequate linguistic representation, contaminates his analogical reading of the world and determines all—including his present writing.

The double loss—of the "full knowledge" of Ligeia's "expression" and the "wisdom . . . divinely precious" (*TS* 314, 316)—implicates Ligeia inextricably in language. Most crucially, Ligeia is invested by the narrator with a significance that cannot be translated into words. The text demonstrates that his attempted recuperation, as soon as he begins to write, must always be cast in a culturally encoded language. (And it shows that the symbol is mute—it does not offer access to the transcendent, but is merely endlessly, frustratingly suggestive, dependent on the subjective will to interpret for its significance.)

When the narrator claims that "there is one dear topic . . . on which my memory fails me not. It is the *person* of Ligeia," he emphasizes the singularity of what he is trying to recapture (*TS* 311). She is, like the symbol, a product or creation of the narrator's desire: self-sufficient and free of originating or attendant context. Yet his phrasing also implies that her significance is constrained by language; she is a "topic" to be opened out. And indeed he does so, addressing part by part. The terms of his description replace the lost context with one that is culturally encoded—one in which any "original" is lost beneath layers of cultural accretion, displacements from model to model. Her beauty was "more wildly divine than the phantasies which hovered about the slumbering souls of the daughters of Delos" (*TS* 311); her hair, "raven-black [and] . . . glossy," set "forth the full force of the Homeric epithet, 'hyacinthine!'" The "delicate outlines" of her

nose compared with those on "the graceful medallions of the He-
brews," and her chin had "the contour which the God Apollo revealed
but in a dream, to Cleomenes, the son of the Athenian" (*TS* 312).

This insistent cataloguing of her parts fragments her and emphasizes the impossibility of his task—that is, the reproduction of the
unity of immediate presence—the "essence" both of his interpretation
of Ligeia and of the symbol—in a medium that is mediatory, arbitrary,
and must proceed consecutively. He must write her in terms of the
already written; her beauty can be phrased only in terms of previous
models already encoded. He cannot get beyond language. When he
cites Bacon—"There is no exquisite beauty . . . without some *strangeness* in the proportion" (*TS* 311–12)—he makes a substitution appropriate to his enterprise—of "exquisite" for "excellent."[46] Excellence
is a quality that in its root meaning of rising above all others, of towering over, would seem to fit the narrator's conception of Ligeia's
transcendental beauty. But "exquisite" implies that the quality he seeks
to describe is not immediately available (from Latin, *exquisire*, "to
search out diligently") and must be sought out, and the narrator attempts to do just that; he tries to "detect" it and "trace [it] home"
(*TS* 312). As we have seen, his detection traces across the surface of
her various parts, her fragments encoded in textual fragments, and
then centers on her eyes—"for which we have no models in the remotely antique" (*TS* 312). This denial of prior models emphasizes the
unique, inner presence, the "secret" within the eyes of Ligeia that he
so desperately wants to penetrate. The strangeness is not in the collocation of forms implied by Bacon's term "proportion," but is, "of
a nature distinct from the formation, or the colour, or the brilliancy
of the features"—it is in the "expression" (*TS* 313). So it has been
traced home. Or has it? His project is to attach the word "strangeness," already a citation to a previous text, to the referential world;
he decides that it "must, after all, be referred to the *expression*." But
the subsequent lament—"Ah, word of no meaning! behind whose vast
latitude of mere sound we intrench our ignorance of so much of the
spiritual" (*TS* 313)—emphasizes that he can refer words to words
only in what promises to be a potentially endless series of displacements. This characteristic is reinforced by the narrator's use of "of"
constructions—as in: "The hue *of* the orbs was the most brilliant *of*
black, and, far over them, hung jetty lashes *of* great length"; "The

expression *of* the eyes *of* Ligeia," etc. (*TS* 313; emphasis mine). Used throughout his opening portrait of Ligeia, this construction recurs obsessively in the paragraph describing her person. It suggests both the struggle to attach Ligeia's uniqueness to language codes and the discontinuities that such strategies fail to overcome.

The relationship between surface features, described in terms of textual codes, and inner essence that cannot be translated, is analogous to that implied in the first paragraph between the "large, old, decaying city near the Rhine" and Ligeia's paternal name, lost beyond recovery. This homology—surface beauty/inner essence; decaying city/paternal (originating) name—in which each second term is irrecoverable has several implications. The most immediate is that in a transitive world we can never recall origins or know essence. Moreover, it establishes a relationship between beauty and death—in the figure of Ligeia we are shown perfection and death inextricably implicated one with another. Third, it implies a link between representation and death, or recomposition and decomposition. Though the narrator claims an original intuition of the essence of transcendent beauty behind or beyond Ligeia's surface appearance, it must be displaced into representation before it is available for translation—which necessarily involves both a loss of the immediacy of the intuition and the death of the object.[47]

The narrator's project in the first part of the tale is thus to recover in his narrative the lost presence of Ligeia whom he has invested with the redemptive qualities of the ideal sign, the symbol. As we have seen, his account is inscribed with the marks of its inevitable failure; moreover, his interpretation of Ligeia as intransitive symbol of infinitude is punctuated and punctured by his description of her death. From this perspective, the subsequent events of the narrative may be considered as analogues of this failure dramatized on the level of action.

The deathbed scene itself has a certain lowering effect on the narrator's account of, for example, "that delicious vista" that opens up before him as Ligeia "bent over me in studies" (*TS* 316). Joel Porte shows that the secret to which the narrator would penetrate has a repressed sexual content,[48] and throughout the text sexuality and understanding are interrelated. What in the first part of his account the narrator depicts in terms of promised revelation of a "wisdom too divinely precious not to be forbidden" (*TS* 316), is now 'implicated in his discovery of her "passionate devotion" to him, her love that "amounted to idolatry" (*TS* 317). This interrelationship is subsequently reaffirmed in the narrator's recollections "of her purity, of her wisdom, of her lofty, her ethereal nature, of her passionate, her idolatrous love [for him]" (*TS* 323). Thus there are hints that the desire for the transcendent is implicitly a displacement of frustrated sexual desire.

The deathbed scene is followed by the narrator's account of his removal to England, his purchase there of an old abbey, and his redecoration of its interior. His description of this episode suggests that it is an ironic analogue for his attempt to recover the lost presence of Ligeia in the first part of his narrative. Whereas Ligeia's death marks his sense of loss of the transcendental, the decayed abbey is associated with an analogous spiritual loss—the "many melancholy . . . memories" connected with it *"had much in unison* with the feelings of utter abandonment" that the narrator feels (*TS* 320; emphasis mine). His decoration project is an attempt to fill and so give significance to a decayed exterior from which a presumed spiritual essence has long departed.

His filling of the abandoned inner "spiritual" space of the abbey is depicted in terms that associate this space with the lost presence of Ligeia and so confirms his identification of her with transcendental loss. The "display of more than regal magnificence" is enabled by her "wealth," inherited by the narrator (*TS* 320). He brings "the fair-haired and blue-eyed Lady Rowena Trevanion, of Tremaine" to the inner "bridal chamber" explicitly as "the successor of the unforgotten Ligeia" (*TS* 321). Moreover, the extended description of the decor of this chamber occupies a position structurally parallel to that of "the person" of Ligeia. The introductory sentence—"There is no individual portion of the architecture and decoration of that bridal chamber which is not now visibly before me"—recalls his image of Ligeia brought "before [his] eyes in fancy," and the "one dear topic . . . on which [his] memory fails [him] not" (*TS* 321, 311). Here, too, he dwells on the vagaries of memory: "I have said that I minutely remember the details of the chamber—yet I am sadly forgetful on topics of deep moment" (*TS* 321). And in this we have another ironic reflection on his initial project. The "topics of great moment"—the origin, the supernal, the transcendental—all those qualities that he has projected onto Ligeia—are resolutely beyond memory. But the details of "the fantastic display" take hold, and he describes the interior fully, in terms that emphasize their materiality and their explicitly cultural provenance.

Whereas in the description of Ligeia he attempts to penetrate her surface beauty to an essence beneath where his terms assert their necessarily cultural, arbitrary nature, here he documents his filling of an inner space by an act of will—yet he can fill it only with explicitly cultural products. His actions, which, he recognizes, could easily be labeled as "madness," comment ironically on his earlier efforts. Implicitly, he is attempting to restore the presence of absolute being to a world that he feels has been "abandoned." Significantly, the room is pentagonal, the shape of the mystic "sacred space" at the heart of the pentacle, which supposedly allows the magus to call up and control the powers of the spiritual world. Yet, again ironically, in each of its angles "stood on end a gigantic sarcophagus of black granite, from the tombs of the kings over against Luxor, with their aged lids full of immemorial sculpture" (*TS* 322). These sarcophagi are emblematic of the problems faced by the narrator in his attempt to recover Ligeia in his narrative. The repository of royal flesh, memorializing in their inscriptions the king within, sarcophagi (from Greek, "flesh-eater"), in fact consume that flesh, and their inscriptions become "immemorial sculpture." Beneath the unreadable lids the monuments are hollow, a space occupied only by the irredeemable absence that is death, memorial only to the loss of memory.[49]

The "chief phantasy of all," though, is provided by a "heavy and massive-looking tapestry" that covers "the lofty walls" and is

> found alike as a carpet on the floor, as a covering for the ottomans and the ebony bed, as a canopy for the bed, and as the gorgeous volutes of the curtains which partially shaded the window. The material was the richest cloth of gold. It was spotted all over, at irregular intervals, with arabesque figures, about a foot in diameter, and wrought upon the cloth in patterns of the most jetty black. But these figures partook of the true character of the arabesque only when regarded from a single point of view. By a contrivance now common, and indeed traceable to a very remote period of antiquity, they were made changeable in aspect. To one entering the room, they bore the appearance of simple monstrosi-

ties; but upon a farther advance, this appearance gradually departed; and step by step, as the visiter moved his station in the
chamber, he saw himself surrounded by an endless succession of
the ghastly forms which belong to the superstition of the Norman,
or arise in the guilty slumbers of the monk. The phantasmagoric
effect was vastly heightened by the artificial introduction of a
strong continual current of wind behind the draperies—giving a
hideous and uneasy animation to the whole. (*TS* 322)

Thompson observes that "the arabesque decor as Poe uses it is not
merely the monstrousness of supernatural things but is a matter of
appearance, of deceptiveness, of perspective and point of view in an
overall design," and notes that this passage is "a kind of allegorical
statement" about this tale and about " 'tales of the grotesque and arabesque,' " suggesting that "the real subject of such tales is subconscious and obsessive delusion."[50] The passage also provides an implicit
commentary on the narrator's endeavors. If we note the parallel between the steps by which the "visitor" advances into the room and the
"progressive paces" of the narrative's first paragraph, suggesting passage through time, this description implies that an "arabesque" view
of the world—even if merely of a repeated pattern of "simple mon-
strosities"—is inevitably transformed through displacements in time
into an "endless succession of the ghastly forms," as haunting and
indeterminate as superstition and nightmare. The passage also comments on the "circle of analogies," in that these "forms" are also animated by "spirit," but in this case literally an "artificial introduction
of a strong continual current of wind behind the draperies—giving
a hideous and uneasy animation to the whole." The shift is significant,
for the narrator is no longer struggling to trace an intuited spiritual
presence in a circle of disparate images but is instead actively imposing a "willed" animation upon the arbitrary collection of forms
with which he seeks to supply an inner "regal magnificence" to the
decayed abbey that is his world.

   This suffocating enclosure—bridal chamber or crypt?—is the site
of the final scene. The narrative maintains the uncertainty of the temporal status of the action as the narrator says that "I revelled in recollections of [Ligeia's] purity, of her wisdom, of her lofty, her ethereal
nature, of her passionate, her idolatrous love. *Now, then,* did my spirit

fully and freely burn" (*TS* 323; emphasis mine). Rowena's death and Ligeia's return to inhabit her corpse have prompted fierce debate: does the narrator poison Rowena? As Thompson points out, he is even supplied with a motive.[51] Is Ligeia's return an opium-induced hallucination? The references to his addiction are clear. Even he is uncertain: "I saw, or may have dreamed . . ." (*TS* 325). Or do we accept the sober-sided supernatural reading? The latter persists implicitly in such recent work as Taylor Stoehr's " 'Unspeakable Horror' in Poe," which claims that "Ligeia" shows the power of names to "produce their referents," that the narrator, "by chanting [Ligeia's] name, . . . has succeeded in reviving not merely her image, but her very body."[52] Stoehr implies that the narrator has closed the gap between signifier and signified, has somehow recovered a motivated sign in which name and thing named are one. However, such a reading ignores, first, the fundamental hesitation of the narrative between natural and supernatural explanations, a hesitancy made all the more acute by the epistemological uncertainty of the narrator. Second, it ignores the fact that from its opening sentence the narrative is predicated on loss, not recovery.

When Rowena died "the hands of her menials prepared her for the tomb," and her body was "shrouded." The narrator sat with "the pallid and rigid figure" (*TS* 326). During the series of revivifications and relapses Rowena's name is dropped out of the narrative to be replaced by "the body," "the corpse," and "the thing." Each relapse is attended by "a sterner and apparently more irredeemable death" (*TS* 328): after the first, "the color disappeared from both eyelid and cheek, leaving a wanness even more than that of marble; the lips became doubly shrivelled and pinched up in the ghastly expression of death; a repulsive clamminess and coldness overspread rapidly the surface of the body; and all the usual rigorous stiffness immediately supervened" (*TS* 327). After the second, "the whole body took upon itself the icy chilliness, the livid hue, the intense rigidity, the sunken outline, and *all the loathsome peculiarities of that which has been, for many days, a tenant of the tomb*" (*TS* 328; emphasis mine). Each episode, he states, "was succeeded by I know not what of wild change in the personal appearance of the corpse" (*TS* 329). The nature of such "wild change" is left open and can be read as Rowena's physical displacement by Ligeia.

However, just as the narrator has introduced an "artificial" "animation" into the decayed abbey by a projection of will, so here, implicitly, he has animated the decayed corpse by a projection of desire. Confronted by the "charnel" figure he shrieks that "these are the full, and the black, and the wild eyes—of my lost love—of the lady—of the LADY LIGEIA!" (*TS* 329, 330). Once more, the "of" constructions function ambiguously, suggesting similarity and hence difference as well as possession and identity. In an ironic fulfilment of the narrator's desires for full presence, the name "Ligeia" is attached not to the pure, the wise, the lofty, the ethereal Ligeia but to a corpse that has undergone the "wild change" of progressive decomposition. The symbol, then, does not offer access to the infinite, but is a blank, or rather, like the corpse, it is mute, accepting a significance imparted to it by the interpreting mind—though the mind be one seized by "inexpressible madness" (*TS* 330).

VI

Voice

and

Text:

Displacements

of

Authority

As the last chapter demonstrates, Poe's skepticism circumscribes the visionary idealism of the romantic symbol by revealing that it exhibits the very disjuncture between signifier and signified that his narrators yearn to escape, and by suggesting that this disjuncture is only apparently overcome by force of a desire that is revealed as monomania. This chapter focuses on how Poe brings this skepticism to bear on the character of the "voice" in written texts—a recurring if indirect issue in several of the previous analyses in this study—addressing specifically the question of the authority of a written record and the degree to which a recovered authorial voice can be used to validate a unitary interpretation of a text. "Ligeia" suggests that the inaccessible supernal and the irrecoverable past are figures for each other, equally ineffable; the following analyses examine tales featuring, first, a voice purporting to speak from the beyond—in "The Facts in the Case of M. Valdemar" (1845)—and, second, a voice recovered from the ancient past—in "Some Words with a Mummy" (1845). In each case, the speaker is presented in terms that suggest he be considered a figure for a written text, and in each case the authority of the voice that speaks is subverted. Moreover, the narrators' interpretations are revealed as deluded appropriations of power over the word, and their accounts themselves undercut the ground on which they base their own authority.

The Philosophy of Decomposition: M. Valdemar's Tongue

The question of the authority of a written record is directly addressed in "The Facts in the Case of M. Valdemar." In this tale, the narrator is supremely confident of his control over his language and its adequacy to convey "facts" ascertained by empirical observation. The announcement contained in the title—that these are unambiguously *the* facts in the *case*—makes no concession and is reinforced in the second paragraph: "the *facts* . . . are, succinctly, these" (*TS* 1233). As a "case" history, the narrative claims kinship with legal and scientific discourse[1] and shares the pretension to adequate circumscription of the world. Appropriately, this sense of circumscription is reflected in the narrator's schematization of his original motives for undertaking the experiment ("first . . . ; secondly . . . ; thirdly . . .") and is maintained throughout the narrative. He emphasizes that he is recording that which was "evident" or "apparent" to the observers present and implicitly effaces both himself and his language, assuming that neither offers any resistance to the reader's access to the events in the phenomenal world. He confidently assumes that his discourse, like the signs of mesmeric influence that he reads in Valdemar's body, is "unequivocal"—unambiguous and fully adequate to the representation of his intended meaning.

These assumptions underpin and provide his justification for the authority of his written record, which he opposes to the "many unpleasant misrepresentations" of public speculation. His narrative is an attempt to regain control over the dissemination of information. He had originally tried to retain such control by silence—"all parties concerned" had desired "to keep the affair from the public," but their endeavours to do so had actually prompted the generation of speculative accounts to fill the silence, the gap in knowledge (*TS* 1233).

Orally transmitted gossip arises without any specifically identifiable human agency—"a garbled or exaggerated account made its way into society" (*TS* 1233)—and its lack of a clear "parent" makes it, from the narrator's point of view, culpably deformed from birth, for there exists no single authority who can vouch for its authenticity or be held responsible for "misrepresentations" in it.

P——'s insistence on the incompatibility of, and clear demarcation between, representation and misrepresentation is also an insistence on the disjunction between fact and fiction. On one level, this strategy can be read in the context of Poe's deliberate exploitation of that convention of fiction whereby, in the words of J. Hillis Miller, "it is presented not as a work of fiction but as some other form of language . . . almost always some 'representational' form rooted in history and in the direct report of 'real' human experience."[2] And in these terms, if we are to judge by the correspondence Poe received—from, for example, the self-proclaimed mesmerist, Robert Collyer—and by the tale's initial publication history and reception in England, where it was printed in the *Popular Record of Modern Science* and in a pirated pamphlet, *Mesmerism "in articulo mortis,"* the alibi was fairly successful.[3] In establishing the alibi, however, the narrator suggests an opposition between authorized writing and irresponsible speech—between an orderly, direct, written report, grounded in empirical observation and unchanging through time, and disorderly, creative, spoken constructions without grounds in the phenomenal world, assuming various forms as they are passed on.

At first, this distinction between gossip and written text appears to present few problems. P—— opposes the groundless and authorless products of the wagging of tongues with his own single-authored, written testimony. Paradoxically, however, this testimony depends strongly on the value of personal voice in the written text, thereby implicitly accepting the privilege of speech over writing. Moreover, whereas P—— objects to the drifting, groundless play of gossip and attempts to interdict it in his writing, it is precisely these qualities of gossip that writing shares.[4] He is attempting to stop with the written word a process characteristic of writing. Further, the central event of the text radically disturbs such distinctions as it presents a figure that may be read as a text that indeed "speaks," but it does so through a blackened tongue that can only announce its own death.

The narrator's claims to veracity are supported by his apparently scrupulous recording of chronology and observed details. Yet frequently those features that contribute to his credibility also undermine it. For example, as G. R. Thompson points out,[5] the methodical and precise depiction of Valdemar's symptoms in medical terminology begins reasonably enough, recording those that would be apparent to an external examination of a still-living subject: his face was "leaden," his eyes "lustreless," his cheekbones protrusive, his expectoration "excessive," and his "pulse was barely perceptible" (*TS* 1235). But then P—— records the "minute account of the patient's condition" given him by Doctors D—— and F——, accounts that have two remarkable features: first, they describe the internal symptoms, such as would have been available only after a post mortem; second, the symptoms are so extreme as to apply only to one already dead.[6] His lungs are almost completely "ossified"; those areas not so are "a mass of purulent tubercles, running one into another." Moreover, the lungs are perforated, and "at one point, permanent adhesion to the ribs had taken place." As if this were not enough, the hapless Valdemar "was suspected of aneurism of the aorta; but on this point the osseous symptoms rendered exact diagnosis impossible" (*TS* 1235). The modest concession of the last clause points amusingly to the absurdity of the whole diagnosis. As Poe puns in his response to the praise of the self-proclaimed mesmerist Collyer, it "may be called a hard case—*very* hard for M. Valdemar."[7]

We can certainly read this, as Thompson does, as one element supporting a hoaxical reading of the tale, evincing "Poe's skeptical attitude toward the nightside, despite his obsessive fascination with it."[8] In the present context, however, we can also note the hesitancy introduced into the narrator's account by the tension between his claim to authority over the medical "facts" in Valdemar's "case" and the bizarre undermining of that case by those same facts.

Another element ostensibly supports P——'s claim for the unambiguous veracity of his version of events while simultaneously disturbing it: his dependence on the "memoranda" of Mr. Theodore L——l, who, according to the narrator, "was so kind as to accede to my desire that he would take notes of all that occurred" (*TS* 1236). From these notes, "what I now have to relate is, for the most part, either condensed or copied *verbatim*." On the one hand, P—— offers this fact as reassurance that he is not relying merely on the resources of his own memory; but on the other, the phrasing indicates the presence in his "relation" of at least three orders of text—L——l's notes copied word for word, the notes "condensed" or edited by P——, and P——'s independently written version.[9] When to this veritable collage we add Valdemar's note, itself copied verbatim, and his puzzling memoranda in his pocket-book (puzzling in that Valdemar knows that he is about to die and will need no aids to memory), the narrator's claim to univocity begins to disintegrate, and the distinction between his text and the multiauthored versions of gossip begins to collapse.

P——'s rigid distinction between his written "truth" and the publicly spoken "falsehood" is further blurred by his claim for a "natural" connection between "unpleasant misrepresentations" and "disbelief"; after all, *his* narrative is certainly not pleasant, and he fears that "every reader will be startled into positive disbelief" by it (*TS* 1240). Is his version, then, representation or misrepresentation? Moreover, he shares a motive with the anonymous public who fill the gap in knowledge by speculation; he undertakes his experiment in order to satisfy his "curiosity," to fill an "omission" in the "series of experiments made hitherto" (*TS* 1233). His own experiment, the event that supposedly authorizes his account, has itself a fictional, constructive quality not different in kind from the subsequent constructions of gossip. This quality, in turn, contaminates his record of the "facts." Moreover, his implicit distinction between written and spoken word, and between the credence to be attached to each is undercut in the conflation of text and tongue in the figure of M. Valdemar.

The issue of the authority of text *and* speech is crucially posed by the central "character" of the tale, M. Valdemar, since there is sufficient evidence to consider him as a figure for a written text. When P—— introduces him as the "good subject" for his "test," he identifies him with particular strategies of control over the written word. First, he is "the well-known compiler of the 'Bibliotheca Forensica'" (*TS* 1234). Whether Valdemar has compiled a bibliography or an actual collection of legal texts, his act involves an assumption of power over the letter as thing, subject to manipulation and control. His second role, that of "author (under the *nom de plume* of Issachar Marx) of the Polish versions of 'Wallenstein' and 'Gargantua,'" has other implications (*TS* 1234). First, just as the narrator assumes the transparency of his own language—that is, he effaces it in the service of prior empirical "facts"—so the act of translation attaches primacy to a meaning that is assumed to exist prior to language and separable from it. The pen name—that index of the authorial function rather than any author—labels such an approach "Issachar Marx," which is an appropriate name, since, as Mabbott notes, "Issachar" means "he brings gifts" (*TS* 1243, n.1); such an approach considers language as merely the bringer of the gift of meaning and the written word as merely "Marx" on a page for its conveyance.[10]

This valorization of meaning over text, of signified over signifier, has parallels in the dualistic soul/body relationship that is implicated in the question of Valdemar's speaking tongue—where we shall see that the passage from signifier to signified is by no means an unequivocal one. Meanwhile, we can observe another parallel—ironically, that between Valdemar's treatment of the inscribed word as object and the narrator's exercise of power over Valdemar's body (increasingly thinglike as it ossifies) in his experiment. P—— "subdues" Valdemar and places him under "mesmeric influence." Then

> with a few rapid lateral passes I made the lids quiver, as in incipient sleep, and with a few more I closed them altogether. I was not satisfied, however, with this, but continued the manipulations vigorously, and with the fullest exertion of the will, until I had completely stiffened the limbs of the slumberer, after placing them in a seemingly easy position. The legs were at full length; the arms were nearly so, and reposed on the bed at a moderate distance from the loins. The head was very slightly elevated. . . . I made a kind of half effort to influence his right arm in pursuit of my own. . . . His arm very readily, although feebly, followed every direction I assigned it with mine. (*TS* 1237, 1238)

As Valdemar's body becomes more subject to the narrator's rituals of control, it also comes to be identified figuratively with the written text. Throughout the narrative he is subject to the "reading" of others—in that the physicians may be said to read the signs of his condition and the narrator to read the "signs of the mesmeric influence" (*TS* 1237)—but as the account progresses, more explicitly textual associations are evoked. Valdemar is first described in terms of the "violent contrast" between the "whiteness of his whiskers" and the "blackness of his hair" (*TS* 1234). As the account of his demise advances his skin coloring also becomes distinctly textlike. In the same paragraph in which the narrator describes Valdemar "penciling memoranda in a pocket-book," he observes that "his face wore a leaden hue" (*TS* 1235). Subsequently, at the critical time at which the narrator implies that Valdemar dies, his "skin generally assumed a cadaverous hue, resembling not so much parchment as white paper" (*TS* 1239). If this change in skin color represents, however tenuously, the fading of the significant marks of a text, leaving only a blank page, what then do we make of the event that immediately follows: "the lower jaw fell with an audible jerk, leaving the mouth widely extended, and disclosing in full view the swollen and blackened tongue" (*TS* 1239)? Out of the cadaverous white paper, the deathly black tongue vibrates and speaks.

When Poe reprinted "The Facts in the Case of M. Valdemar" in the *Broadway Journal,* 20 December 1845, he added an introduction in which he responded to speculation about the "truth or falsity of the statements made" in his "article"; his comment was that "we leave it to speak for itself."[11] The text's tongue does indeed speak for itself, without the usual aid of lips and respiration. This fact, together with Valdemar's identification with the written text, implicitly undermines the narrator's distinction between speech and text by conflating them. The "text" does speak, and it has a powerful and significant effect on the two writer-figures, P—— and L——l. First, it shakes the narrator's confidence in his control over his medium; his discourse comes close to breaking down when he attempts to represent the voice. It was "such as it would be madness in me to attempt describing." He can suggest "two or three epithets which might be considered as applicable to it in part; . . . for example, that the sound was harsh, and broken and hollow; but the hideous whole is indescribable, for the simple reason that no similar sounds have ever jarred upon the ear of humanity" (*TS* 1240). It seems to be a pure, original voice that escapes the common-sense empirical language of the narrator. When he attempts to characterize its "intonation" and convey its "*unearthly* peculiarity" (my emphasis), he can do so only in figures that emphasize their own earthly quality—"the voice seemed to reach our ears . . . from some deep cavern within the earth"—and palpability—"it impressed me . . . as gelatinous or glutinous matters impress the sense of touch"—which magnifies the distance between his language and the unutterable utterance of the tongue (*TS* 1240). In addition, the voice actually causes L——l, ostensibly the primary recorder of these events, to swoon and reduces the others present to silence: "For nearly an hour, we busied ourselves, silently—without the utterance of a word" (*TS* 1241).

What is the cause of such an effect, such a spasm of inarticulation? The narrator has attempted to arrest Valdemar *"in articulo mortis,"* just at the point of the ultimate difference—that between life and death, which is the hidden, the unknown, the secret against which life is defined. While his body is held in suspension, free from decomposition, his tongue speaks in a voice that prompts Daniel Hoffman, among others, to ask "what . . . [is] speaking if not the soul?"[12] And it certainly appears that Valdemar's tongue is occupying the place of the privileged translator of the transcendental Beyond into the local Now—the place, in fact, of the symbol. But the emphasis here is not on the unity of the real and the ideal, but on their discontinuity. The voice speaks from the marginal *in between,* the place of absolute difference, where its "syllabification," its production of sound by difference, is perfect—"wonderfully, thrillingly distinct" (*TS* 1240)—and its utterance—*"I am dead"*—is an articulation of "pure" difference in which the terms are mutually canceling. As Roland Barthes observes, it is *"a speech which is impossible insofar as it is speech."*[13]

The tongue, then, announces the impossibility of the symbol's provision of access to the supernal, or, in other terms, to the secret signified of which death itself is the signifier. And, as voice in the text, which speaks only to say *"I am dead,"* it memorializes its own distance from its object and so subverts the narrator's ideal of a transparent text offering untroubled access to the phenomenal world. Representation is always displacement and, like the image in the mirror held to Valdemar's lips, is always implicated in the death of the object represented.

Representation and misrepresentation, fact and fiction, are here inextricably intertwined. The narrator has assumed that his record of the facts can be pure and uncontaminated by the falsehoods of "misrepresentations." The final scene, however, offers a climactic ironic comment on this assumption, and, implicitly, on his related assumptions of the polar opposition between truth and falsehood, letter and voice. Throughout, P—— has attempted to recompose the facts in the case in the structure of his narrative in order to regain unequivocal authorized control over them and impose the stability of "truth." Analogously, in the final stage of his experiment, he frantically attempts to "recompose" Valdemar,[14] to reestablish him in the stable mesmeric trance that P—— believes he can understand and therefore control. The end of each project coincides as, "beneath [his] hands" the "frame" rots away and, in a figure for all endings, "upon the bed, before that whole company, there lay a nearly liquid mass of loathsome—of detestable putridity" (*TS* 1243). Formless, viscous, and slippery, this is an apt image of the signifier that both resists access to an authentic signified and prompts the production of interpretations that, finally, must all be (mis)representations.

The Voice in the Text:
"the mother-tongue of the mummy"

"Some Words with a Mummy" has attracted little commentary; it has most often merely been cited *en passant* as evidence of Poe's distaste for the contemporary mythology of progress as it was expressed in politics, science, and commerce.[15] In the words of its singular spokesman, the revivified Mummy Allamistakeo, progress "was at one time quite a nuisance, but it never progressed" (*TS* 1193). Those studies that focus on the tale do so to identify its sources and references to contemporary figures like George Robins Gliddon and James Silk Buckingham.[16] Ironically, however, the tale itself implicitly undercuts this very activity, positing a fundamental skepticism toward the accessibility of the past in and through textual representations. It denies the assumption that the interpretation of texts is an enterprise that, as readings accumulate, draws ever closer to the goal of perfect understanding of the original truths they are presumed to embody; and, more generally, it questions any interpretive effort to recover from a text an authentic "voice" with which to reinvest writing with the authority of the spoken word.[17]

At one point, Allamistakeo explains why certain Egyptians chose to be embalmed before the end of their "natural term" of life—eight hundred years—and cites the case of an historian, who having attained the age of five hundred, would write a book with great labor and then get himself carefully embalmed; leaving instructions to his executors *pro tem.*, that they should cause him to be revivified after the lapse of a certain period—say five or six hundred years. . . . He would invariably find his great work converted into a species of hap-hazard notebook—that is to say, into a kind of literary arena for the conflicting guesses, riddles, and personal squabbles of whole herds of exasperated commentators. These guesses, etc., which passed under the name of annotations or emendations, were found so completely to have enveloped, distorted, and overwhelmed the text, that the author had to go about with a lantern to discover his own book. (*TS* 1189)

This complaint about the vulnerability of the written word to misinterpretation is a familiar one. The classic statement is that of Socrates, in *Phaedrus:* "Once a thing is put in writing, the composition, whatever it may be, drifts all over the place, getting into the hands not only of those who understand it, but equally of those who have no business with it; it doesn't know how to address the right people, and not address the wrong. And when it is ill-treated and unfairly abused it always needs its parent to come to its help, being unable to defend or help itself."[18] Allamistakeo seems to be describing a solution to the plight of the orphaned text. The revivified historian must follow a "process of re-scription and personal rectification"; that is, he must first rewrite his text and then correct "from his own private knowledge and experience, the traditions of the day concerning the epoch at which he had originally lived." He speaks as the past in the present and so prevents "history from degenerating into absolute fable" (*TS* 1189).

Such a revival of an authentic voice is paralleled in the case of Allamistakeo, who is represented, in part, as a text that speaks back. He is discovered at the heart of a series of inscribed layers. The outer "large box, or case" is *"papier maché,* composed of papyrus" and "thickly ornamented with paintings, representing funeral scenes, and other mournful subjects" (*TS* 1179). Moreover, among these, "in every variety of position, were certain series of hieroglyphical characters intended, no doubt, for the name of the departed. By good luck, Mr. Gliddon formed one of our party; and he had no difficulty in translating the letters, which were simply phonetic, and represented the word, *Allamistakeo*" (*TS* 1179). The group gathered about this box must open two other boxes, one inside the other, before penetrating to the core, to the body named by the hieroglyphs. The Mummy so discovered is sheathed in papyrus "and coated with a layer of plaster, thickly gilt and painted. The paintings represented subjects connected with the various supposed duties of the soul, and its presentation to different divinities, with numerous identical human figures, intended, very probably, as portraits of the person embalmed. Extending from head to foot, was a columnar or perpendicular inscription in phonetic hieroglyphs, giving again his name and titles, and the names and titles of his relations" (*TS* 1180). They strip off the layers of papyrus and uncover the "flesh" beneath.

The process so far has been an exercise of power, of an "interest" that reduces the sepulchres and their contents to "specimens . . . at our disposal" (*TS* 1179). Such "disposal" initially takes the form of their physical control over the Mummy, which had so far been "subject only externally to public examination," as they remove its outer inscribed layers; their interpretive confidence in similarly "disposing" of the meaning of these outer inscriptions is reflected in the unhesitating descriptions of the nature of the representations (disturbed momentarily by the verbal tics of "no doubt," and "very probably") and in Gliddon's ease in translating the "simply phonetic" letters. Certain elements, however, subvert this approach. Their Mummy has been transferred "from a tomb near Eleithias" and is regarded as a particular "treasure" because such tombs, according to the narrator, "are of higher interest [than those at Thebes], on account of affording more numerous illustrations of the private life of Egyptians" (*TS* 1179). But a project, whether it involves texts or corpses, that seeks to recover "life" from "sepulchres" has an element of perverseness; and the distance between death and the doubly remote "private life" implies that interpretations of that life will bear a tenuous relation to any original.

This sense of subversion is reinforced by Gliddon's translation of the phonetic hieroglyphs. As John T. Irwin points out, Poe might well be alluding here to Champollion's "discovery of the key to the phonetic character of the hieroglyphics through the translation of Egyptian proper names."[19] But because the phonetic is the most complex of the three types of sign that Champollion identified—the other two being the figurative and the symbolic, tropic, or aenigmatic[20]—we should be suspicious of the ease of Gliddon's translation, especially since it yields "*Allamistakeo*." The name appears "in every variety of position" on the outer boxes and extends "from head to foot" on the inner papyrus sheath (*TS* 1180). The examiners assume that it names the Mummy, but the phrasing—"the letters . . . represented the word"—leaves the precise nomination in question; it could easily name their project and, like the word "DISCOVERY" in "MS. Found in a Bottle," mock the very search for meaning from which it issues.[21]

Having reached the flesh, which, the narrator observes, is "in excellent preservation, with no perceptible odor" (*TS* 1180), the examiners search "the corpse very carefully for the usual openings through which the entrails are extracted" but discover none. Before continuing inward by dissection, they decide on "the application of electricity" to the Mummy, in a spirit—"one tenth in earnest and nine tenths in jest"—that emphasizes the sense of contempt that is implicated in the assumption of control (*TS* 1181). When the Mummy is galvanized into life, their interpretive complacency is assaulted: they are faced no longer with the dead letter, the orphaned word open to interpretive abuse, but with an inscription that *talks back*; they have literally revived a presence within the text. Like the revivified historian, Allamistakeo sets about correcting the "traditions of the day concerning the epoch at which he had originally lived" (*TS* 1189).

Many commentators accept the "authority" of Allamistakeo's voice in his refutation of the "fable" of progress and perfectibility, but ironically his remarks and the narrative situation in which they are delivered undercut his own claim to authority; the voice speaking from within the text may indeed be "All a mistake, oh!" When he describes the historian searching for his original book beneath the layers of accumulated commentary, emendation, and annotation, he remarks that "when discovered, it was never worth the trouble of the search" (*TS* 1189). He further states that the historian must rewrite it, implying that this rescription, like the correction of tradition, is somehow a reassertion of an authentic vision. Yet a subsequent statement dismisses much of the authority of the original written version: "The Kabbala [spurious traditions] . . . were generally discovered to be precisely on a par with the facts recorded in the un-re-written histories themselves;—that is to say, not one individual iota of either, was ever known, under any circumstances, to be not totally and radically wrong" (*TS* 1190). The implied homology here—historical fact/subsequent tradition, Torah/Kabbala, in which the first term is temporally prior to and inspires the second—is repeated by the third pair—original text/"un-re-written histor[y]." But the unrewritten history in this third pair obviously contains some portions of the historian's "original book," portions that must be, by definition, "totally and radically wrong." Implicitly, the author's proximity to, or even participation in historical events is no guarantee of the truth of his written statements. Moreover, although the historian feels impelled to rewrite his book, it is unclear how this second version could be anything but a repetition of the (inadequate) first, since his embalmment followed immediately upon its composition.

The frame narrative of the tale recapitulates these issues by offering a parallel instance of a "history," an original text inscribed by a participant in the events it records: the narrator, not unlike the Egyptian mummy-historian, is awakened suddenly from a sound "slumber"; he pens his "memoranda for the benefit of . . . family and of mankind"; and when the writing task is done, he prepares to "get embalmed for a couple of hundred years" (*TS* 1178, 1195). This frame functions, as will be seen, to elaborate both the limitations of authority at the origin of written histories and the problems that language itself poses for efforts to maintain that authority in written texts.

One reason for the implied distance between "facts" and "recorded facts" in Allamistakeo's discussion of the original texts of Egyptian histories is suggested by the ambiguous status of the narrator's experience of events. As in so many of Poe's tales, distinctions between reality and perception blur in epistemological confusion, for experience itself is deceptive and necessarily subjective. The opening paragraph strikes a reasonable tone, a gesture for establishing the narrator's authority: "The symposium of the preceding evening had been a little too much for my nerves. I had a wretched headache, and was desperately drowsy. Instead of going out, therefore, to spend the evening as I had proposed, it occurred to me that I could not do a wiser thing than just eat a mouthful of supper and go immediately to bed" (*TS* 1177). The vaguely intellectual connotations of "symposium" suggest that here speaks a cultured man, perhaps—given the forbearance of the mere "mouthful of supper"—even an ascetic one. But in the light of the next two paragraphs we suspect that the symposium was, quite literally, a drinking party and that his indisposition is a hangover; furthermore, his *"light* supper" consists of several pounds of "Welsh rabbit" washed down with five bottles of Brown Stout. After this "frugal meal" he puts on his night cap, and "with the serene hope of enjoying it till noon the next day, I placed my head upon the pillow, and through the aid of a capital conscience, fell into a profound slumber forthwith" (*TS* 1178). His crapulous sleep is interrupted by a "furious ringing at the street-door bell," an "impatient thumping at the knocker," and his summons to the unswathing of the Mummy.

As Mabbott notes (*TS* 1195, n.1), too much cheese before bedtime was (as it still is) commonly considered to induce nightmares, and, quite apart from the ludicrous nature of the central event, elements of the narrative imply that it could easily be a report of a dream. After such a meal it is appropriate that the narrator arrives at Dr. Ponnonner's to find the Mummy "extended upon the dining table" (*TS* 1178). Moreover, when, after the rude administration of the electric shock to the Mummy's nose, the narrator perceives that its eyelids have moved, he accounts for his own lack of alarm by reference to the Brown Stout but notes that, as in a dream, "Mr. Gliddon, by some peculiar process, rendered himself invisible" (*TS* 1182). A similar dream-logic accounts for Ponnonner's survival of his fall through the window to the street below, and the fact that when the Mummy speaks "no member of our party betrayed any very particular trepidation, or seemed to consider that any thing had gone very especially wrong" (*TS* 1183). The narrative events could, then, be all a dream, in which case, as David Ketterer notes, the narrator has "confused the deceptive line between illusion and reality, making the story an excellent exemplum of the razor-edge on which our awareness of the 'real' both mentally and temporally rests."[22]

More disturbing than this epistemological confusion, however, is the implication that the fundamentally figurative nature of language prevents its use as a controllable medium for representing the historian's version of events and so compounds the problems of interpretation. Allamistakeo implies that the historian loses control over his "original book" because authority for establishing its meaning is transferred over time to readers who treat "history" as "fable" to be explicated, annotated, and emended. But the distinction between history and fable can be maintained only by a faith in the distinction between two levels of language—the literal and the figurative—and in our ability to keep them distinct. And the narrative subverts this faith by repeatedly displaying the tendency of all language to figuration. The narrator draws attention to this tendency even as he implies his own control over it: when Ponnonner pulls Allamistakeo's nose into contact with the electric wire, he says, "Morally and physically—figuratively and literally—was the effect electric" (*TS* 1182). But the tenuous nature of this assumption of control is clear when the narrator unself-consciously repeats an unintentional pun uttered by Allamistakeo, whose first words are "I am as much surprised as I am mortified, at your behaviour" (*TS* 1183). When the narrator subsequently claims that "I could not endure the spectacle of the poor Mummy's mortification" (*TS* 1195), he appears equally unconscious that his own readers could find a similar pun at work. In his written text, the narrator has lost control over such readings, a control that, it is implied, is maintained in speech by the monitoring presence of the speaker. When Allamistakeo's statement that he was embalmed alive because he is "of the blood of the Scarabaeus" (*TS* 1187) is taken literally by Doctor Ponnonner, the Mummy can assume the role of "parent" to his discourse and correct the misinterpretation: "To be 'of the blood of the Scarabaeus,' is merely to be one of that family of which the Scarabaeus is the *insignium*. I speak figuratively" (*TS* 1187).

This potential for interpretive confusion in the interpenetration of the literal and figurative levels—like the deceptive nature of experience—is established at the outset of the tale. The disjunction between the narrator's statement that he would "just eat a *mouthful* of supper" (emphasis mine) and his actual gorging on at least four pounds of "Welsh rabbit" is crudely comic, but it also illustrates the potential for subjective interpretation allowed by figurative language (*TS* 1177). Furthermore, the name of the dish draws attention to the vital role of shared convention in signification—"Welsh rabbit," by convention, is not a Celtic bunny. Yet other elements emphasize that language always oversignifies (in a way that is impossible, for the writer at least, to control), whether by juxtaposition—the "*light* supper," in which "light," usually taken to refer to digestibility, is here measured in pounds weight—or by concealed pun—when the narrator notes that without Brown Stout, "Welsh rabbit is to be eschewed," his intended sense of avoidance is overridden by a hideous play on unlubricated mastication of the glutinous meal.

The opening also draws attention to the interpretive instability of even the simplest kinds of denotative language. When the narrator adopts conventional terms of measurement—of numbers and pounds—to describe his meal, we might seem to be on firm ground but are not: "More than a pound at once . . . may not at all times be advisable. Still, there can be no material objection to two. And really between two and three, there is merely a single unit of difference. I ventured, perhaps, upon four. My wife will have it five; but, clearly, she has confounded two very distinct affairs. The abstract number, five, I am willing to admit; but, concretely, it has reference to bottles of Brown Stout" (*TS* 1178). Abstract numbers, then, gain significance only in conjunction with the units to which they are applied and the objects to which they are referred—pounds or bottles, cheese or stout—and can, as here, be made instruments of blithe prevarication. Moreover, the disagreement between the narrator and his wife over the "two very distinct affairs" of cheese and stout points up the essential arbitrariness of any sign's relationship to a particular referent, an arbitrariness that invites, as in this case, multiple interpretations.

The narrator, happily oblivious to the problems that diet and language pose for the authority of his own history, inscribes in it a dialogue with the revivified Mummy, asking his readers to accept Allamistakeo's "voiced" opinions as authoritative, in part precisely because they are spoken. The narrative makes clear, however, that whatever authority such a voice might have carried in the event, it cannot be recovered from the written text. This loss is dramatized when the narrator describes the series of displacements that underlies his "record" of the "conversation in which the Mummy took a part" (*TS* 1184). It is a "record" of a dubious translation of a language of which he has no knowledge. He relies totally on "the medium . . . of Messieurs Gliddon and Buckingham, as interpreters," claiming that they "spoke the mother-tongue of the mummy with inimitable fluency and grace." But though his unqualified assertion would seem to be supported by Allamistakeo's comment to them that "you speak Egyptian fully as well, I think, as you write your mother tongue" (*TS* 1183),[23] the Mummy's endorsement is in a translation that, paradoxically, is its own only verification. Moreover, the process of communication is beset with difficulties that the narrator attributes to "the introduction of images entirely modern, and, of course, entirely novel to the stranger" (*TS* 1184). He notes that to convey their "particular meaning" they must resort to "the employment of sensible forms"—for example, "the term 'politics' " is linked with a picture "sketched upon the wall, with a bit of charcoal," and "the absolutely modern idea, 'wig,' " is accompanied by Buckingham's removal of his own (*TS* 1184, 1185). But there is no guarantee that the communication is successful: in the first case, the hieroglyph that Gliddon employs—"a little carbuncle-nosed gentleman, out at elbows, standing upon a stump" (*TS* 1185)—is a culturally determined image, far more likely to be recognized by a nineteenth-century American than an ancient Egyptian; and, in the second, the narrator (and the interpreters in whom he places such faith) are mistaken in believing the wig to be "absolutely modern," unknown to the Egyptian (*TS* 1198, n.15); any confusion must be on a far more fundamental level than they assume. The narrator's text, then, even as it claims for itself the authority of a transcription of an original voice, draws attention to its own displacement from Allamistakeo's "primitive Egyptian." The Mummy's "original . . . speech" is finally inaccessible to the reader of the tale.

In sum, the tale strongly identifies the revivified Mummy with the interpretive strategy of attempting to recover, to bring to life as it were, an originating, authenticating voice in a written text; its narrative frame, its punning texture, and the Mummy's own testimony mock the possibility of success. The search for such origins, like the questions put to Allamistakeo about the creation, lead only back to language—"the very word '*Adam*' (or Red Earth)" (*TS* 1190).[24] Thus it is not by coincidence that the language that Allamistakeo speaks is termed "the mother-tongue of the mummy" (*TS* 1184); this is more than an awful play on words, for "mother-tongue" implies, on the one hand, that it is an original language from which subsequent languages have derived and, on the other, that even the Mummy has a mother-tongue—this original is itself merely one in a series of linguistic progenitors, the ur-form of which recedes in infinite regress before efforts to recover it.

VII

Conclusion:
Allegories
of
Reading

Poe's works are filled with texts that resist interpretation, as if they could be items in "the *Directorium Inquisitorum*," the list of forbidden books in Roderick Usher's library (*TS* 409). For various reasons, like the "certain German Book" mentioned at the beginning of "The Man of the Crowd" (1840), they do not permit themselves to be read (*TS* 506). That is, they resist an easy passage from signifier to signified; they seem to promise signification, but defer it. In "The Bargain Lost" (1832), the narrator describes a "voluminous MSS., intended for publication on the morrow," the title of which is "A complete exposition of things not to be exposed" (*TS* 88); and, indeed, they are not exposed, since "this valuable work" has been lost, leaving only its motto: "Brethren, I come from lands afar / To show you all what fools you are" (*TS* 88). A similar, though perhaps more somber, version of this mockery of the reader is implicit in the word "DISCOVERY," which confronts the narrator of "MS. Found in a Bottle" (1833), and which, as Allan Gardner Smith suggests, only gives a name "to the narrator's baffled search for knowledge."[1] The process about which Allamistakeo complains, that of the deformation of a text by the addition of "annotations or emendations" that over time envelop, distort, and overwhelm a text (*TS* 1189), is analogous to that physical distortion or effacement of signifiers over time that renders them quite literally unreadable. They become like the desks in "William Wilson," whose putative "original form" has been lost—"piled desperately with much-bethumbed books, and so beseamed with initial letters, names at full length, grotesque figures, and other multiplied efforts of the knife, as to have utterly lost what little of original form might have been their portion in days long departed" (*TS* 430). As we have seen, characters in Poe's tales approach such signifiers with various degrees of interpretive confidence, and their results evince various degrees of failure—if success is defined as recuperation of an original or intended meaning.

One obviously burlesque example of the interpretive consequences of the loss of context and of the ambiguities of syntax is provided in "Mellonta Tauta" (1849). Here, Pundita, writing in the year 2848 to her "dear friend," describes *"an inscription—a legible inscription"* on a marble slab recently unearthed with other "genuine Amriccan relics" (*TS* 1303, 1304). The letters are clear:

This Corner Stone of a Monument to the
Memory of
GEORGE WASHINGTON,
was laid with appropriate ceremonies on the
19TH DAY OF OCTOBER, 1847,
the anniversary of the surrender of
Lord Cornwallis
to General Washington at Yorktown,
A.D. 1781,
under the auspices of the
Washington Monument Association of the
city of New York.
(*TS* 1304)

Appropriately, the cornerstone signifies the absence of an actual monument as its inscription signifies the absence of the events such a monument would belatedly commemorate. Undeterred, Pundita—whose name, perhaps, could be appropriately rendered "pun-sayer" (reading "dit-a" as a play on the third person singular of French *dire*, "to say")—with wonderful interpretive confidence undertakes to recuperate the signified of the text. "From the few words thus preserved," she claims to be able to glean "several important items of knowledge, not the least interesting of which is the fact that a thousand years ago *actual* monuments had fallen into disuse" (*TS* 1304). She then embarks on an analysis of "the how, as well as the where and the what, of the great surrender in question":

> As to the *where*, it was Yorktown (wherever that was), and as to the *what*, it was General Cornwallis (no doubt some wealthy dealer in corn). *He* was surrendered. The inscription commemorates the surrender of—what?—why, "of Lord Cornwallis." The only question is what could the savages wish him surrendered for. But when we remember that these savages were undoubtedly cannibals, we are led to the conclusion that they intended him for sausage. As to the *how* of the surrender, no language can be more explicit. Lord Cornwallis was surrendered (for sausage) "under the auspices of the Washington Monument Association"— no doubt a charitable institution for the depositing of cornerstones. (*TS* 1304–5)

Thus Poe offers a parody of that interpretive project that, as an archaeology of the text, would recuperate origins. Pundita's interpretation is interrupted just at this moment by the collapse of the balloon in which she is riding (despite the fact that it is made of a material that is an improvement over the "papyrus"-based silk of earlier times), upon which she corks the "MS. up in a bottle . . . and throw[s] it into the sea" (*TS* 1305).

The deflation of Pundita's recovery through the text of an original past in the present is also accomplished by the dizzying series of displacements in the mode of the narrative itself—which emphasizes the play of intertextuality rather than a recoverable prior historical moment. The inscription is transcribed by the "late papers" (*TS* 1302) from the "original" slab beneath which are "coins," "names," and "several documents which appear to resemble newspapers" (*TS* 1304); it is then translated "verbatim" by Pundita's husband, Pundit ("so there *can* be no mistake about it") (*TS* 1304), and then copied into a letter in the form of a journal, which is cast into the sea in a bottle to be found "floating in the *Mare Tenebrarum*" by one Edgar A. Poe who, after having it translated into English by his "friend, Martin Van Buren Mavis," offers it, prefaced by another letter "TO THE EDITORS OF THE LADY'S BOOK" (*TS* 1291). As if this (not quite closed) circle of intertextual relations were not enough, Poe includes long sections from "this very unaccountable if not impertinent epistle" in *Eureka* (1848).[2]

One of Poe's most powerful images of the reader occurs in *The Narrative of Arthur Gordon Pym* (1838). Trapped in the labyrinthine hold of the *Grampus*, in utter darkness, confused by the interrelation of dream, memory, and reality, desperately trying to make sense of his situation, Pym himself embodies Poe's bleak view of the human condition. He discovers tied to his dog Tiger a note written, we subsequently learn, by his friend Augustus, who has been unable to release Pym because he has been captured and confined by a group of brutal mutineers. It is so dark that Pym can discern the "white slip of paper" only "by turning the exterior portions of the retina towards it, that is to say, by surveying it slightly askance" (*IV* 77–78). He has no candles, so he rubs phosphorous into the paper, whereupon "a clear light diffused itself immediately throughout the whole surface; and had there been any writing upon it, I should not have experienced the least difficulty, I am sure, in reading it. Not a syllable was there, however—nothing but a dreary and unsatisfactory blank" (*IV* 78). After he has torn the paper into three pieces and thrown them away, he realizes that he has examined only one side. With Tiger's help, he recovers the pieces, fits them together, and once more applies the phosphorous: "this time several lines of MS. in a large hand, and apparently in red ink, became distinctly visible." He sees that there are three sentences, but "in my anxiety . . . to read all at once, I succeeded only in reading the seven concluding words, which thus appeared: '*blood—your life depends upon lying close*' " (*IV* 80).

Commentators have noted an apparent "mistake" on Poe's part: Pym later learns that the note was written on "the back of a letter—a duplicate of the forged letter from Mr. Ross" (*IV* 92), which should, therefore, have been visible to Pym's first examination. Yet, as John Carlos Rowe has suggested, rather than being merely an error, this offers an important illustration of Poe's conception of the doubleness of writing. Poe's poetic theory seems to argue that human discourse is grounded in a principle of writing that is silence: a paradoxical emptiness and fullness. In *Pym* the act of writing carries the trace of a prior representation, which defers the desired approach to an undifferentiated meaning or central signified. . . . As another reflection on the question of "poetic" writing, the note demonstrates the difficulty of transcending the differential system of language to deliver a unified truth. The note is a palimpsest—*the* palimpsest of language itself, whose messages are always intertexts.[3]

Written in blood on the back of a duplicate of a forged original, this note figures the fundamental displacements from originality that we have seen recurring throughout Poe's work.

Pym seizes on the word *"blood,"* which fills him with "harrowing and yet indefinable horror": "that word of all words—*so rife at all times* with mystery, and suffering, and terror—how trebly full of import did it now appear—how chillily and heavily (*disjointed, as it thus was, from any foregoing words to qualify or render it distinct*) did its vague syllables fall, amid the deep gloom of my prison, into the innermost recesses of my soul!" (*IV* 80; emphasis mine). The fact that the word *"blood"* is "disjointed . . . from any foregoing words," that is, from any defining syntactic context, enables Pym to fill the signifier subjectively. Blind to the arbitrary nature of language, he assumes that the word signifies consistently, "at all times," and reads it symbolically as "rife . . . with mystery, and suffering, and terror." Yet, as he subsequently learns, the word in this case merely refers to the medium in which it is written—*"I have scrawled this with blood"* (*IV* 92). It names only its own materiality.[4]

Poe's work offers many similar examples, and, as we have seen, those characters who confront such signs in the hope of recovering an originally intended meaning are defeated by the mechanisms of displacement and deferral in language itself. Yet in the so-called tales of detection, Poe does seem to offer characters who have achieved a form of mastery over the letter. Legrand in "The Gold-Bug" (1843), Dupin in the detective tales, and the narrator of *Eureka* (the latter playing detective to the universe), all at first reading appear to have developed strategies adequate to the recovery of meaning from signifiers displaced from their signifieds. As we shall see, however, such mastery is in each case heavily qualified, even compromised. "The Gold-Bug" offers perhaps the most vivid, even ostentatious, image of success in the "treasure of incalculable value" that Legrand unearths (*TS* 826). The apparently unequivocal nature of this recovery—together with the perhaps related fact that, of the texts in question, this tale has received relatively little critical attention—warrants the choice of "The Gold-Bug" as exemplary subject of the final extended reading in this study. This analysis will be followed by a brief examination of those factors that critics such as J. A. Leo Lemay and Joseph N. Riddel have identified as qualifying or circumscribing the interpretive mastery of Dupin—his naive conception of the self on the one hand, and the displacement and dissemination of writing on the other. The final section examines *Eureka* to suggest ways in which the narrator's ambitious project—to interpret the universe—is subverted. As the following shows, each of these works entertains the possibility that discourse is predicated on the loss or the absence of original meaning, and that the significance derived from texts is largely a product of interpretive practice.

"The Gold-Bug": "the language of the cipher"

As is well known, whereas Poe's financial position was, in John Ward Ostrom's words, "perpetually precarious," he still generally identified himself with an idealized image of the southern gentry class.[5] There is a certain degree of irony, then, in the fact that an impoverished author should strike it rich (by Poe's standards) by winning a competition organized by the appropriately named *Dollar Newspaper* with a story about a southern aristocrat whom "a series of misfortunes had reduced . . . to want" (*TS* 806) but who remakes his fortune by discovering and deciphering on a sheet of paper a message that leads him to gold.[6]

At one point, Legrand reminds the narrator of "the many stories current—the thousand vague rumors afloat about money buried, somewhere on the Atlantic coast, by Kidd and his associates," and he notes that "the stories told are all about money-seekers, not about money-finders." These stories are generated by absence—of the treasure "entombed"—and loss—of "a memorandum indicating its locality" (*TS* 834). That an analogy is here at work between the lost buried gold and original meaning is clear from Marc Shell's discussion of the tale in the context of the contemporary debate between advocates of paper money ("paper money men") and advocates of gold ("gold bugs").[7] This debate directly raised issues of signification in that it centered on the relationship between sign (inscribed paper) and substance (gold), and, as Shell notes, it encouraged analogies such as "paper is to gold as word is to meaning."[8] Whether the relationship between the first and the second terms should be considered natural or arbitrary was an issue of crucial importance. Legrand's project, then, which follows a movement from paper to gold, can be seen as an attempt to recover a lost significance buried in the word; his account of his procedure entertains and examines the possibility of such a recovery, which, implicitly, would halt the generation of "stories . . . [and] rumors" just as the discovery of singular meaning would close the play of language (*TS* 834).

In a commentary that stresses how "the text requires and defines the kind of reading which can decipher its workmanship," Jean Ricardou provides a useful starting point for an examination of this tale's exploration of interpretive strategies: "It is by their way of reading [that is, of interpreting signs, linguistic and otherwise] that the nature of each of the three characters is determined. Only Legrand is capable of decoding. Jupiter and the narrator, for their part, are on bad terms with language."[9] As the following demonstrates, Jupiter and the narrator are entrapped in their opposed but equally inadequate assumptions about language; in contrast, Legrand is an apparently exemplary interpreter by whose practice the reader can gauge the shortcomings of his companions. He is aware that the relationship between word and referent is ultimately arbitrary, and alert to the consequent semantic implications of changing contexts. Legrand's interpretive strategy depends on a sensitivity to the possibilities of intention, which allows him to restore words to those contexts in which they convey significant meaning, contexts in which an essential consistency can be perceived.[10] Because his approach to context remains flexible, he eventually reconstitutes the "links of a great chain" leading to the treasure (*TS* 831)—the tale's ostensible validation of his reading.

Throughout the tale, the contingent nature of the sign is repeatedly implied. The narrative's shifting terminology for its central image, the gold-bug, emphatically illustrates the arbitrariness of the relationship between word and referent. Legrand introduces the insect by its genus, "*scarabaeus*," but he and the other characters soon fall back on the even more inclusive term, "bug" (*TS* 808). The physical absence of the bug and the lack of a specific classification make general description necessary, but words prove inadequate to capture the attributes of this nameless insect; of the quality of the color, the mysteriously "brilliant metallic lustre," the narrator "cannot judge till to-morrow," when he will be able to see it (*TS* 809). Meanwhile, a sketch must suffice to give him some idea of its shape. When the narrator eventually sees the bug for himself, he refers to it indiscriminately as "*scarabaeus*," "bug," "beetle," and "insect" (*TS* 815–16). The synonyms circumscribe a still unnamed center; the connection of names to that referent is obviously arbitrary and unstable. In most cases, the narrator's terms merely point to the bug as a physical object rather than describe or classify it in a stable context.

The drawing of the shape of the bug bears a "remarkable similarity of outline" to the representation of the death's-head on the back of the parchment (*TS* 829). Although this similarity of form creates the possibility of confusion, the drawings have distinctive meanings, discernible, however, only by "reading" them in their intended frames of reference. The drawings are thus analogous to homophones, which also must be taken in context to be understood. A parallel instance of homophonic confusion occurs, in fact, at a crucial point in the narrative. Jupiter, out of sight in the tulip tree, signals a discovery after following Legrand's instructions to crawl out along the seventh branch:

> "—o-o-o-o-oh! Lor-gol-a-marcy! What *is* dis here pon de tree?"
> "Well!" cried Legrand, highly delighted, "what is it?"
> "Why taint noffin but a skull—somebody bin lef him head up de tree, and de crows done gobble ebery bit ob de meat off."
> (*TS* 820–21)

Jupiter's comments (punning on absentmindedness) establish one meaning of the word "left." When Legrand tells Jupiter to "find the left eye of the skull," Jupiter is unable to shift his usage of "left" to the new context, replying "Hum! hoo! dat's good! why dar aint no eye lef at all." Struggling to impose his own context on Jupiter so that the servant can drop the bug through the appropriate eye socket of the skull, Legrand relates the abstraction to a practical function, that of chopping wood: " 'To be sure! you are left-handed; and your left eye is on the same side as your left hand. Now, I suppose, you can find the left eye of the skull, or the place where the left eye has been. Have you found it?' " (*TS* 821). The process of instruction is beset with ambiguities of reference: " 'Is de lef eye of de skull pon de same side as de lef hand of de skull, too?—cause de skull aint got not a bit ob a hand at all—nebber mind! I got de lef eye now' " (*TS* 821). But, we learn later, he has not. What he believes to be his left eye is actually his right: " 'Oh, my golly, Massa Will! aint dis here my lef eye for sartain?' roared the terrified Jupiter, placing his hand upon his *right* organ of vision" (*TS* 824). Comically displaying the absence of necessary relationship between word and referent, the tale again stresses that meaning is created by conventions of use and context, which alone stabilize the interpretation of signs.

The text similarly dramatizes the obstacles to communication that arise when words are considered to be naively referential, as if word and thing were indissolubly linked. Such extreme referentiality characterizes Jupiter's use of an elemental vocabulary; he fixes on a single referent in the speech of others, recognizing familiar sounds rather than understanding meaning in context. For example, when he hears Legrand refer to the gold-bug's "*antennae*," he interrupts: "Dey aint *no* tin in him, Massa Will, I keep a tellin on you, . . . de bug is a goole bug, solid, ebery bit of him" (*TS* 808–9). Jupiter believes that the middle syllable has only one referent—the metal, tin.[11] Similarly, when the narrator asks "What cause have you?" for thinking Legrand has been bitten by the bug, Jupiter replies, "Claws enuff, massa, and mouff too" (*TS* 812). His lexical economy admits only one name for each object in his world; when he is asked, "Did you bring any message from Mr. Legrand?" he replies, "No, massa, I bring dis here pissel" (*TS* 813). Legrand has given him a name for what he carries, and because his language use precludes synonyms, he does not recognize "message" as an alternate signifier.

Such a linguistic practice also inhibits abstraction, as illustrated by Jupiter's struggles with the concepts of left and right. Discovering a scythe and three spades in the bottom of the boat bound from Charleston to Sullivan's Island, the narrator asks, "What is the meaning of all this, Jup?"; "Him syfe, massa, and spade," Jupiter replies (*TS* 814). He can go no further than the meaning contained in naming. Thus, when the narrator ponderously asks, "To what fortunate circumstance am I to attribute the honor of a visit from you to-day?" Jupiter, bewildered, replies "What de matter, massa?" (*TS* 813); the formulaic words, without reference to any object that Jupiter can identify, do, in one sense, lack "matter" for him.

By contrast, the narrator illustrates the dangers of language dependent upon a single, inflexible framework for controlling the relationship of word and referent. Because the narrator's language strategies are linked to a fairly broadly defined perspective and cognitive style, it is necessary to consider his character in some detail. In a tale that on one level demonstrates the value of heightened intellectual powers, the narrator's laziness of mind is marked. His conversation with Legrand, in which he learns of the discovery of the "totally new" *scarabaeus*, is characteristic. In response to Legrand's regret that he could not show him the bug that evening, the narrator thinks only of the chill from which he suffers and wishes "the whole tribe of *scarabaei* at the devil" (*TS* 808). The same intellectual torpor underlies his approach to language (typical of what Poe calls in *Eureka* "the common understanding of words"), and gives rise to contextual confusion:

> [Legrand:] "Stay here tonight, and I will send Jup down for it at sunrise. It is the loveliest thing in creation!"
> [Narrator:] "What?—sunrise?"
> [Legrand:] "Nonsense! no!—the bug."
> (*TS* 808)

Significantly, the narrator misidentifies the referent of "it," the understanding of which demands, of course, that distant syntactic elements be held in mind in order to be linked correctly.[12] We discover as the tale progresses that the narrator's lapse is emblematic: he is irremediably obtuse to the possibilities of fixing words in displaced or alternate contexts.

Unlike Legrand, the narrator's thoughtless acceptance of the conventions of his class limits both his own use of language and his understanding of others. He recognizes only one context in which to place words, the societal, and when words and behavior violate the expectations it establishes, he is simply bewildered. The first sentence neatly establishes his manner with words: "Many years ago, *I con-tracted an intimacy* with a Mr. William Legrand. He was *of an ancient Huguenot family*, and had once been wealthy; but a series of misfor-tunes had *reduced him to want*. To *avoid the mortification consequent upon his disasters*, he left New Orleans, the *city of his forefathers*, and *took up his residence* at Sullivan's Island, near Charleston, South Carolina" (*TS* 806; emphasis mine). The narrator's discourse is little more than a series of clichés and formulaic expressions that keep harsh realities at a comfortable distance. The "residence" so formally taken up is, we soon learn, a hut, and the effete nature of merely social "mortification" is exposed later in the tale by a confrontation with the results of literal mortification—the skull and the skeletons. Even his admiration of Legrand is tempered with the condescension of a so-cially secure urbanite for a displaced peer, as seen in his measured evaluation that "there was much in the recluse to excite interest and esteem" (*TS* 807). This condescension is made explicit in his immedi-ate reaction to Legrand's note demanding his company: "What 'busi-ness of the highest importance' could *he* possibly have to transact?" (*TS* 814).

The world of socially defined value sharply delimits the narrator's reactions to the unpredictable. The first part of the narrative shows his inability to comprehend events that violate his expectations as other than symptomatic of the "otherness" of insanity—a convenient catch-all for the mysterious or the ostensibly irrational. He interprets Le-grand's "moods of alternate enthusiasm and melancholy" accordingly, speculating that his relatives have contrived Jupiter's guardianship of a man "somewhat unsettled in intellect" (*TS* 807). The narrator can describe Legrand's enthusiasms only as "fits." Unlike Jupiter, he clearly has a vocabulary to generate alternate names for the behavior, and by the very question, "How else shall I term them?" he, or rather the text, lays open the possibility of other interpretations (*TS* 808). He actually reacts, however, by withdrawing into the security of "pru-dent" silence; subsequently, he withdraws physically, having "deemed it proper to take leave" for his own world of Charleston (*TS* 810, 811). His incomprehensions, at the outset innocent enough, fore-shadow his later settled conviction of Legrand's lunacy.

The narrator's growing persuasion of his friend's "aberration of mind" (*TS* 817) springs from the assumption that a man who has fallen from wealth and social prominence to unrelieved poverty and obscurity is likely to go mad: "I dreaded lest the continued pressure of misfortune had, at length, fairly unsettled the reason of my friend" (*TS* 814). His criterion for madness is whether behavior is readily comprehensible in the context of social convention. If it is not, then such behavior can be appropriated to that context only by being named as "mad"; once so labeled, it cannot threaten or force the readjustment of the narrator's point of view. The arbitrary nature of this defensive strategy is implied by the narrator's reaction to the proposed nocturnal expedition—"The man is surely mad!"—a conventional expression of astonishment that can be translated as "I do not understand you" (*TS* 816). For the narrator, then, words have become mere signals of social approval or disapproval. Such a use of language allows him to reserve for himself the stance of sane judgment and reaffirms the adequacy of his settled perspective in the face of experience that it cannot accommodate. Such an approach is, of course, as limited in the face of complexity as Jupiter's obsessively referential use of language, for it presupposes a meaning, alternative possibilities to which are severely constrained by premature closure.[13] Apparently, Legrand offers an eclectic and flexible alternative.

Legrand's task is doubly difficult; he has not only to cope with the unreliability of language, but also to recover meaning from a text that human ingenuity has deliberately rendered obscure. That meaning, which conveniently in this instance can be validated by empirical investigation, lies beneath a series of obfuscating layers: on the underside of the sketch of the bug is a text concealed by its invisibility; once the text is made visible, its words are concealed by its being in code; once the code has been broken and the words made manifest, their meaning is obscured by their use of pirate conventions and by their distance from their referents. Under such conditions, the interpreter (like the cosmologist in *Eureka*) must proceed largely on faith in the existence of some final order to which the apparently arbitrary can be reconciled.

Legrand's belief in that process of discovery by which nature appears to conform to man's need for order is clear. Having found "an unknown bivalve, forming a new genus," Legrand displays his awareness of how conventional taxonomy establishes likenesses, makes connections, and thus establishes meaning in the natural world. Having

"hunted down and secured . . . a *scarabaeus* which he believed to be
totally new," he recognizes that taxonomy must also be flexible (*TS*
808). He can make the accommodations that new circumstances require, an ability that is tested to the full by the cipher. In confronting
the concealed text, he follows a process of reification, recognizing displacements and concealments in order to reach through them to a putative original meaning. Just as he is able to reify the form of the boat
at the seashore, he is able to reconstitute the text and its purposes in
order to rediscover its meaning. The original form of each is hidden:
one has suffered disintegration by the forces of nature so that "the resemblance to boat timbers could scarcely be traced" (*TS* 830); the
other has been disguised by the agency of man. Legrand is successful
in each instance. That his successful strategy for reading a disguised
text derives from a particular way of looking at the world is implied by
a crucial juxtaposition in Legrand's account of his capture of the gold-
bug and his coincident discovery of the parchment with the concealed
text: "Upon my taking hold of it, it gave me a sharp bite, which caused
me to let it drop. Jupiter, with his accustomed caution, before seizing
the insect, which had flown towards him, looked about him for a *leaf*,
or something *of that nature*, by which to take hold of it. It was at this
moment that his eyes, and mine also, fell upon the scrap of *parchment*,
which I then supposed to be paper" (*TS* 830; emphasis mine). "Leaf"
is here a middle term with a double reference, both to leaves of the
natural world and to leaves of paper or parchment. This possibility is
kept in view as Legrand details his pursuit of the "*rationale*" of the cipher and refers to "the natural alphabet" and "the natural division intended by the cryptographist" (*TS* 837, 840).

Legrand believes in an order that lies beneath the surface of apparent coincidence; he describes the struggle of the mind to discover a
"connexion—a sequence of cause and effect" (*TS* 829) that establishes
the one significant context among the many possibilities. When this attempt meets resistance, his mind lapses into a "species of temporary
paralysis." Yet even then, faced with the sudden mysterious appearance of the image of the skull, "there seemed to glimmer, faintly, within
the most remote and secret chambers of [Legrand's] intellect, a glow-
worm-like conception of that truth which last night's adventure brought
to so magnificent a demonstration" (*TS* 829). His methodical examination of the circumstances in which he found the document leads him

to establish a connection between "two links of a great chain," for the boat and the parchment are conjoined by the death's-head, "the well-known emblem of the pirate." He reasserts his belief in the existence of such a chain when he claims, "My steps were sure, and could afford but a single result" (*TS* 831). His steps are governed by thoughtful common sense, intuition, and an insistence that the meaning of words and signs is contingent on a multiplicity of possible contexts.

The sequence in which the elements of the message emerge from the parchment reflects a hierarchy of increasing complexity and privacy of language requiring radical shifts of perspective on the part of the interpreter. When the narrator perceives the shape on the paper as that of "a skull, or a death's-head" (*TS* 809), he proves himself blind to the possibility of other meanings: " 'It is a very *excellent* skull, according to the vulgar notions about such specimens of physiology. . . .' The whole *did* bear a very close resemblance to the ordinary cut of a death's-head" (*TS* 810). Beyond the social labels "vulgar" and "ordinary," the narrator contemplates no other frame of reference in which to interpret the sketch. Legrand, however, immediately tests for other possibilities: "There was a boat lying on a sea-coast, and not far from the boat was a parchment—*not a paper*—with a skull depicted on it. You will, of course, ask 'where is the connection?' I reply that the skull, or death's-head, is the well-known emblem of the pirate" (*TS* 831). The next element to emerge, "diagonally opposite" the skull, appears to be the figure of a goat; a "closer scrutiny," however, suggests to Legrand "that it was intended for a kid" (*TS* 832–33). To the narrator, goats and kids are "pretty much the same thing," and in labored humor he asserts that "pirates, you know, have nothing to do with goats; they appertain to the farming interest" (*TS* 833). Legrand, however, recognizes that a sign's significance changes according to the context in which it is read, and his sensitivity to alternate possibilities for the intentions of the design enables him to place the kid in the appropriate one. Thus he hypothesizes, first, that the figure is a hieroglyph and, second, that it is a "punning . . . signature" of the pirate, Captain Kidd.[14] The death's-head and the kid on opposite corners of the sheet are no longer for Legrand merely images; their positions follow the conventions of letter writing: they are "stamp" and "signature," suggesting that additional texts might emerge from the space between them. After a narrative delay, detailing Legrand's procedural difficulties, the last and most obscure elements emerge on the parchment: "figures arranged in lines" (*TS* 834). The narrator is lost, "as much in the dark as ever," and immediately admits his own inability to solve "this enigma." Though he sees merely numbers, Legrand recognizes that they could "form a cipher—that is to say, they convey a meaning" (*TS* 835).

Even after Legrand successfully decodes the numbers so that English words are distinguishable, the narrator cannot imagine how to "extort a meaning from all this jargon about 'devil's seats,' 'death's-heads,' and 'bishop's hotels.' " He remains "in the dark" (*TS* 840), for the language that emerges from the cryptograph is in another kind of code in which the meanings of some words are established by convention and those of others by reference to a particular landscape. To interpret the first group, Legrand must place them in the context of the specialized jargon of sailors, reading, for example, "good glass" as "nothing but a telescope" (*TS* 841). The second group of meanings is more difficult to discover, for though the features of the landscape might remain stable, the words naming them drift away from their referents, as the search for the "bishop's hostel" illustrates. The phrase modulates: "hostel," a recognizable archaism, changes to "hotel" (the narrator has already made this shift but not, like Legrand, consciously, with an awareness of the implications); Legrand changes "Bishop's" to "Bessop's," making it conform with the locality to which he hopes the message refers (*TS* 840). The phrase when finally linked to the landscape becomes *"Bessop's Castle,"* which only remotely resembles the original "bishop's hostel," and which, moreover, refers not to a castle at all but to "an irregular assemblage of cliffs and rocks—one of the latter being quite remarkable for its height as well as for its insulated and artificial appearance" (*TS* 841).

Legrand's final superimposition of the decoded text upon the landscape presupposes, in his terms, a "definite point of view, *admitting no variation*" by which meaning can be discovered (*TS* 841). The conditions of the realm of the referent, at this last stage, impose "but one interpretation" upon the text (*TS* 842). Separate, landscape and text would remain indeterminate—the first, a wilderness "excessively wild and desolate" (*TS* 817), the second, obscure—and this indeterminacy opens them to misreading. Without the limits provided by the landscape, the deciphered text remains a series of floating signifiers that, like the single word "blood" that Arthur G. Pym reads in the hold of the *Grampus,* can be variously and subjectively interpreted. Furthermore, without the significance conveyed to it by the text, the landscape is merely "infinitely . . . dreary" and sternly solemn (*TS* 817). But as text and topography are superimposed, it becomes clear, despite the fact that "no trace of a human footstep was to be seen," that the landscape is not simply unencoded wilderness; it, as well as the text, has been previously structured by Kidd so that the conformity between them will yield the meaning that is, finally, the recovery of the treasure. But landscape and text remain "meaningful" only to the extent to which their arbitrary linkages have remained determinate. Legrand is able to establish relations between the two by virtue of his sensitivity both to the multiple conventions that govern the formation of texts and to the arbitrary relationship between the conventions and the referential world. To a great extent, this sensitivity depends upon his ability to generate hypotheses about Kidd's intentions. When he claims that "it may well be doubted whether human ingenuity can construct an enigma of the kind which human ingenuity may not, by proper application, resolve" (*TS* 835), the phrasing emphasizes the identity of the activities of construction and resolution.[15] This identification enables Legrand, once he has consciously resisted the inherent instability of language by clarifying the various contingencies affecting text and referent, to establish an ultimate determining context within which the words may be mapped in a one-to-one way onto the realm of the signified.

Legrand's recovery of the gold seems a triumphant validation of his method of interpretation: the identification of context, of authorial intention, and of appropriate reference—no one of which is adequate independently. It is as if he had read the text of "Marginalia," restored the original texts to which they had been contexts, and recovered the gold of their original meaning (at one point, having discovered the death's-head and the kid—"seal" and "signature"—he was "sorely put out by the absence of all else . . . of the text for my context" [*TS* 833]). The narrative establishes, however, significant qualifications to his project.

First, Legrand's success cannot be read as the assertion of a natural necessary relationship between signifier and signified. The "links of a great chain" are quite fortuitously established (*TS* 831); the series of happy "accidents and coincidences" are, in Legrand's word, "extraordinary"—so much so as to verge on the ridiculous; as Legrand comments: "Do you observe how mere an accident it was that these events should have occurred on the *sole* day of all the year in which it has been, or may be, sufficiently cool for fire, and that without the fire, or without the intervention of the dog at the precise moment in which he appeared, I should never have become aware of the death's-head, and so never the possessor of the treasure?" (*TS* 833). When Legrand declares that "Fortune" has given him the bug that will make his "fortune," and confesses to feeling "a presentiment of some vast good fortune impending" (*TS* 815, 833), his terms suggest that the fortunate series of events are themselves related arbitrarily by a kind of punning play analogous to that of the verbal puns that riddle the text, exemplifying the *dis*connection between word and meaning.[16]

Second, as Ricardou has noted, the text presents Legrand in the role of encoder of his own text as well as decoder of Kidd's. This is seen most clearly in what he calls his "sober mystification" of the narrator, who complains of Legrand's "grandiloquence . . . [and insistence] on letting fall the bug, instead of a bullet, from the skull" (*TS* 843–44). Having recognized the nature of the narrator's reading of events—that he, Legrand, is insane—Legrand creates a set of signs that reinforce that interpretation, thus dramatizing its arbitrary nature. His confession of this authorial role recalls his earlier statements that link his interpretive project to his "desire" for "vast good fortune," and to an intellectual quality that, Marc Shell suggests, has a "generative power": "Even at that early moment, there seemed to glimmer, faintly, within the most remote and secret chambers of my intellect, a glow-worm-like conception of that truth which last night's adventure brought to so magnificent a demonstration" (*TS* 829).[17] The "glow-worm"/"gold-bug" analogy suggests that Legrand actually creates the meaning/substance in the process of reading the collection of arbitrary signs. Barton Levi St. Armand traces the alchemical images in the tale and concludes that Legrand does not recover but generates the gold: "It is actually Legrand's Romantic imagination that helps to accomplish the multiplication of the gold-bug into Captain Kidd's treasure."[18] Clearly, then, Legrand's interpretive recovery of meaning is implicated with the generation of meaning, and the motifs compromise each other.

Third, Legrand's assertion that the gold-bug bears only a tenuous relation to the reading of the cipher and to his own actions is surely sub-versive of a text called "The Gold-Bug," whose most obtrusive sign is that bug. Throughout the tale, the narrator invests the bug with poeti-cal significance; it, to paraphrase Ricardou, consumes his interest just as it consumed the corner of the parchment. Yet the gold-bug proves to be an empty sign, with no necessary relationship to any referent; it is an index only to itself. As Marc Shell points out, Jupiter's redefinition of "antennae" as having "*no* tin in him" offers (at least) three possi-bilities: first, that there is no *tin* in the bug—which is important to the alchemical reading; second, that there is no *thing* in[side] the bug—it is physically hollow; third, that there is nothing in it, or nothing to it.[19] The bug is, as Legrand's explanation confirms, an empty sign manipu-lated by an artist, gaining significance only in relationship to other signs to be interpreted by a reader—in this case, the rather obtuse narrator.

It is not merely the narrator, however, who has been distracted by a sign that proves to be empty. Poe swings the gold-bug before the eyes of the reader right from the point of entry into the story—the title—and the possibility is thus raised that Poe, like Legrand, is offering a "sober mystification" that encourages a recuperative reading while subverting its possibility.

Such considerations suggest a way to account for those violations of verisimilitude that have disturbed readers such as J. Woodrow Hassell, who points out that Legrand's explanations, while pretending to com-prehensiveness, actually contain notable inconsistencies and elementary mistakes in, for example, his specification of the ink used for the ci-pher, his listing of letter frequencies in cryptography, and his calcula-tions determining the location of the treasure.[20] Given Poe's generally meticulous approach to detail, it is surely inadequate to write such er-rors off as mere carelessness. Poe is most careful to provide that infor-mation by which the reader can judge him careless—as, for example, in the case of the muddled triangulation. These "violations" subvert the attempt to authorize Poe's fiction by reference to conditions outside it-self. As Ricardou has shown, the text establishes a logic of its own, one aspect of which is the subversion of the priority of an *"extra-textual subject."*[21] Just as it is Poe, not "Fortune," who has set up the "series of accidents and coincidences . . . so *very* extraordinary" by which Legrand becomes aware of the existence of the death's-head (*TS* 833), so it is Poe who wills the solutions posited by Legrand, despite any lapses in verisimilitude. Legrand's interpretive strategy—whereby he recuperates meaning by clarifying definition, establishing a determining context, and intuiting authorial intention—only *seems* to offer a reassuring paradigm of the reading process. It can work only inside a closed, mutually validating system arbitrarily established. Even if the reader shares Legrand's faith in an ultimate order to which the text may be reduced, in "The Gold-Bug" he is faced, as Poe's disruptive "errors" remind us, with a text lacking an external "landscape" against which to measure it: the implied realm of the referent is whatever Poe wills it to be, and our access to his intentions is limited to the models we can construct but cannot test.

The text, then, like the sign of the gold-bug, resists a reading that would recuperate a "lost" or "entombed" meaning from it. Implicitly, meaning is a function of the arbitrary play of signifiers the extreme form of which is punning. And this, perhaps, suggests why the ending of the tale is so disconcerting. As noted above, "the many stories" and "thousand vague rumors" are generated by the burial of the gold and the loss of the "memorandum"—that is, by analogy, the loss of original meaning (*TS* 834). The recovery of such meaning, which, implicitly, would be singular, would silence such stories and stop the play of language. Legrand unearths the treasure, but in doing so he also unearths "a mass of human bones, forming two complete skeletons, intermingled with several buttons of metal, and what appeared to be the dust of decayed woollen" (*TS* 825). Indeed, the language of death pervades the narrative—from the obvious images of the "death's-head" on the parchment and "the ominous insignium" that is "*the skull*" nailed to the tree (*TS* 843) to apparently innocuous statements like the narrator's "dying with impatience for a solution" (*TS* 828). At the close of Legrand's "solution of this extraordinary riddle," the narrator asks "What are we to make of the skeletons found in the hole?" (*TS* 844). Legrand speculates on the possibilities of murder, but finally can ask only, "Who shall tell?" Most obviously this suggests that mortality is a mystery that evades "accounting," but it also suggests that there is always a mysterious surplus in signification (like the surplus that enables the pun), which both resists the closure of single meanings and generates new versions, new rumors, new stories.

"the supposititious Dupin"

C. Auguste Dupin, according to the narrators of "The Murders in the Rue Morgue" (1841) and "The Purloined Letter" (1844), is a master of interpretation—of disentanglement and "re-solution" (*TS* 528). Dupin himself boasts "that most men, in respect to himself, wore windows in their bosoms" (*TS* 533). His power of analysis is grounded in his ability to identify himself with another's consciousness, like the analyst who in a game of draughts "throws himself into the spirit of his opponent, identifies himself therewith, and not unfrequently sees thus, at a glance, the sole methods . . . by which he may seduce into error or hurry into miscalculation" (*TS* 529). In "The Purloined Letter," Dupin offers an analogy for his method in the case of the schoolboy who always won at the game of "even and odd" by "*thorough* identification" of "his intellect with that of his opponent" (*TS* 984). According to David Halliburton this suggests that in interpreting a text we comprehend it "by going back into the consciousness that made it, in order to relive its signifying acts."[22] As a self-declared phenomenologist, Halliburton is content with this model. However, though the detective tales on one level do dramatize Dupin's apparent mastery over the letter, such mastery, as a number of critics in recent years demonstrate, is as carefully circumscribed as Legrand's.

In "The Murders in the Rue Morgue," for example, the narrator attempts to convey the "character of [Dupin's] remarks" by offering an "example" of Dupin's "intimate knowledge" of the narrator's "bosom" (*TS* 533). On this occasion Dupin breaks fifteen minutes of silence during which they had been walking, "both, apparently, occupied with thought," by demonstrating that he knows the narrator to be thinking of one Chantilly, "a *quondam* cobbler of the Rue St. Denis, who, becoming stage-mad, had attempted the *rôle* of Xerxes, in Crébillon's tragedy so called, and been notoriously Pasquinaded for his pains" (*TS* 533, 534). The narrator is astonished, and demands to know "the method . . . by which you have been enabled to fathom my soul in this matter" (*TS* 534). Dupin obliges by tracing "the larger links of the chain" of the narrator's thought—"Chantilly, Orion, Dr. Nichol, Epicurus, Stereotomy, the street stones, the fruiterer" (*TS* 535)—and beginning with the fruiterer he traces the connections to Chantilly. His account makes it clear that whereas the narrator has been "occupied with thought," Dupin has been occupied with observation, attempting to follow the associative chain of that thought and memorizing it. As a demonstration of Dupin's "fathom[ing]" the narrator's "soul" it is less than satisfactory, being riddled, as Burton R. Pollin shows, with coincidences, jokes, strained connections, and at least one missing link—that of Dr. Nichols.[23] To account for the narrator's admiration for such a performance we must assume with Pollin that "the 'stooge' of Dupin must be able to forget almost everything, and Dupin nothing."[24] Whereas Dupin's reading depends on a one-for-one reading of possible signifiers,[25] the clues themselves demonstrate both the actual surplus of meaning in those signifiers and their tendency to change over time—for example, in the "stereotomy"/"atomies" shift, or in the Latin line "Perdidit antiquum litera prima sonum" ("the first letter has lost its original sound") (*TS* 536, 571, n.22)—thus emphasizing the fortuitous and arbitrary nature of his reading.

In fact, as Pollin's analysis shows, the whole tale is built around a series of "strained coincidences" designed "to 'spoof' the serious and frolic with the knowing."[26] Those who take Dupin's approach as a model for interpretive practice are open to the same critical question that Poe, in a letter to Philip P. Cooke, levels at readers who think the "tales of ratiocination . . . more ingenious than they are—on account of their method and *air* of method. In 'The Murders in the Rue Morgue', for instance, where is the ingenuity of unravelling a web which you yourself (the author) have woven for the express purpose of unravelling? The reader is made to confound the ingenuity of the supposititious Dupin with that of the writer of the story" (*L* 328). Appropriately, the term "supposititious" carries strong connotations of the fraudulent, spurious, or counterfeit.

Dupin's declared procedure of identification with the psyche of the criminal other paradoxically involves both self-effacement and self-consciousness—since he must transform himself into the object of his own scrutiny. In the analogy of the game of "even and odd" that Dupin describes in "The Purloined Letter," the victorious schoolboy achieved a "*thorough* identification" with his opponent by fashioning "the expression of [his] face, as accurately as possible, in accordance with the expression" of the other, and then waiting "to see what thoughts or sentiments arise in [his] mind or heart, as if to match or correspond with the expression" (*TS* 984–85). Two assumptions exposed elsewhere in Poe's work as fallacious are here related. First, the self so considered is a sign in which a perfect correspondence exists between outside and inside, between surface "expression" and inner "thoughts or sentiments." Second, such a method is grounded in the power of adequate self-reflection, the impossibility of which this study has examined in "Morella." Dupin lays claim to mastery both of language and of himself.

Gregory S. Jay, in his discussion of "The Purloined Letter," locates one series of risks the existence of which Dupin does not acknowledge: "Identification with another may be perilous if human subjectivity is heterogeneous or multiple. Which of the other's selves do we identify with, and with which one of ourselves do we do it? Through identification we might take into ourselves the others within the other, and deposit them unknowingly within our own consciousness."[27] Clearly, Dupin believes that such a process can be controlled; in "The Murders in the Rue Morgue" he is blind to the ironic and threatening implications of the fact that his identification of/with the criminal leads him to indict a maddened "brute," the orangutan. In his fine examination of "The Psychology of 'The Murders in the Rue Morgue,'" J. A. Leo Lemay has carefully traced the motifs of repressed sexuality in the narrative.[28] One of the implications of this analysis is that Dupin is complicit in the denial of the culturally forbidden power of sexuality in human life. Such power is *"excessively outré"* in that it is "altogether irreconcilable with our common notions of human action, even when we suppose the actors the most depraved of men" (*TS* 557). The linguistic problem—whereby "denizens of the five great divisions of Europe could recognize nothing familiar" in the "shrill" voice (*TS* 550)—is resolved into "the fiendish jabberings of the brute" (*TS* 568). Yet, as Lemay points out, the details that suggest to Dupin a nonhuman cause "are the ones caused by the *humanness* of the orangutan's response when he sees the face of the sailor at the window"—"fear, shame, and consciousness."[29] The potentially disruptive brute in man is displaced, named as other, as "Ourang-outang"; but Dupin's doubling with the orangutan, following as it does the narrator's early admission that "the world" ("denizens of . . . Europe"?) should have regarded him and Dupin as "madmen," and his hint that Dupin's "intelligence" was "diseased," operates to expose this enterprise. To the

extent that Dupin insists that there are "no *secret* issues . . . *no* secret issues" (*TS* 551), he is as culpable as the Prefect of Police in his
denial of what is, and explanation of what is not (*TS* 568). As Jay's
analysis shows, Dupin repeats this pattern of repression in "The Purloined Letter." The diversion he arranges—in which a "frantic" man
discharges a musket "among a crowd of women and children" (*TS*
992)—has clear sexual implications,[30] and his admission that "the pre-
tended lunatic was a man in my own pay" expresses his confidence in
his own mastery over the illicit in himself. However, such mastery is
placed in question by his identification with his double, the Minister
D——,[31] and by the signature he leaves inside the "*fac-simile*" of the
(by now) doubly purloined letter as a clue to "the identity of [his]
person" (*TS* 993). The signature takes the form of a quotation from
"Crébillon's 'Atree' " (*TS* 993), a version of a bloody myth about murder, revenge, and adultery. Dupin thus signs himself as that "*monstrum
horrendum*" he would exclude by denial and displacement onto the
Minister D——.[32]

Dupin's signature also derogates from his claim to mastery over the
letter. As Joseph N. Riddel, following Jacques Derrida, has pointed
out, the signature as a quotation is made up of purloined letters themselves originating in "a myth about origins the origin of which is un-
locatable."[33] The fact that this authentic citation within the facsimile
letter recalls the stage-mad, name-changing cobbler who, in "The Murders in the Rue Morgue," had "attempted the role of Xerxes, in Crébillon's tragedy" (*TS* 534) might be a concealed joke at Dupin's expense,
but it also contributes to the pervasive intertextuality that undermines
Dupin's claim to authority and his ostensible return of the letter to its
"proper" place.

"The document in question," which, according to Prefect G——,
gives power to its purloiner, is "a letter, to be frank" (*TS* 977). Just
as "frank" punningly evokes the superscription that enables letters to
be sent free of charge, so "letter" is both epistle and character—the
(phonemic) difference that makes meaning possible. To the extent that
its content is never disclosed, it is a signifier without a signified.[34] As
Derrida has noted, its "origin" is in the usurpation of the King's power
by the Queen's adultery, and the movement of the letter demonstrates
the displacement of meaning from its "proper" home.[35] Yet it is this
displacement that ensures the power of the letter, and enables the gen-

eration of interpretation and conjecture. Implicitly, the inauguration of
the letter is always adulterous—in that it involves the transgression of
an absent "royal" identity—and in this sense it has no proper place to
which it can be returned; as we have seen in "The Gold-Bug," revelation of univocal meaning would implicitly stop the circulation of the
letter, halt the game of language, be no meaning at all.[36]

The title of the tale, "The Purloined Letter," names both text and
letter; in Derrida's formulation, "it names itself and thus includes itself while pretending to name an object described in the text."[37] Thus
the vagaries of the purloined letter are shared by "The Purloined Letter"—both are of necessity pilfered and displaced. In the Prefect's account, we learn only that the letter "had been received" by the Queen—
its author is effaced; the letter is already "purloined" in the sense of
being displaced, or put at a distance from an origin before it is pilfered. Beneath the title of the tale, the epigraph also suggests both
distance—it is in Latin, and credited to "Seneca"—and pilferage, the
latter with a wry twist since it has already been "purloined" in "The
Murders in the Rue Morgue" (which raises the question of the location
of a "proper" place).[38] As Derrida observes, the opening of the tale is
not really a beginning point but "a scene of writing—its access or border undeterminable—whose boundaries are blurred."[39] The narrative
is situated in relation to other texts by reference—"the affair of the
Rue Morgue, and the mystery attending the murder of Marie Rogêt"—
and by the fact that this beginning scene is located in the "little back
library, or book-closet" of C. Auguste Dupin (*TS* 974).

Riddel remarks on Derrida's marking of this "beginning that in every way refuses the proper notion of beginning."[40] Referred back to
"The Murders in the Rue Morgue" we find there, too, the library—the
"obscure library" where narrator and Dupin meet, "both being in
search of the same remarkable volume" (*TS* 531–32)—and a frame
to the narrative that denies it is a "treatise," claiming it is merely
"prefacing . . . by observations very much at random" (*TS* 528),
but which then offers the following "narrative" as "a commentary on
the propositions just advanced" (*TS* 531).[41] And if we look to the epigraph—"What song the Syrens sang, or what name Achilles assumed
when he hid himself among women, although puzzling questions, are
not beyond *all* conjecture" (*TS* 527)—we find a further undercutting
to Dupin's claim to have restored the letter to its proper place. Just as

Dupin's signature at the end of the last tale in which he appears locates him in a maze of inscriptions without locatable origins, so also does this epigraph to his first appearance: citation leads to citation, from "Sir Thomas Browne" to "Suetonius" to "Tiberius," but they issue only in questions about the power of seductive song and deceptive naming, questions that cannot be answered, but that, like the skeletons in "The Gold-Bug," prompt the generation of "conjecture."[42]

Eureka: *"fondle the phantom of the idea"*

This study began with Poe's double-edged compliment to Coleridge's poetry, in which he imagined himself standing "upon a volcano, conscious, from the very darkness bursting from the crater, of the fire and the light that are weltering below" (*CW* 7:xlii). It will end with a brief consideration of *Eureka* (1848), in which "E. A. P." attempts to read the "uniqueness" of the work of another author—God—and likens the project to that of standing "on the summit of Aetna" and "by a rapid whirling on his heel . . . comprehend[ing] the panorama in the sublimity of its *oneness*" (*EAP* 1261). The fact that Aetna was an active volcano in Poe's time ironically foreshadows the simultaneity of Oneness and annihilation that is the culmination of the work, and already raises the question of its *tone*—the focus of much debate.[43] The present concern, however, is not to offer an extended analysis of *Eureka* but merely to suggest in general terms the ways in which it raises those issues of authority and displacement that, as we have seen, are articulated throughout Poe's work.

The outlines of the cosmic narrative offered in *Eureka* can be summarized briefly. In the beginning, "Godhead" by his "Volition" made—out of "Nihility"—"Matter in its utmost conceivable state of . . . *Simplicity*": that is, a "particle" characterized only by *"Oneness"* (*EAP* 1276, 1277). This was the primary *"conception,"* which was immediately followed by "the primary *act*" by which this infinitely divisible particle was willed by the "Thought of God" into atomic diffusion (*EAP* 1300, 1301). Thus the One became many, no-difference became difference, the "normal" became "abnormal" (*EAP* 1282, 1298). Upon the "discontinuance of the Divine Volition" the atoms, seeking to satisfy their desire for their "normal" condition, began to return according to the principle of gravity or "Attraction" to their original center—conceived not as a location but as "the principle, Unity" (*EAP* 1287). To prevent their frustration of "the general design"— "*that of the utmost possible Relation*" (*EAP* 1280)—they are delayed by the force of electricity or "repulsion," which allows them only to "approximate" each other without absolutely coalescing.

As the atoms tend to the center they form "nebulae," then "agglomerate" by "condensation" to form masses, of which our solar system is but a "*generic instance*" (*EAP* 1323) in the galaxy or "cluster" that is a member of the "cluster of clusters" that is the universe. In the "awful Future" the systems and galaxies will themselves coalesce to form "amid unfathomable abysses . . . glaring unimaginable suns," which, in their "passion for oneness" will rush toward "their own general centre" and "flash . . . into a common embrace" (*EAP* 1353). Since this "absolutely consolidated globe of globes would be *object-less*," the two principles "'by which Matter . . . exists" would cease to exist and matter would be "*Matter no more*": "In sinking into Unity, it will sink at once into that Nothingness which, to all finite perception, Unity must be—into . . . Material Nihility" (*EAP* 1354, 1355). Yet, based on "the law of periodicy," the narrative offers a "hope—that the processes we have here ventured to contemplate will be renewed forever, and forever, and forever; a novel Universe swelling into existence, and then subsiding into nothingness, at every throb of the Heart Divine" (*EAP* 1356).

As was noted in chapter 1, *Eureka* at crucial points identifies the universe with a literary work; in the process a curious effect is established whereby the "plot" of the universe and the "discourse" of the text are mutually implicated. In its symmetry the universe is "the most sublime of poems" (*EAP* 1349); in the "absolute *reciprocity of adaptation*" of elements it fulfills Poe's criteria for the perfect plot, by which we should "not be able to determine, of any one [incident], whether it depends from any one other or upholds it. . . . The plots of God are perfect. The Universe is a plot of God" (*EAP* 1342). Moreover, its ending cannot be arbitrary, since in that case

we should have been forced to regard the Universe with some such sense of dissatisfaction as we experience in contemplating an unnecessarily complex work of human art. Creation would have affected us as an imperfect *plot* in a romance, where the *dénoûment* is awkwardly brought about by interposed incidents external and foreign to the main subject; instead of springing out of the bosom of the thesis—out of the heart of the ruling idea—instead of arising as a result of the primary proposition—as inseparable and inevitable part and parcel of the fundamental conception of the book. (*EAP* 1352)

The narrator is, of course, evoking the long tradition of reading the natural world as God's book—though in this case the book is vastly expanded, since in it "the Earth [is] considered in its planetary relations alone" (*EAP* 1262). Perhaps the analogy should be that of universe as corpus, or as library, in which the infinite complexity of intertextual relationships makes up the single plot of their putative author. More immediately, however, the characterization of the universe as poem and romance recalls the terms of the preface in which "E. A. P." declares that he wants the following book to be read "as an Art-Product . . . as a Romance; or . . . as a Poem" (*EAP* [1259]). They also evoke the opening paragraphs of the text, in which its "ruling idea" or "general proposition" is explicitly set out—"*In the Original Unity of the First Thing lies the Secondary Cause of All Things, with the Germ of their Inevitable Annihilation*"—which, the narrator says, "throughout this volume, I shall be continually endeavoring to suggest" (*EAP* 1261). The implicit correlation of universe and discourse continues as, for example, the narrative calls attention to its own strategy as it moves first from "centre" to "outskirts" in describing diffusion (*EAP* 1272–83) and then reverses the process in describing attraction (*EAP* 1283–88).

The preface not only contributes to this intermingling of universe and discourse but also introduces the central problem posed by each. "E. A. P." concludes by declaring that "it is as a Poem only that I wish this work to be judged after I am dead" (*EAP* [1259]). In so doing, he registers his anxiety about the fate of his text at the hands of future interpreters and attempts to control future readings by placing constraints upon them. But in attributing an independent existence to the work as he announces his own death, and by offering the cryptic signature "E. A. P." he emphasizes the displacement of the writing "I" by an inscribed self. The letters declare their own particularity and their distance from an originating authorial presence that is located in the "position" of the irrecoverably absent author. Thus he places the reader in the same relationship to his text as he bears to the universe. In the system of *Eureka,* the narrator as reader is confronted by particularity in which "Godhead" is nowhere present; the word "God," like "infinity" and "spirit," only identifies "a certain *tendency* of the human intellect" (*EAP* 1272); of "Godhead, *in itself,* he alone is not imbecile . . . who propounds—nothing" (*EAP* 1276).

The narrator's reading purports to be a systematic explanation of the universe and confirmation of its transcendental origin, yet it repeatedly reveals its explanation as a fictional construct and reaffirms the absolute displacement of the universe from such an origin. The narrator declares that "we know absolutely *nothing* of the nature or essence of God" (*EAP* 1276), and repeatedly denies the present "agency" of God in the universe (*EAP* 1279, 1313, 1312)—asserting that "Nature and the God of Nature are distinct" (*EAP* 1313). Yet he grounds his reading of the text of the universe displaced from its author in "Him" (*EAP* 1276). "Let us," he announces in terms that suggest the subjective and constructed nature of what follows, "let us content ourselves with supposing" that Godhead made matter out of Nothing. And of the *"nothing"* that he knows of God, he proceeds to make the "matter" of his discourse. Supposition becomes "irretrievably by-gone *Fact*" (*EAP* 1288–89) authorized by *"Intuition,"* which arises by processes *"so shadowy as to escape our consciousness, elude our reason, or defy our capacity of expression"* (*EAP* 1276–77). Yet, as Peter C. Page demonstrates, the text subversively derogates from the authority of intuition in various ways, among them the immediate juxtaposition of this claim with the saying of Baron de Bielfeld—*"Nous ne connaissons rien . . . Nous ne connaissons rien de la nature ou de l'essence de Dieu"*—in which lurks a concealed pun on the Greek *nous,* by means of which the repeated clause may be rendered: "Intuition knows nothing" (*EAP* 1276).[44]

The suggestion is constantly kept before us that the narrator, confronted by a text absolutely displaced from origin and author and characterized by multiplicity and difference, constructs a reading to satisfy his desire for a single unified meaning. The universe in *Eureka* is the universe as he writes it, and the self-enclosed nature of the project is suggested by the narrator's definitions of, for instance, the original "particle" as "positively a particle at all points," or the "Beginning" as *"that which it was"* (*EAP* 1277, 1304). He constantly cites his own "introspective analysis" as evidence (as in *EAP* 1274, 1275, 1277, 1286, 1288, 1289), but he unwittingly taints such evidence when he suggests that the human "leaning to the *'Infinite,'* " may to "a class of superior intelligences . . . wear all the character of monomania" (*EAP* 1329), and subsequently warns against the "monomaniac grasping at the infinite" (*EAP* 1342). The introduction of the possibility that the narrator's enterprise may itself be a product of monomania is one aspect of *Eureka*'s satiric subversion of man's attempts to conceive a universal explanation.[45] And his postulation of "superior intelligences" to whom, from a point outside his system, this monomania would be apparent implicitly acknowledges that perpetual inadequacy to which such attempts are condemned. The universe is only God's "plot" as it is plotted by readers who themselves project both origin and end.

The end projected by *Eureka* comments ironically on the narrator's "monomaniac grasping" for the *"Essence," "Origin,"* and *"Destiny"* of the universe. The climax of matter's "passion" for primal unity, once achieved in the final mutual "embrace," issues in "Nothingness," "Nihility," or void. The yearning for the author and origin of the universe can be "fulfilled" only when text and readers cease to exist. The displacement is total. Just as "difference" produces "consciousness and *Thought*" (*EAP* 1282)—implicitly produces *Eureka* itself—so absolute Unity annihilates them. Nothing would *"matter no more"* (*EAP* 1355).[46]

The narrator's final citation of the voice of *"Memories"* attempts to ameliorate this disquieting prospect by subsuming "individual identity" into "identity with God" (*EAP* 1358). It declares that when All becomes One, "Man . . . will at length attain that awfully triumphant epoch when he shall recognize his existence as that of Jehovah" (*EAP* 1358). Furthermore, a note appended to this passage declares that "the pain of the consideration that we shall lose our individual identity, ceases at once when we further reflect that the process, as above described, is, neither more nor less than that of the absorption, by each individual intelligence, of all other intelligences (that is, of the Universe) into its own. That God may be all in all, *each* must become God" (*EAP* 1359). The note confirms that the origin of this discourse on the "*Origin*" lies in the narrator's absorptive desire for unity. In his attempt to construct an all-embracing explanation he has, throughout the narrative, questioned "the sagacity, of many of the greatest and most justly reverenced of men" (*EAP* 1261); that is, he has tried to absorb "other intelligences" and absorb other versions, other interpretations into his own. But the note also undercuts his aspirations to universal explanation since as a note—that is, as a supplement to the quoted voice itself appended to his own discourse—it indicates that potentially there is always something more to be added, that there is always a surplus that escapes. The universe that such a discourse depicts is implicitly only the universe that it depicts. And, as the inset "remarkable letter" from the future implies, it is always open to interpretation and reinterpretation and resists the closure of a univocal reading for which "E. A. P." demonstrates such concern in his preface and for which he yearns in his narrative.

Eureka thus confirms that fundamental skepticism regarding the interpretive recuperation of origin, author, or unequivocal meaning that is consistently manifested in Poe's work. At this point it should not be necessary to document this claim explicitly—for instance, it should by now be clear that *Eureka*'s identification of Absolute Unity with "Nihility" and annihilation explicitly articulates the consequences of Morella's aspiration to absolute "*Identity*," or that it provides a context in which we can place Legrand's double discovery of gold and skeletons. More than this, however, *Eureka* asserts that human existence is irreducibly inscrutable, and that language both allows us what we know of the world and paradoxically displaces us from it—inaugurating a desire that it necessarily frustrates.

Yet this is too solemn a note on which to end a discussion of Poe. Perhaps we should instead recall that linguistic playfulness apparent in the juxtaposition of *Eureka* and "X-ing a Paragrab," written almost immediately afterward. The former is thickly populated with "spheres" and "globes," culminating in the narrator's celebration of the "*One*." The latter too is "as O-wy as O-wy could be" (*TS* 1371); Touch-and-go Bullet-head eulogizes the *O* as "beautiful vowel—the emblem of Eternity" (*TS* 1371). But when Bob the printer's devil comes to set up the *O*-wy text, "Not a single little-*o* was in the little-*o* hole," and in what might be taken as a humorous description of Poe's strategy in *Eureka*, Bob declares, "I can't never set up nothing without no o's" (*TS* 1372).[47] He must be content with the letter *X*, a sign for a sign; and so, Poe's texts imply, must we all.[48]

Notes

Preface

1 Cited by Eric W. Carlson, *The Recognition of Edgar Allan Poe: Selected Criticism since 1829* (Ann Arbor: Univ. of Michigan Press, 1966), 73. For an informative account of the fate of Poe's remains, see John C. Miller, "The Exhumations and Reburials of Edgar and Virginia Poe and Mrs. Clemm," *Poe Studies* 7 (1974), 46–47.

2 *American Renaissance: Art and Expression in the Age of Emerson and Whitman* (1941; rpt. New York: Oxford Univ. Press, 1968), xv, xii.

3 "Poe and the Marginalia of American Criticism: A Review Essay," *Poe Studies* 17 (1984), 24.

4 "An Interview with Claude Richard," *Iowa Review* 12 (1981), 12.

5 "Inescapable Poe," *The New York Review of Books*, 11 October 1984, 24.

6 Thompson's "Perspectives," *Poe's Fiction: Romantic Irony in the Gothic Tales* (Madison: Univ. of Wisconsin Press, 1973), chap. 1, is a well-documented discussion of the traditional views of Poe and the problems they present, though it does not mention the influential "visionary" reading in John F. Lynen's *The Design of the Present: Essays on Time and Form in American Literature* (New Haven: Yale Univ. Press, 1969), 205–71. The most recent full-length version of this reading is that of David

Ketterer, who, in *The Rationale of Deception in Poe* (Baton Rouge: Louisiana State Univ. Press, 1979), claims that Poe "on balance . . . belongs primarily with the Transcendentalists" (222). Douglas Robinson, in his review of studies of *Pym*, offers a classification of approaches that could be extended to more general treatments of Poe's work—"Reading Poe's Novel: A Speculative Review of *Pym* Criticism, 1950–1980," *Poe Studies* 15 (1982), 47–54.

7   Jacques Lacan, "Seminar on 'The Purloined Letter,'" trans. Jeffrey Mehlman, *Yale French Studies* 48 (1972), 38–72; Jacques Derrida, "The Purveyor of Truth," trans. Willis Domingo, James Hulbert, Moshe Ron, and M.-R. L., *Yale French Studies* 52 (1975), 31–113.

8   "Destin, Design, Dasein: Lacan, Derrida and 'The Purloined Letter,'" *Iowa Review* 12 (1981), 1.

9   Irwin, *American Hieroglyphics: The Symbol of the Egyptian Hieroglyphics in the American Renaissance* (New Haven: Yale Univ. Press, 1980), 41–235; Rowe, *Through the Custom-House: Nineteenth-Century American Fiction and Modern Theory* (Baltimore: Johns Hopkins Univ. Press, 1982), 91–110; Riddel, "A Somewhat Polemical Introduction: The Elliptical Poem," *Genre* 11 (1978), 459–77, and "The 'Crypt' of Edgar Poe," *Boundary 2* 8 (1979), 117–44.

10 This characterization of Poe's texts is supported—with different emphases— by, for example, Robert Crosley, "Poe's Closet Monologues," *Genre* 10 (1977), 215–32; Gregory S. Jay, "Poe: Writing and the Unconscious," *Bucknell Review* 28 (1983), 144–69; Jean Ricardou, "Gold in the Bug," trans. Frank Towne, *Poe Studies* 9 (1976), 33–39, and "'The singular character of the water,'" trans. Frank Towne, *Poe Studies* 9 (1976), 1–6; Allan Gardner Smith, "'Discovery' in Poe," *Delta* 12 (1981), 1–10. See also the studies by Riddel and Rowe cited above. Recent studies of romantic texts have generally shifted their attention away from the previous focus on the creative power of the imagination, the organic unity of the work of art, and the possibility of transcendence supposedly offered by the romantic symbol, to scrutinize the degree to which those texts examine their own signifying practices. The exchange between Jonathan Culler and M. H. Abrams in *High Romantic Argument: Essays for M. H. Abrams*, ed. Lawrence Lipking (Ithaca: Cornell Univ. Press, 1981) offers a convenient emblem of this shift; see "The Mirror Stage" (149–63) and "A Reply (164–75). Michel Foucault argues that the self-awareness embodied in romantic texts is part of a larger cultural development: "From the nineteenth century, language began to fold in upon itself, to acquire its own particular density, to deploy a history, an objectivity, and laws of its own. It became an object of knowledge among others, on the same level as living beings, wealth and value, and the history of events and men"—*The Order of Things*, trans. Alan Sheridan (New York: Pantheon, 1970), 296. Cf. Hans Aarsleff, *From Locke to Saussure: Essays on the Study of Lan-*

guage and Intellectual History (Minneapolis: Univ. of Minnesota Press, 1982), and, for the American context, Philip Gura, *The Wisdom of Words: Language, Theology, and Literature in the New England Renaissance* (Middletown, Conn.: Wesleyan Univ. Press, 1981).

11   "Al Araaf" (*P* 104).

12   Allan Gardner Smith, " 'Discovery' in Poe," 6.

13   John C. Miller, "Exhumations and Reburials," 46.

Chapter I

1   Coleridge, like Byron, has long been considered a major early influence on Poe. See Floyd Stovall, "Poe's Debt to Coleridge," *University of Texas Studies in English* 10 (1930), 70–127; Edward H. Davidson, *Poe: A Critical Study* (Cambridge: Belknap Press of Harvard Univ. Press, 1957), chap. 2. For important qualifications, see Robert D. Jacobs, *Poe: Journalist and Critic* (Baton Rouge: Louisiana State Univ. Press, 1969), and Glen A. Omans, " 'Intellectual Taste and the Moral Sense': Poe's Debt to Immanuel Kant," *Studies in the American Renaissance* (Boston: Twayne, 1980), 123–68.

2   "Poe's Debt to Coleridge," 74, 73.

3   *Biographia Literaria . . . with the Aesthetical Essays*, 2 vols., ed. J. Shawcross (1907; rpt. London: Oxford Univ. Press, 1954), 1:102.

4   Poe repeats the paragraph in his 1845 essay on N. P. Willis (*CW* 12:37). Jacobs convincingly documents the influence on Poe of Scottish Common-Sense philosophy, and comments on this passage that Poe "was attempting to refute Coleridge on eighteenth-century premises"—*Poe: Journalist and Critic*, 236. Jacobs also notes the influence of Lockean psychology, and observes that the example of the griffin was a common one going back at least to Hobbes. A typical Common-Sense definition of the imagination is that of Dugald Stewart: "The province of the Imagination is to select qualities and circumstances from a variety of different objects; and, by combining and disposing these, to form a new creation of its own"—*Outlines of Moral Philosophy* (1793), in *The Works of Dugald Stewart* (Cambridge: Hilliard and Brown, 1829), 6:394. As we shall see in the next chapter, Poe seriously questioned the fundamental assumption of Common-Sense philosophy—that of a stable, unified, personal identity.

5   Cf. Michael Davitt Bell, *The Development of American Romance: The Sacrifice of Relation* (Chicago: Univ. of Chicago Press, 1980), 93–94.

6   See Davidson's chapter 4, "Death, Eros, and Horror," in *Poe: A Critical Study*, for a thematic discussion of Poe's "dramaturgy of death" in a cultural context. In a suggestive article, Gregory S. Jay writes of "The Philosophy of Composition" that "the opening references to Godwin and Dickens alert us that this is a murder mystery: the narrator of it turns out to be both culprit and detective"—"Poe: Writing and the Unconscious,"

Bucknell Review 28 (1983), 157. For a determinedly cheerful view of the position of death in Poe's aesthetics, see Joseph J. Moldenhauer, "Murder as a Fine Art: Basic Connections between Poe's Aesthetics, Psychology, and Moral Vision," *PMLA* 83 (1968), 284–97. Note also the response by G. R. Thompson, "Unity, Death, and Nothingness—Poe's 'Romantic Skepticism,'" *PMLA* 85 (1970), 297–300. See also Michael Davitt Bell, *The Development of American Romance*, 96–101. In my discussion I am indebted to Joseph N. Riddel's "A Somewhat Polemical Introduction: The Elliptical Poem," *Genre* 11 (1978), 464–67.

7 According to Omans, Poe is here following Kant in departure from, for example, Shelley, Keats, Carlyle, Emerson, Longfellow, and Bryant who, under the influence of Schelling, "fused beauty, truth, and goodness into one supreme ideal"—" 'Intellectual Taste and the Moral Sense,'" 129. For Poe's skeptical questioning of Schelling's Absolute "Identity," see my discussion of "Morella" in chapter 2.

8 Compare the phrasing of the passage from "The Poetic Principle" (*CW* 14:273–74) quoted above with the following "Marginalia" entry on music: "When music affects us to tears, seemingly causeless, we weep *not*, as Gravina supposes, from 'excess of pleasure;' but through excess of an impatient, petulant sorrow that, as mere mortals, we are as yet in no condition to banquet upon those supernal extasies of which the music affords us merely a suggestive and indefinite glimpse" (*M* 6). Poe registers his scorn for imitation in music in a "Marginalia" note of December 1884 (*M* 32).

9 Among Poe's many scornful dismissals of representation is the following: "The defenders of this pitiable stuff, uphold it on the grounds of its truthfulness. Taking the thesis into question, this truthfulness is the one overwhelming defect. An original idea that—to laud the accuracy with which the stone is hurled that knocks us in the head. A little less accuracy might have left us more brains. And here are critics absolutely commending the truthfulness with which only the disagreeable is conveyed! In my view, if an artist must paint decayed cheeses, his merit will lie in their looking as little like decayed cheeses as possible" (*CW* 16:28).

10 An amusing footnote is provided by Poe's first choice, a parrot, which was "superseded forthwith by a Raven, as equally capable of speech, and infinitely more in keeping with the intended *tone*" (*CW* 14:200). As Kevin M. McCarthy has noted, Poe's parrot has a Lockean progenitor—"a very intelligent rational *Parrot*"—who, in a chapter of *An Essay Concerning Human Understanding* cited by Poe in "Morella," talks quite eloquently in *"Brasilian"*—"Another Source for 'The Raven': Locke's *Essay Concerning Human Understanding*," *Poe Newsletter* 1 (1968), 29. See my discussion of "Morella" in chapter 2.

11 My discussion of this point is indebted to Joseph N. Riddel's "The 'Crypt' of Edgar Poe," *Boundary 2* 8 (1979), 117–44.

12 The lyrical moment is thus the obverse of the Poe protagonist's horrified vacant stare into the void. See Robert Martin Adams's brief but insightful discussion of Poe's work in *NIL: Episodes in the Literary Conquest of Void During the Nineteenth Century* (New York: Oxford Univ. Press, 1966), 41–50.

13 *The Design of the Present: Essays on Time and Form in American Literature* (New Haven: Yale Univ. Press, 1969), 264.

14 "Language and Victorian Ideology," *American Scholar* 52 (1983), 366.

15 As in Emerson's view of language as fossil poetry; Aarsleff calls this trend "Adamicism."

16 Tzvetan Todorov writes: "Without exaggerating, we could say that if we had to condense the romantic aesthetic into a single word, it would certainly be the word 'symbol' as A. W. Schlegel introduces it here ['the beautiful is a symbolic representation of the infinite . . . making poetry (in the broadest sense of the poetic that is at the root of all the arts) is nothing other than an eternal symbolizing']"—*Theories of the Symbol*, trans. Catherine Porter (Ithaca: Cornell Univ. Press, 1982), 198–99.

17 " 'Unspeakable Horror' in Poe," *South Atlantic Quarterly* 78 (1979), 324.

18 For example, see "The Question of Poe's Narrators," *College English* 25 (1963), 177–81.

19 Allan Gardner Smith makes a related contention that "Poe's supernaturalism is testament to the prison house of language and of thought: the apparent intrusions from beyond are either reflections of the self and its desires or repressed knowledge, or are ironic denials of their own possibility"—" 'Discovery' in Poe," *Delta* 12 (1981), 8.

20 Taylor Stoehr, " 'Unspeakable Horror,' " 318.

21 Taylor Stoehr, " 'Unspeakable Horror,' " 324.

22 These "angelic" names carry a freight of prior usage. In *Politian*, Lalage reads of Cleopatra's handmaidens—"two gentle maids / With gentle names—Eiros and Charmion!" (*P* 261, ll. 26–27). In Shakespeare's *Antony and Cleopatra*, they consult a soothsayer who can "read" in "nature's infinite book of secrecy" (1. 2. 8–9). Their bawdy badinage makes a humorous contrast to the tenor of the "Conversation."

23 Joseph Riddel writes: "Poe's so-called colloquys reflect on a Romantic commonplace, the provisional non-presence of language and the possibility of recuperation of presence in the poetic void"—"The 'Crypt' of Edgar Poe," *Boundary 2* 8 (1979), 121.

24 David Halliburton, *Edgar Allan Poe: A Phenomenological View* (Princeton: Princeton Univ. Press, 1973), 388.

25 " 'Unspeakable Horror,' " 327.

26 "The 'Crypt' of Edgar Poe," 122.

27 *The Development of American Romance*, 94.

28 "The 'Crypt' of Edgar Poe," 131.

29 "Unity, Death, and Nothingness," 300.

Chapter II

1 *The Instructed Vision: Scottish Common Sense Philosophy and the Origins of American Fiction* (Bloomington: Indiana Univ. Press, 1961).

2 A. D. Nuttall notes that Reid, at first a disciple of Berkeley, began his own work as a result of "the skeptical despair he had fallen into as a result of reading Berkeley and Hume"—"The Sealing of the Doors," chap. 1 of *A Common Sky: Philosophy and the Literary Imagination* (London: Chatto & Windus, 1974), 29. For the brief summary that appears in my text I am indebted to Nuttall and, particularly, to Stephen D. Cox, *"The Stranger within Thee": Concepts of the Self in Late–Eighteenth-Century Literature* (Pittsburgh: Univ. of Pittsburgh Press, 1980), 13–34. See also W. B. Carnochan, *Confinement and Flight: An Essay on English Literature of the Eighteenth Century* (Berkeley: Univ. of California Press, 1977).

3 "Of Identity," *Essays on the Intellectual Powers of Man,* ed. A. D. Woozley (London: Macmillan, 1941), pp. 202–4. On Reid's influence on American orthodoxy see Martin, *Instructed Vision,* and Allan Gardner Smith, *The Analysis of Motives: Early American Psychology and Fiction* (Amsterdam: Editions Rodolphi, 1980), 135ff. I choose to cite Reid here, and below in my discussion of "A Predicament," not as one of Poe's "sources" but as the most influential of those whose work provided the philosophical ground for the assumptions that Poe's tales question.

4 The tale contains a series of attacks on the transcendentalists. Toby Dammit suffers from an attack of "transcendentalism," the symptoms of which include his "now shouting out, and now lisping out, all manner of odd little and big words" indiscriminately and the stile/style leaping at which, we are told, Mr. Carlyle excels (*TS* 627). The literalization of the figure of speech brings Toby back to earth. David Ketterer notes the pun in the narrator's being able to recall only "the heads of [Dammit's] discourse," which, he says, "suggests that it is the basic abstract assumptions of the Transcendentalists that Poe wishes to demolish"—*The Rationale of Deception in Poe* (Baton Rouge: Louisiana State Univ. Press, 1979), 99. More interesting is the interpretation by Eliot Glassheim, who identifies three targets for the satire: "the Transcendental Idealist position (Toby), the materialist and literalist position (the devil), and the conventional social or moralistic position (the narrator)"—"A Dogged Interpretation of 'Never Bet the Devil Your Head,'" *Poe Newsletter* 2 (1969), 45.

5 I give here the *Broadway Journal* (1845) title with the date of original publication. The *American Museum* (1838) titles were "Psyche Zenobia" and "The Scythe of Time"; see Burton R. Pollin, "Poe's Tale of Psyche Zenobia: A Reading for Humor and Ingenious Construction," in *Papers on Poe: Essays in Honor of John Ward Ostrom,* ed. Richard P. Veler (Springfield, Ohio: Chantry Music Press, 1972), 92. Pollin's is the only worthwhile full-length treatment of this tale; in the course of his larger argument G. R. Thompson notes the parody of literary styles in "How to

Write a Blackwood Article"—*Poe's Fiction: Romantic Irony in the Gothic Tales* (Madison: Univ. of Wisconsin Press, 1973), 36–38. Other studies are Kenneth Leroy Daughrity, "Notes: Poe and Blackwood's," *American Literature* 2 (1930), 289–92; Walter F. Taylor, "Israfel in Motley," *Sewanee Review* 42 (1934), 330–40; Thomas H. McNeal, "Poe's *Zenobia*: An Early Satire on Margaret Fuller," *Modern Language Quarterly* 9 (1950), 215–26; Ben Harris McClary, "Poe's 'Turkish Fig-Pedlar,'" *Poe Newsletter* 2 (1969), 56; Pollin, "Figs, Bells, Poe and Horace Smith," *Poe Newsletter* 3 (1970), 8–10; Richard Schuster, "More on 'The Fig-Pedlar,'" *Poe Newsletter* 3 (1970), 22; Gerald Gerber, "The Coleridgean Context of Poe's *Blackwood* Satires," *ESQ: A Journal of the American Renaissance* 60 (1970), 87–91, and "Milton and Poe's 'Modern Woman,'" *Poe Newsletter* 3 (1970), 25–26; and Joseph L. McElrath Jr., "Poe's Conscious Prose Technique," *NEMLA Newsletter* 2 (1970), 34–43.

6 *Poe: A Critical Study* (Cambridge: Belknap Press of Harvard Univ. Press, 1957), 144.

7 *Poe's Fiction*, 85.

8 William Whipple first marshaled significant evidence to identify Johnson as a target—"Poe's Political Satire," *University of Texas Studies in English* 35 (1956), 81–95; he is followed by Thompson, *Poe's Fiction*, 83, and Ketterer, *Rationale of Deception*, 80. Ronald Curran identified Scott— "The Fashionable Thirties: Poe's Satire in 'The Man That Was Used Up,'" *Markham Review* 8 (1978), 14–20; he is followed by Daniel Hoffman, *Poe Poe Poe Poe Poe Poe Poe* (New York: Doubleday, 1972), 197, and Richard A. Alekna, "'The Man That Was Used Up': Further Notes on Poe's Satirical Targets," *Poe Studies* 12 (1979), 36. See also Elmer Pry, "A Folklore Source for 'The Man That Was Used Up,'" *Poe Studies* 8 (1975), 46.

9 "Poe's Other Double: The Reader in the Fiction," *Criticism* 24 (1982), 345.

10 As well as Auerbach (346), see Mabbott (*TS* 377), and Sidney P. Moss, *Poe's Literary Battles: The Critic in the Context of His Literary Milieu* (Carbondale: Southern Illinois Univ. Press, 1969), 55–56, 58, 93.

11 Moss, *Poe's Literary Battles*, 57, 55.

12 There are echoes here of the "Clothes Philosophy" of Carlyle's *Sartor Resartus*—specifically of "the Dandiacal Body," which, like the General, is a product of a crass and materialistic society.

13 The epigraph from Corneille offers further support to this assertion:

> Pleurez, pleurez, mes yeux, et fondez-vous en eau!
> La moitié de ma vie a mis l'autre au tombeau.

Poe had earlier noted these lines in "Pinakidia" (1836), where he translated them thus:

> Weep, weep my eyes! it is no time to laugh
> For half myself has buried the other half. (*CW* 14:44)

The address to the eyes as separate from the self who speaks introduces the motif of fragmentation, which is reinforced by the substitution in the second line of "half my*self*" (emphasis mine) for "half my life."

14   Such a reading makes sense out of an otherwise baffling parallelism—first noticed by Richard Wilbur and developed by Thompson (*Poe's Fiction*, 83–85)—between "The Man That Was Used Up" and "Ligeia."

15   Other tales in which this theme has been noted include "Metzengerstein," "A Tale of the Ragged Mountains," and "Ligeia."

16   G. R. Thompson, *Poe's Fiction*, 168. Other readings of the tale include Lee J. Richmond, "Edgar Allan Poe's 'Morella': Vampire of Volition," *Studies in Short Fiction* 9 (1972), 93–94; Martin Bickman, *The Unsounded Centre: Jungian Studies in American Romanticism* (Chapel Hill: Univ. of North Carolina Press, 1980), 67–75; David Halliburton, *Edgar Allan Poe: A Phenomenological View* (Princeton: Princeton Univ. Press, 1973), 219–23.

17   Cf. the protestations of the narrator of "Ms Found in a Bottle" (1833).

18   *Edgar Allan Poe*, 219.

19   "Of Identity and Diversity," book 2, chap. 27, of *Essay*, ed. Peter H. Nidditch (Oxford: Oxford Univ. Press, 1975), 343. Further references will be cited parenthetically.

20   Cf. Antony Flew, "Locke and the Problem of Personal Identity," in *Locke and Berkeley: A Collection of Critical Essays*, ed. C. B. Martin and D. M. Armstrong (Notre Dame: Notre Dame Univ. Press, 1968), 155–78; John J. Richetti, *Philosophical Writing: Locke, Berkeley, Hume* (Cambridge: Harvard Univ. Press, 1983), 110. On Poe's use of Locke here and elsewhere, see Margaret Alterton, *Origins of Poe's Critical Theory* (Iowa City: Univ. of Iowa Press, 1925), 99–102; S. Gerald Sandler, "Poe's Indebtedness to Locke's *An Essay Concerning Human Understanding*," *Boston University Studies in English* 5 (1961), 107–21; Kevin M. McCarthy, "Another Source for 'The Raven': Locke's *Essay Concerning Human Understanding*," *Poe Newsletter* 1 (1968), 29.

21   Part 3, chap. 38; Mabbott, *TS* 236–37, n.3. Mabbott notes that Poe follows Hobbes's misspelling, Hinno*n*, in all published versions of "Morella," correcting it in the Whitman copy (1848). The motif of child sacrifice provides thematic support for the murder theory suggested by Thompson.

22   *Unsounded Centre*, 67.

23   The narrator's sense of otherness from himself, this doubleness in his own identity that he attempts to familiarize and so negate by naming "demon" or "fiend" is already lodged within that reasonable definition of personal identity to which he subscribes. The definition attempts to establish a discrete "identity" by defining "person" as "an intelligent *essence* having reason" (*TS* 231; emphasis mine); yet this self is distinguished from "other beings that think" by a "consciousness which always accompanies thinking." The "identity" of the self at any moment is thus doubled, on the assumption that the motives and thought processes of the self are avail-

able to the monitoring scrutiny of the consciousness. Moreover, the fundamental "sameness of a rational being" suggests a crucial identification of consciousness with memory, to which the past actions of the self offer themselves in a coherent and unchanging narrative that constitutes the present personal identity. Thus the self is conceived of as both identical to and different from itself. Cf. John T. Irwin, *American Hieroglyphics: The Symbol of the Egyptian Hieroglyphics in the American Renaissance* (New Haven: Yale Univ. Press, 1980), 121–22.

24 F. W. J. von Schelling, *Vorlesung über der akademische Studium* (1802), in *Werke*, ed. Manfred Schoter, 6 vols. (Munich, 1927–28), 3:290. Cited by Marc Shell, *Money, Language, and Thought: Literary and Philosophical Economies from the Medieval to the Modern Era* (Berkeley: Univ. of California Press, 1982), 164; the translation is Shell's.

25 Previously "A Decided Loss" (1832); this quote is from material added in 1835 and excised in 1845. Henry A. Pochmann suggests that though there is no evidence that Poe "was familiar with the whole of Schelling's philosophy," he could have gained the ideas he uses indirectly through the work of Novalis—*German Culture in America: Philosophical and Literary Influences 1600–1900* (Madison: Univ. of Wisconsin Press, 1957), 401.

26 Palmer C. Holt has shown that Poe probably found this in H. N. Coleridge's *Introduction to the Study of the Greek Classic Poets* (rpt. Philadelphia, 1831); in early versions of the tale Poe used Coleridge's translation ("Itself—alone by itself—eternally one and single") changing it in the *Broadway Journal* (1845) text—"Poe and H. N. Coleridge's *Greek Classic Poets* 'Pinakidia,' 'Politian,' and 'Morella' Source," *American Literature* 34 (1962), 8–10.

27 " 'Unspeakable Horror' in Poe," *South Atlantic Quarterly* 78 (1979), 322.

28 "Poe's 'Morella': A Note on Her Name," *American Literature* 47 (1975), 261–62. Mabbott mentions other deathly associations of the name (*TS* 222).

29 Roman Jakobson calls such elements "shifters"; they signify only by reference to a particular message or enunciation—*Selected Writings* (The Hague: Mouton, 1971), 2:130–47. Jacques Derrida argues that "the signifying function of the *I* does not depend on the life of the speaking subject," but that "my death is structurally necessary to the pronouncing of the *I*"—*Speech and Phenomena*, trans. David B. Allison (Evanston: Northwestern Univ. Press, 1973), 96. See also my discussion in chapter 4 of M. Valdemar's "I am dead."

30 In "The Black Cat" the imp appears as "the spirit of PERVERSENESS" (*TS* 852). James W. Gargano suggests that in this tale, the narrator offers this spirit in an attempt to evade moral responsibility for his own actions, and that if we "grant Poe's protagonist his belief in an uncontrollable and enigmatic imp of the perverse," we "agree with him" that any "moral rationale of life" is "naive and illogical"—" 'The Black Cat': Perverseness Reconsidered," *Texas Studies in Literature and Language* 2 (1960), 172.

In voicing this concern, Gargano echoes the moral urgency of the Common-Sense philosophers who feared the unstable self: for example, Beattie, in his *Essay on Truth* (1770), writes that "to a man who doubts the individuality or identity of his own mind, virtue, truth, religion, good and evil, hope and fear, are absolutely nothing"—quoted by Cox, *The Stranger Within Thee*, 21. I strategically avoid dealing with this problem here, but note the arguments offered by Joseph J. Moldenhauer, "Murder as a Fine Art: Basic Connections between Poe's Aesthetics, Psychology, and Moral Vision," *PMLA* 83 (1968), 284–97; and, less convincingly, Victor J. Vitanza, " 'The Question of Poe's Narrators': Perverseness Considered Once Again," *American Transcendental Quarterly* 38 (1978), 137–49.

31   " 'Nests of Boxes': Form, Sense, and Style in Poe's 'The Imp of the Perverse,' " *Studies in Short Fiction* 17 (1980), 307. See also Eugene R. Kanjo, " 'The Imp of the Perverse': Poe's Dark Comedy of Art and Death," *Poe Newsletter* 2 (1969), 41–44.

32   Many commentators have discussed the parallels between this passage and that in *Pym*, chap. 24. John T. Irwin notes that "in each instance the injunction not to think is symptomatic of that self-dissolving abyss of thought about thought, of thought seeking its own origin by trying to conceive of the condition of nonthought that preceded it"—*American Hieroglyphics*, 194. See also Burton R. Pollin, "The Self-Destructive Fall: A Theme from Shakespeare Used in *Pym* and 'The Imp of the Perverse,' " *Études Anglaises* 29 (1976), 199–202.

33   " 'Nests of Boxes,' " 313.

34   See Quinn, " 'That Spectre in My Path,' " *The French Face of Edgar Allan Poe* (Carbondale: Southern Illinois Univ. Press, 1954), chap. 7. Henry A. Pochmann briefly discusses the relationship between Poe's use of the *doppelgänger* motif and that of the German romanticists—*German Culture in America: Philosophical and Literary Influences 1600–1900* (Madison: Univ. of Wisconsin Press, 1957), 397–98. See also Otto Rank, "The Double as Immortal Self," *Beyond Psychology* (1941; rpt. New York: Dover, 1958), chap. 2; Marianne Wain, "The Double in Romantic Narrative: A Preliminary Study," *Germanic Review* 36 (1961), 257–68; and Claire Rosenfield, "The Shadow Within: The Conscious and the Unconscious Use of the Double," *Daedalus* 92 (1963), 326–44.

35   Thompson, *Poe's Fiction*, 172.

36   According to Daniel Hoffman, in Poe's work the "vulture is associated with TIME, and time is associated with our mortality, our confinement in a body"—*Poe Poe Poe Poe Poe Poe Poe* 229. See Richard Wilbur, "The Poe Mystery Case," *Responses: Prose Pieces: 1953–1976* (New York: Harcourt Brace Jovanovich, 1976), 132; David Ketterer, *The Rationale of Deception*, 103–6; and particularly James W. Gargano, "The Theme of Time in 'The Tell-Tale Heart,' " *Modern Fiction Studies* 5 (1968), 378–82. Apart from Gargano's essay, the most interesting treatments of the tale remain those by E. Arthur Robinson, "Poe's 'The Tell-Tale Heart,' " *Nine-*

teenth-Century Fiction 19 (1965), 369–78, and John E. Reilly, "The Lesser Death-Watch and 'The Tell-Tale Heart,'" *American Transcendental Quarterly* 2 (1969), 3–9. Other studies are John W. Canario, "The Dream in 'The Tell-Tale Heart,'" *English Language Notes* 7 (1970), 194–97; E. Arthur Robinson, "Thoreau and the Deathwatch in Poe's 'The Tell-Tale Heart,'" *Poe Studies* 4 (1971), 14–16; David Halliburton, *Edgar Allan Poe*, 333–38; Robert McIlvaine, "A Shakespearean Echo in "'The Tell-Tale Heart,'" *American Notes and Queries* 15 (1976), 38–40; Edward W. Pitcher, "The Physiognomical Meaning of Poe's 'The Tell-Tale Heart,'" *Studies in Short Fiction* 16 (1979), 231–33.

37 Or, in John E. Reilly's convincing interpretation, it is identified with the sound of the "lesser death-watch" insect noted earlier in the tale: "the innocuous sound of an insect becomes a measure of time under the aspect of death, a kind of metaphor binding together three tokens of man's mortality: the process of nature, the beating of the human heart, and the ticking of a watch"—"The Lesser Death-Watch and 'The Tell-Tale Heart,'" 8.

38 Cf. Psyche Zenobia's eye, above.

39 Cf. the fiend in "Morella." See also Robinson, "Poe's 'The Tell-Tale Heart,'" 377.

40 *Edgar Allan Poe*, 335.

41 Evoking the analogy with the *camera obscura*, Locke writes: "the *Understanding* is not unlike a Closet wholly shut from light"—"Of Discerning, and other Operations of the Mind," book 2, chap. 11, of *Essay*, 163.

42 It is also "at midnight, when all the world slept" that the narrator has groaned "the groan of mortal terror" (*TS* 794).

43 Examples of such readings in general studies of the double in literature are: Robert Rogers, *A Psychoanalytic Study of the Double in Literature* (Detroit: Wayne State Univ. Press, 1970), 25, and C. F. Kepler, *The Literature of the Second Self* (Tucson: Univ. of Arizona Press, 1972), 104–6. Among studies primarily devoted to "William Wilson," that by Ruth Sullivan reverses the usual psychoanalytical reading by suggesting that "William Wilson's superego tells the story of William Wilson's id"— "William Wilson's Double," *Studies in Romanticism* 15 (1976), 254. The most interesting fully developed discussions of the tale are those by James W. Gargano, "'William Wilson': 'The Wildest Sublunary Visions,'" *Washington and Jefferson Literary Journal* 1 (1967), 9–16, and "Art and Irony in 'William Wilson,'" *Emerson Society Quarterly*, no. 60 Suppl. (1970), 18–22; and Thomas F. Walsh, "The Other William Wilson," *American Transcendental Quarterly* 10 (1971), 17–26. See also Edward H. Davidson, *Poe: A Critical Study*, 198–201; Donald B. Stauffer, "Style and Meaning in 'Ligeia' and 'William Wilson,'" *Studies in Short Fiction* 2 (1965), 316–30; James M. Cox, "Edgar Poe: Style as Pose," *Virginia Quarterly Review* 44 (1968), 81–83; David Halliburton, *Edgar Allan Poe*, 299–308; Robert Coskren, "'William Wilson' and the Disintegration of

Self," *Studies in Short Fiction* 12 (1975), 155–62; Eric W. Carlson, "'William Wilson': The Double as Primal Self," *Topic* 30 (1976), 35–40; Sam B. Girgus, "Poe and R. D. Laing: The Transcendent Self," *Studies in Short Fiction* 13 (1976), 299–309; Ottavio Cassale, "The Dematerialization of William Wilson: Poe's Use of Cumulative Allegory," *South Carolina Review* 11 (1978), 70–79; Marc Leslie Rovner, "What William Wilson Knew: Poe's Dramatization of an Errant Mind," in *Poe at Work: Seven Textual Studies*, ed. Benjamin Franklin Fisher IV (Baltimore: The Edgar Allan Poe Society, 1978), 73–82; William West, "Staying Alive: Poe's 'William Wilson,'" *Enclitic* 2 (1978), 34–49; Leonard Orr, "The 'Other' and 'Bad Faith': The Proto-Existentialism of Poe's 'William Wilson,'" *Studies in the Humanities* 9 (1981), 33–38; Nicholas Canady, "Poe's 'William Wilson,'" *Explicator* 40 (1982), 28–29.

44 "Edgar Allan Poe: Style as Pose," 81.
45 Gargano, "Art and Irony," 18.
46 "The Double as Immortal Self," 99.
47 "'William Wilson' and the Distintegration of Self," 155.

Chapter III

1 Part of the paragraph reads: "Does your mother *know* you're out? Oh, no, no!—so go home at once, now, John, to your odious old woods of Concord" (*TS* 1371).
2 According to the *Oxford English Dictionary*, "to cabbage" has long been slang for "to pilfer"; and one entry from *Blackwood's Edinburgh Magazine* (1830) has the usage, "to plagiarize." Cabbages are prolific in "The Devil in the Belfry" (1839).
3 The quote above in n.1 is thus rendered: "Dxes yxur mxther *knxw* yxu're xut? Xh, nx, nx!" etc.
4 "Editorial Miscellanies," *Broadway Journal*, 20 September 1845, rpt. in *Edgar Allan Poe: Essays and Reviews*, ed. G. R. Thompson (New York: Modern Library of America, 1984), 1068.
5 For an excellent analysis of Poe's precarious finances throughout his career, see John Ward Ostrom, "Edgar A. Poe: His Income as Literary Entrepreneur," *Poe Studies* 15 (1982), 1–7.
6. "Editorial Miscellanies," 1068. Compare his uncharacteristically temperate comments in his "Literati" sketch of James Aldrich (*CW* 14:62–63).
7 Plagiarism was, of course, one of the main issues of the so-called Longfellow War. See Sidney P. Moss, *Poe's Literary Battles: The Critic in the Context of His Literary Milieu* (1963; rpt. Carbondale: Southern Illinois Univ. Press, 1969), chap. 5.
8 "Hawthorne's 'Plagiary'; Poe's Duplicity," *Nineteenth-Century Fiction* 25 (1970), 281–98. Note also that in "A Reviewer Reviewed," under the pseudonym of Walter G. Bowen, he charged *himself* with plagiarism (*TS* 1384–86).

9   See particularly Michael Allen, *Poe and the British Magazine Tradition* (New York: Oxford Univ. Press, 1969) ; and Jonathan Auerbach, "Poe's Other Double: The Reader in the Fiction," *Criticism* 24 (1982), 347–48. Michael T. Gilmore examines the ways in which the marketplace influenced the work of American writers in the nineteenth century (without, however, considering Poe) in *American Romanticism and the Marketplace* (Chicago: Univ. of Chicago Press, 1985).

10   Also relevant here is Poe's career-long desire for mastery and control of the system of journal publication within the constraints of which he had to work throughout his career. His resentment of "the nod of a master" was one motive for his desire to found his own journal. In 1848 he solicited George W. Eveleth to make an early subscription to *The Stylus* in terms that suggest his attitude: "I am resolved to be my own publisher. To be controlled is to be ruined. My ambition is great" (*L* 356). Certainly his plans for the production quality and content of both *The Stylus* and the earlier *Penn Magazine* were ambitious, perhaps unrealistic. *The Stylus*, he declared grandly in an 1843 letter to Thomas, would be "the most magnificent Magazine as regards externals, ever seen" (*L* 224; cf. 152, 247) ; and the *Penn* was to have had *"no articles but from the best pens"* (*L* 152). Neither magazine ever appeared. See Burton R. Pollin, "Poe's Iron Pen," *Discoveries in Poe* (Notre Dame, Ind.: Notre Dame Univ. Press, 1970), 206–29.

11   See Moss, *Poe's Literary Battles.*

12   On Poe's relationship to a readership, see Michael Allen, *Poe and the British Magazine Tradition*, and, implicitly, G. R. Thompson, *Poe's Fiction: Romantic Irony in the Gothic Tales* (Madison: Univ. of Wisconsin Press, 1973).

13   Presumably this is what he means by the infelicitous phrase, "meaningful oral exchanges"—*Edgar Allan Poe: A Phenomenological View* (Princeton: Princeton Univ. Press, 1973), 252. Robert Crosley has taken this observation as a starting point for his essay "Poe's Closet Monologues," *Genre* 10 (1977), 215–32.

14   The dates of publication given here are deceptive. A shorter version of "Loss of Breath," entitled "A Decided Loss," appeared in the *Philadelphia Saturday Courier*, 10 November 1832.

15   *Poe's Fiction*, 47.

16   On the Folio Club project, see particularly Alexander Hammond, "A Reconstruction of Poe's 1833 *Tales of the Folio Club:* Preliminary Notes," *Poe Studies* 5 (1972), 25–32; "Further Notes on Poe's Folio Club Tales," *Poe Studies* 8 (1975), 38–42; "Edgar Allan Poe's *Tales of the Folio Club:* The Evolution of a Lost Book," in *Poe at Work: Seven Textual Studies*, ed. Benjamin Franklin Fisher IV (Baltimore: The Edgar Allan Poe Society, 1978), 13–43.

17   "Further Notes," 41.

18   Richard Broxton Onians, *The Origins of European Thought about the*

Body, the Mind, the Soul, the World, Time, and Fate (Cambridge: Cambridge Univ. Press, 1951), 46–60; C. A. Van Peursen, *Body, Soul, Spirit: A Survey of the Body-Mind Problem* (London: Oxford Univ. Press, 1966), 88–89.

19   Bonaparte reads the tale as Poe's "Confession of Impotence"—*The Life and Works of Edgar Allan Poe: A Psycho-Analytic Interpretation*, trans. John Rodker (London: The Hogarth Press, 1949), 373–410.

20   Ketterer, *The Rationale of Deception in Poe* (Baton Rouge: Louisiana State Univ. Press, 1979), 92–93.

21   From the original 1835 version; retained in *Tales of the Grotesque and Arabesque* (1840); dropped from the abbreviated 1846 version. Alexander Hammond notes that this "story takes the reader on a tour of the bizarre landscape of *Blackwood's* fiction"—"Further Notes," p. 39.

22   *TS* 82, n.8; see also Hammond, "Further Notes," 40. This passage is also from the 1835 version.

23   Marc Shell, *Money, Language, and Thought: Literary and Philosophical Economies from the Medieval to the Modern Era* (Berkeley: Univ. of California Press, 1982), 18.

24   Cf. Helene Cixous, "Fiction and Its Phantoms: A Reading of Freud's *Das Unheimlich* (The 'uncanny')," *New Literary History* 7 (1975), 542–43.

25   "The Source of Terror in Poe's 'Shadow—A Parable,'" *Studies in Short Fiction* 6 (1969), 643.

26   Frank Kermode, *The Genesis of Secrecy: On the Interpretation of Narrative* (Cambridge: Harvard Univ. Press, 1979), 23–24.

27   Ibid., 24.

28   Cf. "The Conversation of Eiros and Charmion": "The popular prejudices and vulgar errors in regard to pestilences and wars . . . were now altogether unknown . . . reason had at once hurled superstition from her throne" (*TS* 459).

29   *Edgar Allan Poe*, 316. Burton R. Pollin notes correspondences between the two tales, suggesting that "Shadow" can be read as a "dress rehearsal" for the later tale—"Poe's 'Shadow' as a Source of his 'The Masque of the Red Death,'" *Studies in Short Fiction* 6 (1969), 104.

30   As Stuart and Susan Levine point out, Zoilus "bears the name of a grammarian famous as a critic who castigated Homer for 'introducing fabulous and incredible stories in his poems'"—"History, Myth, Fable, and Satire: Poe's Use of Jacob Bryant," *ESQ: A Journal of the American Renaissance* 21 (1975), 209. According to *The Oxford Classical Dictionary*, Zoilus attacked two scenes of particular relevance to this tale: *Iliad* 1.50 (when Apollo strikes the Greeks with plague) and *Iliad* 23.100 (in which Achilleus tries without success to embrace the shade of Patroklos).

31   Morella on her deathbed tells her husband, "Thou shalt no longer, then, play the Teian with time" (*TS* 233); see *TS* 237, n.10.

32   John T. Irwin is but one critic who makes this observation—*American

Hieroglyphics: The Symbol of the Egyptian Hieroglyphics in the American Renaissance (New Haven: Yale Univ. Press, 1980), 200.

33   The juxtaposition of corpse and shadow here invites comparison with "Sonnet—Silence" and the "two-fold *Silence*": "the corporate Silence" and "his shadow" (*P* 322, ll. 5, 10, 13).

34   In the first published version the pause was marked by a comma; Poe inserted the semicolon in his revision for PHANTASY-PIECES (1842) and retained it thereafter—*TS* 188.

35   Cf. Eugenio Donato, "The Ruins of Memory: Archaeological Fragments and Textual Artifacts," *MLN* 93 (1978), 575–96.

36   See, respectively, Burton R. Pollin, "Light on 'Shadow' and Other Pieces by Poe; Or, More on Thomas Moore," *ESQ: A Journal of the American Renaissance* 18 (1972), 170; Stuart and Susan Levine, *The Short Fiction of Edgar Allan Poe* (Indianapolis: Bobbs-Merrill, 1976), 110; and G. R. Thompson, *Poe's Fiction*, 169.

37   Whereas Mabbott acknowledges that "the word for wine is also *oinos* in Greek," he prefers the translation "one," even though it is much rarer (*TS* 188). There are, however, clear indications that Oinos and his companions are drunk on the "flasks of red Chian wine" (*TS* 189). The symptoms he describes could as well be those of bibulosity as those of metaphysical malaise. Moreover, they sing "the songs of Anacreon—which are madness" (*TS* 190). It is possible, as Pollin suggests ("Light on 'Shadow,' " 169), that Poe is here slyly insulting Thomas ("Anacreon") Moore (see *CW* 15:120); but Poe is also evoking that ancient writer of drinking songs whom he elsewhere calls "the disgusting old *débauché* of Teos"—*CW* 16: 164; *M* 198. See also Herbert G. Eldridge, "Anacreon Moore and America," *PMLA* 83 (1968), 54–62.

Chapter IV

1   "Maelzel" has not attracted much commentary. Readings include W. K. Wimsatt, Jr., "Poe and the Chess Automaton," *American Literature* 11 (1939), 138–51; Leroy L. Panek, " 'Maelzel's Chess-Player,' Poe's First Detective Mistake," *American Literature* 48 (1976), 370–72.

2   See, notoriously, "The Philosophy of Composition" (*CW* 14:193–95). Jonathan Auerbach makes a similar observation—"Poe's Other Double: The Reader in the Fiction," *Criticism* 24 (1982), 342; he mistakenly suggests that Poe wants to reveal a "dwarf" at the heart of the machine, whereas this is one of the possibilities Poe rejects.

3   Robert Regan, "Hawthorne's 'Plagiary'; Poe's Duplicity," *Nineteenth-Century Fiction* 25 (1970), 281–98.

4   Whereas throughout this study references to "Marginalia" items are to *Marginalia*, ed. John Carl Miller, references to the preface to "Marginalia" are to the text in *TS* 1112–18.

5 Mabbott points out a probable printer's error, the substitution of *z* for *g* in *overgezet* (*TS* 1118, n.14).

6 "The Marginal Gloss," *Critical Inquiry* 3 (1977), 610.

7 G. R. Thompson has discussed the "double effect" of the tale—*Poe's Fiction: Romantic Irony in the Gothic Tales* (Madison: Univ. of Wisconsin Press, 1973), 14–16. The tale is *at least* double.

8 Cf. Mr. Blackwood's advice to Psyche Zenobia: "There was '*The Dead Alive*,' a capital thing!—the record of a gentleman's sensations, when entombed before the breath was out of his body—full of taste, terror, sentiment, metaphysics, and erudition. You would have sworn that the writer had been born and brought up in a coffin" (*TS* 339).

9 *The Life and Works of Edgar Allan Poe: A Psycho-Analytic Interpretation*, trans. John Rodker (London: The Hogarth Press, 1949), 585–87.

10 *Poe Poe Poe Poe Poe Poe Poe* (New York: Doubleday, 1972), 221.

11 *Studies in Classic American Literature* (1923; rpt. New York: Viking, 1964), 79.

12 *Poe's Fiction*, 182.

13 In his discussion of Balzac's *Le Colonel Chabert*, Peter Brooks suggests that "the fascination exercised by burial alive on the literary imagination may point to a specifically literary obsession with the buried utterance: the word, the tale, entombed without a listener"—*Reading for the Plot: Design and Intention in Narrative* (New York: Alfred A. Knopf, 1980), 221.

14 "Poe's Other Double," 350.

15 "Poe and Magazine Writing on Premature Burial," *Studies in the American Renaissance* (Boston: Twayne, 1977), 175.

16 These parallels can be clarified thus:

   A. Introductory narrative apparatus: objective "histories"
   B. Narrator's own account: subjective
      a. "practical" apparatus
      b. subjective account
      c. narrator as victim; b revealed as delusion
   C. Reader as victim; B revealed as "bugaboo tale"

17 *The Rhetoric of Fiction* (Chicago: Univ. of Chicago Press, 1961), 201.

18 For another prurient reader who "derived positive pleasure even from many of the legitimate sources of pain" (*TS* 507), see "The Man of the Crowd" (1840).

19 "Poe and Magazine Writing," 174.

20 See Kennedy, "Poe and Magazine Writing," 166–74, for instances such as "The Lady Buried Alive," "The Buried Alive," and "Living Inhumation." Note also Lucile King, "Notes on Poe's Sources," *University of Texas Studies in English* 10 (1930), 128–34; W. T. Bandy, "A Source of Poe's 'The Premature Burial,'" *American Literature* 19 (1947), 167–68.

21 Cf. James W. Gargano, "The Distorted Perception of Poe's Comic Narrators," *Topic* 30 (1976), 23–34.

22 See Robert Shulman, "Poe and the Powers of the Mind," *English Literary History* 37 (1970), 252–53, for his discussion of the tale as embodying "one of modern literature's most moving versions of the tortured, alienated artist."

23 Since the lamp is a traditional image for imaginative creativity, perhaps the flaming corpses dangling from the chandelier can be read as representing that capacity perverted by abuse. A similar image appears in "King Pest" (1835): "Overhead was suspended a human skeleton, by means of a rope tied round one of the legs. . . . In the cranium of this hideous thing lay a quantity of ignited charcoal, which threw a fitful but vivid light over the entire scene" (*TS* 248). In "King Pest," too, the "authority of the king" is violated, but with different implications. On the relation of chandeliers to the powers of the imagination, see Richard Wilbur, "The House of Poe," in *The Recognition of Edgar Allan Poe*, ed. Eric W. Carlson (East Lansing, Mich.: Univ. of Michigan Press, 1966), 273.

24 *Edgar Allan Poe: A Phenomenological View* (Princeton: Princeton Univ. Press, 1973), 229.

25 *Poe: A Critical Study* (Cambridge: Belknap Press of Harvard Univ. Press, 1957), 144—subsequently discounted most directly by Burton R. Pollin, "Poe's Mystification: Its Source in Fay's *Norman Leslie*," *Mississippi Quarterly* 25 (1972), 111, 126. Pollin, reading the tale in the context of Poe's ongoing conflict with the literary clique surrounding the *New York Mirror*, identifies Hermann with Theodore S. Fay. See also Sidney P. Moss, *Poe's Literary Battles: The Critic in the Context of his Literary Milieu* (1963; rpt. Carbondale: Southern Illinois Univ. Press, 1969), chap. 2.

26 See particularly G. R. Thompson, *Poe's Fiction*. In his discussion of Poe's "grotesque," Thompson offers this comment: "As Harry Levin has suggested, the tale seems almost an analysis of Poe's own *psychology*" (119).

27 Late eighteenth-century affective rhetoricians emphasized the power of what was often called "the Living Voice," claiming that specific verbal devices necessarily corresponded to particular mental states. This not only enabled the speaker to prompt specific responses in his audience, but also allowed them to discern his psychology and judge his sincerity. Geoffrey Hartman notes the "smooth consensual calculus of means and ends," whereby "specific verbal devices are isolated as if they effectively corresponded to specific mental or affectional states"—*Saving the Text: Literature/Derrida/Philosophy* (Baltimore: Johns Hopkins Univ. Press, 1981), 120.

28 The joke is compounded, not weakened, by the fact that this attribution results from Poe's own distortion/misreading of a chapter in Isaac D'Israeli's *Curiosities of Literature* called "Literary Follies." See *TS* 305, n.11.

Chapter V

1   "Sign and Symbol in Hegel's *Aesthetics*," *Critical Inquiry* 8 (1982), 771.
2   *The Complete Works of Samuel Taylor Coleridge*, ed. W. G. T. Shedd (New York: Harper & Bros., 1884), 4:45. This passage, from "The Drama generally, and Public Taste," immediately follows a description of "the language of man," in which "the sound *sun*, or the figures *s*, *u*, *n*, are purely arbitrary modes of recalling the object." On romantic concern with the revelatory sign, see Gerald Bruns, *"Energeia:* The Development of the Romantic Idea of Language," in *Modern Poetry and the Idea of Language* (New Haven: Yale Univ. Press, 1974), 42–67. Also see Hans Aarsleff, "Language and Victorian Ideology," *American Scholar* 52 (1983), 365–72, for an historical account of the nineteenth-century renewal of interest in Adamic language.
3   *The Collected Works of Samuel Taylor Coleridge*, Bollingen Series LXXV, ed. K. Coburn (Princeton: Princeton Univ. Press, 1972), 6:30.
4   *Philosophy of the Literary Symbolic* (Tallahassee: Univ. Presses of Florida, 1983), 18–19, 70–75.
5   *The Collected Works*, ed. Coburn, 29.
6   On the etymology of "symbol," see James A. Coulter, *The Literary Microcosm: Theories of Interpretation of the Later Neoplatonists* (Leiden: E. J. Brill, 1976), 61.
7   See Tzvetan Todorov, *Theories of the Symbol*, trans. Catherine Porter (Ithaca: Cornell Univ. Press, 1982), esp. chap. 6, "The Romantic Crisis"; also Thomas McFarland, *Romanticism and the Forms of Ruin: Wordsworth, Coleridge, and Modalities of Fragmentation* (Princeton: Princeton Univ. Press, 1981), esp. 27–31.
8   "The Rhetoric of Temporality," in *Interpretation: Theory and Practice*, ed. C. S. Singleton (Baltimore: Johns Hopkins Univ. Press, 1969), 191.
9   Ibid., 190, 191.
10   Paul de Man's translation in "Sign and Symbol," 763.
11   Ibid., 771.
12   Ibid., 772.
13   "Hegel on the Sublime," in *Displacement: Derrida and After*, ed. Mark Krupnick (Bloomington: Indiana Univ. Press, 1983), p. 152.
14   *The Instructed Vision: Scottish Common Sense Philosophy and the Origins of American Fiction* (Bloomington: Indiana Univ. Press, 1961), 70.
15   Note, however, the contemporary authority for this monomania; see Allan Gardner Smith, *The Analysis of Motives: Early American Psychology and Fiction* (Amsterdam: Editions Rodopi, 1980), 42–44. Cf. David E. E. Sloane, "Gothic Romanticism and Rational Empiricism in Poe's "Berenice," *American Transcendental Quarterly* 19 (1973), 19–26. Other readings that focus on the teeth tend to emphasize the vampire motif: James B. Twitchell, *The Living Dead: A Study of the Vampire in Romantic Literature* (Durham: Duke Univ. Press, 1981), 58–61; Hal Blythe and

Charlie Sweet, "Poe's Satiric Use of Vampirism in 'Berenice,'" *Poe Studies* 14 (1981), 23–24. No one has commented at length on the comic potential of the tale in such absurdity as: "The teeth!—the teeth!—they were here, and there, and everywhere, and vividly and palpably before me; long, narrow, and excessively white, with the pale lips writhing about them, as in the very moment of their first terrible development," etc. (*TS* 215).

16 Roger Forclaz, claims that the "'moral'" of the tale is that of "the dangers of the imagination"—"'Berenice' and a Note on Poe's Reading," *Poe Newsletter* 1 (1968), 26.

17 *Edgar Allan Poe: A Phenomenological View* (Princeton: Princeton Univ. Press, 1973), 199–206. "What we are given is an enclosed state of being in which consciousness is alienated from everything, including the intentionality of its own acts" (206).

18 "Poe's Revisions in 'Berenice': Beyond the Gothic," *American Transcendental Quarterly* 24 Suppl. 2 (1974), 19.

19 *Edgar Allan Poe*, 201.

20 Note that her entry is completely silent and, if we pursue the analogy ruthlessly, the "inner apartment of the library" in which Egaeus sits in introspection can be identified with "the chamber of [his] brain."

21 Richard Wilbur observes the representational relationship between scene and state of mind throughout Poe's work in his seminal essay, "The House of Poe," *Anniversary Lectures, 1959* (Washington, D.C.: Library of Congress, 1959). Rpt. in *The Recognition of Edgar Allan Poe*, ed. Eric W. Carlson (Ann Arbor: Univ. of Michigan Press, 1966), 255–77. See also Clark Griffith, "Poe and the Gothic," in *Papers on Poe: Essays in Honor of John Ward Ostrom*, ed. Richard P. Veler (Springfield, Ohio: Chantry Music Press, 1972), 21–27, and the exchange between Patrick F. Quinn—"A Misreading of Poe's 'The Fall of the House of Usher,'" "Usher Again: Trust the Teller!"—and G. R. Thompson—"Poe and the Paradox of Terror: Structures of Heightened Consciousness in 'The Fall of the House of Usher'"—in *Ruined Eden of the Present: Hawthorne, Melville, and Poe*, ed. G. R. Thompson and Virgil L. Lokke (West Lafayette, Ind.: Purdue Univ. Press, 1981), 303–12, 341–53, 313–40.

22 "The House of Poe," 260.

23 Joseph Riddel makes a similar point—"The 'Crypt' of Edgar Poe," *Boundary 2* 8 (1979), 128.

24 The denial of the father possibly ties in with his search for the symbol— as quest for and claim to originality. Fatherless, *he* would be the father, the origin. (Mabbott notes that Egeus is the name of Hermia's father in *A Midsummer Night's Dream* [*TS* 208]; Aegeus is the name of Theseus's father, who became a father in defiance of the gods, with unfortunate results for him.) The futility of Egaeus's claim is implicit in that his "noon of manhood" still finds him in "the mansion of [his] fathers" (*TS* 210). See also Gregory S. Jay, "Poe: Writing and the Unconscious," *Bucknell Review* 28 (1983), 148–49.

25   Halliburton argues that the first paragraph shows "an emergent identity . . . [that] appears only through an act of consciousness," and that this consciousness is reflexive, aware of itself but not of the external world—*Edgar Allan Poe*, 199–200.

26   Poe's 1845 revisions emphasize the "as" construction.

27   *Edgar Allan Poe*, 205.

28   *The Rationale of Deception in Poe* (Baton Rouge: Louisiana State Univ. Press, 1979), 186.

29   Joel Porte explores the sexual implications of Egaeus's fears in *The Romance in America: Studies in Cooper, Poe, Hawthorne, Melville, and James* (Middletown, Conn.: Wesleyan Univ. Press, 1969), 79–84.

30   Many humorous juxtapositions could be made here—among them that with Hegel's definition of beauty: "the sensory appearance (manifestation) of the idea." Also note the narrator's comment in "The Fall of the House of Usher" (1839) that "if ever mortal painted an idea, that mortal was Roderick Usher" (*TS* 405).

31   James Schroeter, "A Misreading of Poe's 'Ligeia,' " *PMLA* 76 (1961), 397–406, and "Poe's 'Ligeia,' " *PMLA* 77 (1962), 675; John Lauber, " 'Ligeia' and its Critics: A Plea for Literalism," *Studies in Short Fiction* 4 (1966), 28–32.

32   Roy P. Basler, "The Interpretation of 'Ligeia,' " *College English* 5 (1944), 363–72, and "Poe's 'Ligeia,' " *PMLA* 77 (1962), 675; James W. Gargano, "Poe's 'Ligeia': Dream and Destruction," *College English* 23 (1962), 335–42; G. R. Thompson, *Poe's Fiction: Romantic Irony in the Gothic Tales* (Madison: Univ. of Wisconsin Press, 1973), 77–87.

33   Thompson, *Poe's Fiction*, 77–87; Clark Griffith, " 'Ligeia' and the English Romantics," *University of Toronto Quarterly* 24 (1954), 8–25.

34   "A Misreading of Poe's 'Ligeia,' " 397.

35   *The Fantastic: A Structural Approach to a Literary Genre*, trans. Richard Howard (Cleveland: Case Western Reserve Univ. Press, 1973), 33.

36   *Yale French Studies* 55/56 (1977), 285.

37   Ibid., 282.

38   "Edgar Allan Poe," in *Responses: Prose Pieces 1953–1976* (New York: Harcourt, Brace, Jovanovich, 1976), 51.

39   See Thompson, *Poe's Fiction*, 81–82.

40   See discussions by Bryan Jay Wolf, *Romantic Re-vision: Culture and Consciousness in Nineteenth-Century Painting and Literature* (Chicago: Univ. of Chicago Press, 1982), 69–70; Eugenio Donato, "The Ruins of Memory: Archaeological Fragments and Textual Artifacts," *Modern Language Notes* 93 (1978), 575–96.

41   Cf. "Letter to B——" (*CW* 7:xxxix).

42   Joel Porte thoroughly explores the eroticism of the tale—*Romance in America*, 69–76.

43   Which makes him an encyclopedophiliac.

44   *Literary Transcendentalism: Style and Vision in the American Renaissance* (Ithaca: Cornell Univ. Press, 1973), 169.
45   Ibid., 180.
46   Mabbott, *TS* 331, n.4.
47   Cf. Paul de Man, "Intentional Structure of the Romantic Image," in *Romanticism and Consciousness*, ed. Harold Bloom (New York: W. W. Norton, 1970), 65–77; Eugenio Donato, "The Ruins of Memory."
48   *Romance in America*, 69–76.
49   Cf. Jean Starobinski, *The Invention of Liberty 1700–1789* (Geneva: Skira, 1964), 180–81; Donato, "The Ruins of Memory."
50   *Poe's Fiction*, 81.
51   Ibid., 82.
52   *South Atlantic Quarterly* 78 (1979), 321.

Chapter VI

1   Roland Barthes, "Textual Analysis of a Tale by Edgar Poe," *Poe Studies* 10 (1977), 4. Translated by Donald G. Marshall from "Analyse textuelle d'un conte d'Edgar Poe," in *Semiotique narrative et textuelle*, ed. Claude Charbrol (Paris: Librairie Larousse, 1973), 29–54. There is a certain defensiveness about the legalistic tenor of P——'s account, which hints at the tantalizing possibility of criminal activity underlying it: he remarks *en passant* that Valdemar "had no relatives in America who would be likely to interfere" (*TS* 1234), emphasizes his own care to obtain reliable witnesses, and carefully documents Valdemar's permission to proceed with the experiment.
2   "Narrative and History," *ELH* 41 (1974), 456. The hostility of moralistic critics toward the "falsity" of fiction in the early years of the nineteenth century has been clearly documented by Terence Martin in *The Instructed Vision: Scottish Common Sense Philosophy and the Origins of American Fiction* (Bloomington: Indiana Univ. Press, 1961). Poe's exploitation of the ludic possibilities inherent in the claims to credibility prompted by such a climate needs no demonstration here.
3   See the correspondents listed by Mabbott (*TS* 1229–32); for the receptive climate and background information on Robert Collyer, a mesmerist himself duped by the tale, see Taylor Stoehr, *Hawthorne's Mad Scientists: Pseudoscience and Social Science in Nineteenth-Century Life and Letters* (Hamden, Conn.: Archon, 1978), 32ff.; for an examination of Poe's verisimilitude in his treatment of mesmerism, see Doris V. Falk, "Poe and the Power of Animal Magnetism," *PMLA* 84 (1969), 536–46. See also Poe's remarks in *M* 159.
4   Cf. Homer Obed Brown, "The Errant Letter and the Whispering Gallery," *Genre* 10 (1977), 591.

5 *Poe's Fiction: Romantic Irony in the Gothic Tales* (Madison: Univ. of Wisconsin Press, 1973), 159–60.

6 Note Poe's comment: "I represented the symptoms of M. Valdemar as 'severe,' to be sure. I put an extreme case; for it was necessary that I should leave on the reader's mind no doubt as to the certainty of death without the aid of the Mesmerist—but such symptoms *might* have appeared—the identical symptoms *have appeared*, and will be presented again and again" (*M* 159).

7 *Broadway Journal*, 27 December 1845; cited by Mabbott (*TS* 1230–31).

8 *Poe's Fiction*, 160.

9 Note also Poe's repetition of one of the classic accusations against writing—that it destroys memory: "the making of mere *memoranda* . . . has its disadvantages. . . . if you wish to forget anything on the spot, make a note that this thing is to be remembered" (*TS* 1113–14).

10 Mabbott also remarks of "Wallenstein" and "Gargantua" that "Schiller's tragedy, and the work of Rabelais, in Poe's opinion, were burdensome" (*TS* 1243, n.1). Thompson, on the other hand, appropriately suggests that "the thrust is clearly at Valdemar rather than at them"—*Poe's Fiction*, 233, n.18. All thrusting apart, however, there is a possible thematic justification for the choice of "Wallenstein": the historical Wallenstein suffered from a disintegrative disease during the last year or so of his life, by which his body was "falling to pieces"; yet his corpse was "allegedly found to be quite undecomposed two years after his death"—F. J. Lamport, "Introduction" to *The Robbers and Wallenstein* (New York: Penguin, 1977), 14.

11 Cited by Mabbott (*TS* 1231).

12 *Poe Poe Poe Poe Poe Poe Poe* (New York: Doubleday, 1972), 167.

13 "Textual Analysis," 9.

14 Note that Poe remarks of puns that "the goodness of your true pun is in the direct ratio of its intolerability" (*TS* 1116).

15 See, for example, Daniel Hoffman, *Poe Poe Poe Poe Poe Poe Poe*, 195–96, 209. David Ketterer notes that "Poe intends attacking man's misconception that the passing of time brings political, architectural, metaphysical, and scientific improvements"—*The Rationale of Deception in Poe* (Baton Rouge: Louisiana State Univ. Press, 1979), 20. G. R. Thompson cites the ironic satire of the tale to support his case that "the 'sincerity' of Poe's use of the occult sciences in his 'serious' tales is questionable," and as further evidence that Poe's attitudes are "always presented as ambivalent, skeptical, detached"—*Poe's Fiction*, 143.

16 See particularly Burton R. Pollin, "Poe's 'Some Words with a Mummy' Reconsidered," *ESQ*, No. 60 Suppl. (Fall 1970), 60–67. Pollin lists earlier studies.

17 Jonathan Auerbach addresses, from a different perspective, the issues of voice and authority in Poe's tales—"Poe's Other Double: The Reader in the Fiction," *Criticism* 24 (1982), 341–61.

18 *Plato: The Collected Dialogues*, Bollingen Series LXXI, eds. Edith Hamil-

ton and Huntington Cairns, trans. R. Hackforth (New York: Pantheon, 1961), 521.

19 *American Hieroglyphics: The Symbol of the Egyptian Hieroglyphics in the American Renaissance* (New Haven: Yale Univ. Press, 1980), 56.

20 Ibid., 6.

21 Cf. Allan Gardner Smith, " 'Discovery' in Poe," *Delta* 12 (1981), 1–10.

22 *The Rationale of Deception*, 22.

23 Allamistakeo's double-edged comment could also easily be Poe's gibe at the prose of Gliddon and, particularly, Buckingham. Cf. Pollin, "Poe's 'Some Words with a Mummy,' " 62–64.

24 Cf. *American Hieroglyphics*, 57–58.

Chapter VII

1 " 'Discovery' in Poe," *Delta* 12 (1981), 2.

2 *EAP* 1263–70. On the "curious" history of the publication of "Mellonta Tauta" and *Eureka*, see Mabbott (*TS* 1290).

3 *Through the Custom-House: Nineteenth-Century American Fiction and Modern Theory* (Baltimore: Johns Hopkins Univ. Press, 1982), 102. The chapter on Poe, "Writing and Truth in Poe's *The Narrative of Arthur Gordon Pym*," originally published in *Glyph* 2 (1977), 102–21, is the most interesting study on *Pym* in recent years. For a convenient listing of works, see Douglas Robinson, "Reading Poe's Novel: A Speculative Review of *Pym* Criticism, 1950–1980," *Poe Studies* 15 (1982), 47–54.

4 Cf. the words—"No Chalk"—"scored over the doorway by means of that very mineral whose presence they purported to deny" (*TS* 241) in "King Pest" (1835), and note Alexander Hammond's comments in "Further Notes on Poe's Folio Club Tales," *Poe Studies* 8 (1975), 41.

5 "Edgar A. Poe: His Income as Literary Entrepreneur," *Poe Studies* 15 (1982), 1–7. By Ostrom's calculation, Poe's "lifetime earnings as a professional author, editor, and lecturer" amounted to "about $6200."

6 Poe had originally sold the story in 1842 to George R. Graham—for fifty-two dollars—but withdrew it, subsequently entering it in the *Dollar* competition and winning the first prize of a hundred dollars (*TS* 803–4). Cf. Marc Shell, *Money, Language, and Thought: Literary and Philosophical Economics from the Medieval to the Modern Era* (Berkeley: Univ. of California Press, 1982), 9, 13, and Barton Levi St. Armand, "Poe's Sober Mystification: The Uses of Alchemy in 'The Gold-Bug,' " *Poe Studies* 4 (1971), 6.

7 *Money, Language, and Thought*, 5–23.

8 Ibid., 18.

9 "Gold in the Bug," trans. Frank Towne, *Poe Studies* 9 (1976), 36.

10 On the relationship between consistency and truth, see *EAP* 1269.

11 Mabbott points out that the southern pronunciation of "antennae" would have been "Ann-tinny" (*TS* 845, n.9).

12 See Emile Benveniste, *Problems in General Linguistics*, trans. Mary Elizabeth Meek (Coral Gables: Univ. of Miami Press, 1971), 219.

13 The narrator is in this way similar to the prefect in "The Purloined Letter"; see Sergio L. P. Bellei, "The Purloined Letter': A Theory of Perception," *Poe Studies* 9 (1976), 40–42.

14 John T. Irwin, "The Symbol of the Hieroglyphics in the American Renaissance," *American Quarterly* 26 (1974), 103–26. In his discussion of Champollion's deciphering of the hieroglyphics of the Rosetta Stone, Irwin notes that the symbols could operate on one of three levels of increasing complexity—1. figurative, in which the hieroglyph stood for the thing it represented; 2. symbolic, in which it represented simple ideas associated with the objects represented; 3. phonetic, in which the hieroglyph represented sounds (106–7). The narrator of "The Gold-Bug" can make only the most elementary associations and does not recognize that the hieroglyph is phonetic. In *American Hieroglyphics: The Symbol of the Egyptian Hieroglyphics in the American Renaissance* (New Haven: Yale Univ. Press, 1980), Irwin notes Poe's emphasis of the distinction between ideogram and phonetic hieroglyph in this tale.

15 "The Gold-Bug" here echoes Poe's July 1841 article in *Graham's Magazine* (*CW* 14:116).

16 The puns are most obvious in the transcriptions of Jupiter's speech—where visual as well as aural puns are at work—but they also pervade the narrative: for example, when Jupiter silences the Newfoundland dog, he got "out of the hole with a dogged air of deliberation, tied the brute's mouth up with one of his suspenders, and then returned, with a grave chuckle, to his task" (*TS* 823).

17 *Money, Language, and Thought*, 14.

18 "Poe's Sober Mystification," 5.

19 *Money, Language, and Thought*, 21.

20 "The Problem of Realism in 'The Gold-Bug,'" *American Literature* 25 (1953), 171–92. Also note the literalistic complaints about flaws in the tale's cryptographic methodology—Cortell Holsapple, "Poe and Conradus," *American Literature* 4 (1932), 62–65; Alfred Allan Kern, "News for Bibliophiles," *Nation* 97 (22 Oct. 1913); W. K. Wimsatt, Jr., "What Poe Knew About Cryptography," *PMLA* 58 (1943), 778–79.

21 "Gold in the Bug," 33.

22 *Edgar Allan Poe: A Phenomenological View* (Princeton: Princeton Univ. Press, 1973), 240. For an extension of Halliburton's reading, see Sergio L. P. Bellei, " 'The Purloined Letter': A Theory of Perception."

23 "Poe's 'Murders in the Rue Morgue': The Ingenious Web Unravelled," *Studies in the American Renaissance* (Boston: Twayne, 1977), 239–40.

24 Ibid., 239.

25 Smith, " 'Discovery' in Poe," 5.

26 "Poe's 'Murders in the Rue Morgue,' " 239, 248.

27 "Poe: Writing and the Unconscious," *Bucknell Review* 28 (1983), 159–60.

28 *American Literature* 54 (1982), 165–88. See also Jay, "Poe: Writing and the Unconscious," 159.

29 "The Psychology of 'The Murders in the Rue Morgue,' " 187.

30 Jay identifies it as a "violent primal scene" by which Dupin "hopelessly entangles himself in representations of transgression, castration, ejaculation, and dissemination" (all at once!)—"Poe: Writing and the Unconscious," 160.

31 On doubling in the text see Jacques Derrida, "The Purveyor of Truth," trans. Willis Domingo, James Hulbert, Moshe Ron, and M.-R. L., *Yale French Studies* 52 (1975), 100–112; Joseph Riddel, "The 'Crypt' of Edgar Poe," *Boundary 2* 8 (1979), 136–38; Liahna Klenman Babener, "The Shadow's Shadow: The Motif of the Double in Edgar Allan Poe's 'The Purloined Letter,' " *The Mystery and Detection Annual* (Beverly Hills: Donald Adams, 1972), 21–32.

32 On the contemporary interest in the monstrous and the deviant, see Tony Tanner, *Adultery in the Novel: Contract and Transgression* (Baltimore: Johns Hopkins Univ. Press, 1979), 193–96, n.6, and his reference to François Jacob, *The Logic of Life: A History of Heredity* (1973; rpt. New York: Pantheon, 1982).

33 "The 'Crypt' of Edgar Poe," 140. Note also Derrida: "at the Minister who 'is well acquainted with my MS.,' Dupin strikes a blow signed brother or confrère, twin or younger brother or older brother (Atreus/Thyestes). This rival and duplicitous identification of the brothers . . . carries it off infinitely far away in a labyrinth of doubles without originals, of facsimile without an authentic, an indivisible letter, of casual counterfeits . . . imprinting the purloined letter with an incorrigible indirection"—"The Purveyor of Truth," 109–10.

34 Jacques Lacan makes much of this in his "Seminar on 'The Purloined Letter,' " trans. Jeffrey Mehlman, *Yale French Studies* 48 (1972), 38–72. For Lacan, the tale is a "fable" of the relationship between the subject and signification—of "the *insistence* of the signifying chain"—in which each displacement of the letter forces the holder to repeat the symbolic situation: the "displacement [of the subjects] is determined by the place which a pure signifier—the purloined letter—comes to occupy" (39, 45). Lacan's argument is primarily an appropriation of the tale as a metaphor for his own psychoanalytic discourse. This appropriation prompted Derrida's deconstruction in "The Purveyor of Truth," in which he discusses "the disseminal structure, i.e., the no-possible-return of the letter" of writing (100). The commentary on this exchange includes: Barbara Johnson, "The Frame of Reference: Poe, Lacan, Derrida," *Yale French Studies* 55/56 (1977), 457–505; Jeffrey Mehlman, "Poe Pourri: Lacan's Purloined Letter," *Aesthetics Today*, ed. Morris Philipson and Paul J. Gudel (New York: New American Library, 1980), 413–32; Claude Richard, "Destin, Design, Dasein: Lacan, Derrida and 'The Purloined Letter,' " *Iowa Review* 12 (1981), 1–10 ("Interview," 12–22) ; Donald Pease, "Marginal Politics

and 'The Purloined Letter': A Review Essay," *Poe Studies* 16 (1983), 18–23.

35 See also Jay, "Poe: Writing and the Unconscious," 160.

36 Ibid., 160–61.

37 "The Purveyor of Truth," 110.

38 In the version in *Prose Romances* (1843) —*TS* 568.

39 "The Purveyor of Truth," 101.

40 "The 'Crypt' of Edgar Poe," 135.

41 Cf. "The Purveyor of Truth," 103.

42 The epigraph is appropriately taken from chapter 5 of Browne's *Hydriotaphia* (1658), in which he meditates on "the oblivion of names."

43 Contrast, for example, Joseph J. Moldenhauer, "Murder as a Fine Art: Basic Connections Between Poe's Aesthetics, Psychology, and Moral Vision," *PMLA* 83 (1968), 284–97, and G. R. Thompson, "Unity, Death, and Nothingness," *PMLA* 85 (1970), 297–300.

44 "Poe, Empedocles, and Intuition in *Eureka*," *Poe Studies* 11 (1978), 24. Among other studies that corroborate the ironic reading of this work are: Harriet R. Holman, "Hog, Bacon, Ram, and Other 'Savans' in *Eureka*: Notes toward Decoding Poe's Encyclopedic Satire," *Poe Newsletter* 2 (1969), 49–55, and "Splitting Poe's Epicurean Atoms: Further Speculations on the Literary Satire of *Eureka*," *Poe Studies* 5 (1972), 33–37; Erich W. Sippel, "Another of Poe's 'Savans': Edward Tatham," *Poe Studies* 9 (1976), 16–21.

45 On *Eureka* as "Encyclopedic Satire" see Holman, "Hog, Bacon, Ram."

46 For a detailed discussion of Nothingness in *Eureka* see Thompson, "Unity, Death, and Nothingness."

47 What can we make of the fact that when Bob made "a plunge into the capital S-hole [he] came out in triumph with a capital S" (*TS* 1372)?

48 J. Hillis Miller, "Ariadne's Thread: Repetition and the Narrative Line," *Critical Inquiry* 3 (1976), 75.

Index

Aarsleff, Hans, 9
Adams, Hazard, 81
Annihilation: and ideal sign, 12, 150;
    and identity, 31; and perverseness,
    35–36; universal, 147
Aristotle: *Rhetoric*, 8, 18
Auerbach, Jonathan, 22, 23, 67
Authorial anxiety, xv, xvi, 45–61
    passim, 62–79 passim

Bacon, Francis, 30, 98
Barthes, Roland, 112, 173 n.1
Beattie, James, 17
Bell, Michael Davitt, 15
Berkeley, George, 17
Bickman, Martin, 29
Bloom, Harold, xiv
Bob, Captain, 151–52, 178 n.47
Bonaparte, Marie, 51, 66
Booth, Wayne C., 69
Brooks, Peter, 91

Buckingham, James Silk, 113
Buell, Lawrence, 96–97

Champollion, Jean-François, 116, 176
    n.14
Coleridge, H. N., 31
Coleridge, Samuel Taylor, 1–3, 80–81,
    146, 155 n.1
Collyer, Robert, 107, 108
Common-Sense philosophy, 3, 17–18,
    155 n.4, 161 n.30
Cooke, Philip P., 142
Coskren, Robert, 40
Cox, James M., 39

Davidson, Edward H., xiv, 20, 71
Death, 4, 32, 54–61 passim, 88–89,
    101–4, 107–8, 112–13, 140, 155 n.6;
    and beauty, 5, 99; and ideal sign,
    12; as motive for poetry 5. *See also*
    Annihilation; Language: and death

DeFalco, Joseph M., 55
de Man, Paul, 80–82
Dentophilia, 84, 89–90
Derrida, Jacques, xv, 144, 145, 177
   n.33, 177 n.34
Dismemberment, 18–24
Disraeli, Benjamin: *Vivian Grey*, 53
Doppelgänger, 36, 38–40, 50, 163 n.43

Emerson, Ralph Waldo, xiv, 46

Fisher, Benjamin Franklin IV, 84
Folio Club, 50, 165 n.16

Gargano, James W., 9, 32
Gliddon, George Robins, 113
Gossip, 21, 23, 106–13, 128

Halliburton, David, 27, 37, 49, 57, 71,
   83, 87–88, 141
Hammond, Alexander, 50
Hassell, J. Woodrow, 139
Hegel, Georg Wilhelm Friedrich, 82
Hobbes, Thomas, 28
Hoffman, Daniel, 66, 112
Hume, David, 17

Imagination, 1–4, 23, 62–63. *See also*
   Coleridge, Samuel Taylor
Intertextuality, xv, 52, 63, 79, 91, 98,
   125, 144
Irwin, John T., xv, 115, 176 n.14

Jacobs, Robert D., xiv, 3
Jay, Gregory S., 143, 144
Johnson, Richard M., 21

Kennedy, J. Gerald, 69, 70
Kermode, Frank, 56
Ketterer, David, 51–52, 88, 118, 174
   n.15

Lacan, Jacques, xv, 177 n.34
Language, xv–xvi; allegory, 6; arbitrariness of, xvi, 9, 12, 15, 71, 76,
   79, 80, 82, 86, 128–29, 140, 151–52;
   belatedness of, 6, 85, 93; and death,
   13, 32, 54–61, 99, 101, 140; and
   dismemberment, 18–24; figurative,
   8, 14, 86, 93, 118–20; and ideal

sign, 7, 9, 12, 31, 73–74, 80, 82, 86,
   91, 143; materiality of, 7, 60, 126;
   and money, 127–28; of reason and
   perversity, 34–36; and self, 17–44;
   and time, 6, 7, 88; of truth and
   poetry, 5–9. *See also* Romantic
   symbol; Writing
Lawrence, D. H., 66
Lemay, J. A. Leo, 127, 143
Levine, Stuart and Susan, 166 n.30
Lipking, Lawrence, 65
Locke, John, 9, 26, 27–29, 30, 38, 156
   n.10, 160 n.20, 163 n.41
Lowell, James Russell, 15, 28
Lynen, John F., 7

Mabbott, Thomas Ollive, 50, 53, 63,
   76, 110, 118, 167 n.37, 171 n.24,
   174 n.10, 175 n.11
Martin, Terence, 17, 83
Matthiessen, F. O., xv
Memory, 84–85, 87–88, 91–94, 100
Mesmerism, 107, 173 n.3
Metempsychosis, 25
Miller, J. Hillis, 107
Miller, John C., 63

Origins, xv, xvi, 86, 94, 124–25, 144,
   150–51
Ostrom, John Ward, 127

Page, Peter C., 149
Parables, 55–56
Personal identity, xv, xvi, 17–44
   passim, 88–89, 143, 160 n.23
Perverseness, 33–36 passim, 161 n.30.
   See also Annihilation: and perverseness; Language: of reason and
   perversity
Phrenology, 33, 74–75
Plato: *Phaedrus*, 114; *Symposium*, 31
Poe, Edgar Allan: attitude to progress, 113, 174 n.15; attitude to
   readers, 62–79; burlesque/hoax
   technique of, 21, 48, 52, 66, 71; on
   creativity, xvi, 3, 14–15; as editor,
   45–46; exhumation and reburial
   of, xiii, xvii; finances of, 127, 175
   n.5; and Folio Club, 50; on genius,

3–4; on heresy of didactic, 6, 47–48; as journalist, 46–47; literary reputation of, xiii–xv; and plagiarism, 46–47, 63; plans for own journal, 165 n.10; on rhetoric of effect, 4, 7, 8, 65; on supernal beauty, 4–5; on transcendentalism, 50, 96–97, 158 n.4
—*criticism:* "A Chapter of Suggestions," 1; Drake-Halleck review, 2; "Letter to B——," 1, 47, 63; Longfellow review, 3–4, 23; "Maelzel's Chess-Player," 62; "Marginalia," 10, 15, 63–65, 137, 156 n.8; "Peter Snook" review, 51; "The Philosophy of Composition," 5, 7; "Pinakidia," 46–47; "The Poetic Principle," 4, 5, 6; Thomas Moore review, 2–3
—*cosmology: Eureka*, xvi, 15–16, 125, 126, 127, 131, 133, 146–51, 152, criticism on, 178 n.44
—*fiction:* "The Bargain Lost," 122; "Berenice," xv, 82, 83–90, criticism on, 170 n.15; "The Black Cat," 12, 32; "The Colloquy of Monos and Una," 55; "The Conversation of Eiros and Charmion," 11–13; "The Facts in the Case of M. Valdemar," 105, 106–13; "The Gold-Bug," 126, 127–40, 145, 146, criticism on, 175 n.6, 176 n.20; "Hop-Frog," 70–71; "How to Write a Blackwood Article," 19, 50, criticism on, 158 n.5; "The Imp of the Perverse," 18, 32–36, criticism on, 162 n.31; "Ligeia," xv, 2, 3, 55, 82, 90–104, 105, criticism on, 172 n.31, 172 n.32, 172 n.33; "Loss of Breath," 30, 49, 50–54, 66; "The Man of the Crowd," 70, 122; "The Man That Was Used Up," 18, 21–24, 49, 51, criticism on, 159 n.8; "The Masque of the Red Death," 57, 166 n.29; "Mellonta Tauta," 123–25; "Mesmeric Revelation," 54; "Morella," xv, 18, 25–32, 143, criticism on, 160 n.16; "MS. Found in a Bottle," 116, 122; "The Murders in the Rue Morgue," 2, 141–46; *The Narrative*

of Arthur Gordon Pym, 54, 55, 125–26, 137, criticism on, 154 n.6, 175 n.3; "Never Bet the Devil Your Head," 18–19, 47; "The Oblong Box," 70; "The Power of Words," 13–15; "A Predicament," 19–21, 37, 50, 51, criticism on, 158 n.5; "The Premature Burial," 55, 66–70, criticism on, 168 n.15, 168 n.20; "The Purloined Letter," xv, 9, 46, 141–46, criticism on, 176 n.22, 176 n.23, 176 n.31; "Shadow.—A Parable," 49, 54–61; "Silence—A Fable," 55; Some Words with a Mummy," 105, 113–21, criticism on, 174 n.15; "The Spectacles," 70; "The Sphinx," 70; "The System of Doctor Tarr and Professor Fether," 70; "The Tell-Tale Heart," 36–38, 42, criticism on, 162 n.36; "Thou Art the Man," 49; "Von Jung, the Mystific," 70–79, criticism on, 169 n.25; "William Wilson," 18, 38–44, 123, criticism on, 163 n.43; "X-ing a Paragrab," 45, 48–49, 151–52, 178 n.47
—*letters:* to Frederick W. Thomas, 46; to James Russell Lowell, 15; to Joseph Evans Snodgrass, 45; to Philip P. Cooke, 142
—*poetry:* "Al Aaraaf," 10; "The Raven," 7
Pollin, Burton R., 142
Porte, Joel, 99
Premature burial, 66–70, 168 n.13

Quinn, Patrick F., xiv, 36

Rank, Otto, 40
Regan, Robert, 47
Reid, Thomas, 17–18, 19–20
Renza, Louis A., xiv
Ricardou, Jean, 128, 138, 139
Richard, Claude, xiv, xv
Riddel, Joseph N., xv, 14–15, 127, 144, 145
Romantic symbol, xv, 9–10, 80–104 passim, 156 n.16, 170 n.2, 170 n.6, 170 n.7
Rowe, John Carlos, xv, 125–26

St. Armand, Barton Levi, 138
Schelling, Friedrich Wilhelm Joseph
   von, 30, 156 n.7, 161 n.25
Schroeter, James, 90
Scott, Winfield, 21–22
Shell, Marc, 128, 138, 139
Sloane, David E. E., 84
Smith, Allan Gardner, 122, 157 n.19
Snodgrass, Joseph Evans, 72
Socrates, 114
Spanier, Sandra Whipple, 33, 34
Stoehr, Taylor, 9, 10, 14, 31, 103
Stovall, Floyd, 2

Thomas, Frederick W., 73
Thompson, G. R., xiv, 16, 21, 50, 66,

102, 103, 108
Todorov, Tzvetan, 91
Translation, 109–10

Voice, 33, 49, 50, 52–55, 105–21
   passim, 169 n.27

Whitman, Walt, xiii
Wilbur, Richard, 84, 92
Writing, xv, 10–11, 18, 48; cryptographic, 135–36, 139, 176 n.20;
   and gossip, 106–13; hieroglyphic,
   115–16, 121, 176 n.14; letters, 135,
   144–45; as memorial, 60, 64, 91,
   123–24; orphaned, 114; unreadable, 122–23. *See also* Language

About the Author

Michael J. S. Williams is Instructor in English,
Washington State University. He is Editorial
Associate for *Poe Studies* and Editorial
Associate for *Emerson Society Quarterly:
Journal of the American Renaissance.*

Library of Congress Cataloging-in-Publication
Data
Williams, Michael J. S.
A world of words.
Bibliography: p.
   1. Poe, Edgar Allan, 1809–1849—Language.
2. Poe, Edgar Allan, 1809–1849—Fictional
works.   I. Title.
ps2644.w55   1988   813′.3   87–30331
isbn 0–8223–0780–4